THE END OF AN ERA

MARK FIELD

THE END OF AN ERA

The Decline and Fall
of the Tory Party

\B^b\

Biteback Publishing

First published in Great Britain in 2025 by
Biteback Publishing Ltd, London
Copyright © Mark Field 2025

978-1-78590-975-7

10 9 8 7 6 5 4 3 2 1

A CIP catalogue record for this book is available from the British Library.

Set in Minion Pro

Printed and bound in Great Britain by
CPI Group (UK) Ltd, Croydon CR0 4YY

FSC
www.fsc.org
MIX
Paper | Supporting
responsible forestry
FSC® C013604

To Vicki, Frederick and Arabella

CONTENTS

PREFACE

In the immediate aftermath of leaving Parliament, my feelings were too raw to have contemplated writing this book. The sheer intensity of almost two decades at Westminster and the endless dramatic turbulence of my final years there made it impossibly difficult to place events into a proper perspective.

Five years have now passed since I left public life. My reflections on those times have been the cause of melancholy, unease and even a sense of guilt that it was somehow wrong to have walked away when I did, in the midst of a crisis of governance for the nation.

I was born a matter of weeks before the fabled baby boom came to an end. Ours was a golden generation that, especially in the eyes of those who have followed us, has apparently had it all. Peace in our time – not for us wartime military conscription or even being compelled to sacrifice our late teenage years to national service. Higher education almost entirely subsidised by the state, leading to plenty of graduate-level opportunities in stable, well-remunerated and fulfilling careers. Levels of economic prosperity and affluence almost unimaginable to our parents, enabling us to accumulate housing, wealth and personal capital from early adulthood onwards. Rapid advances in technology and progressive social changes – ensuring that we reached middle age in an era before the strains on welfare and pensions began to overwhelm the entire post-war settlement.

Yet the legacy my generation is about to pass on is lamentable. Renewed economic, political and military insecurity; living standards that are stagnating at best; the racking up of levels of collective debt that are unimaginable outside of wartime; and a sense that public utilities and services are in a state of deep crisis.

This has been an era characterised by instant gratification and short termism. Shamefully few of our political or commercial leaders make a virtue of patient accumulation, prudent investment or delayed consumption. But perhaps this lack of serious intent to address many of our nation's structural problems is shared by all too many of us. As I witnessed first hand in the world of politics, shallowness and performative grandstanding counted for more than diligence and competent administration. Social media, and all too often its better-established cousin, the internet, encourages a constant sense of crisis, division and hysteria at a time when we need to work together.

My time in public service featured a moderate level of conventional attainment and prominence without my ever threatening to reach the upper rungs of the political ladder. Occasionally I am still stopped in the street by former constituents. Some thank me for specific assistance that I gave them (in truth this was invariably the work of my ever-attentive private office); others wish to acknowledge more generally my years of service to the local community. But without fail, each and every person I encounter observes with more than a hint of sympathy, 'You must be glad to be out of it.'

• • •

I have read enough political memoirs over the years to take with a huge pinch of salt any author's exaggerated claim this will be a 'totally different sort of biography'.

So, in the hope that you may either be a little more trusting or credulous, let me explain at the outset how I have structured this book. Each of the eight chapters starts with a key event in my life that helped shape my future. In avoiding a slavish chronology, I have tried to scatter within this account some underlying themes that reflect the changes that have taken place in the UK over the last six decades, almost half of which I have spent in public office.

None of this story has needed embellishment, but I also hope to have interspersed some of the more serious messages with anec-dotes which, sometimes at least, make clear the sheer absurdity that is part and parcel of political life.

I remain immensely proud to be English and British. In the lot-tery of life that is citizenship, I still regard myself as hugely fortu-nate to have been able to make my life here. Perhaps we should all reflect a little more on this in trying to understand the desperation of so many migrants who risk everything to reach and breach our borders.

But this is no longer the exceptional country that so often lies at the heart of our national narrative. The sooner our political and ruling class comes fully to terms with this fact, the better it will be for policy formulation at home and building relationships abroad.

I would go further still. The century since the end of the Second World War may still have two decades left to run, but when, in twenty years' time, we reflect on Britain's place in the world since 1945, I believe we shall look back on a period of almost consistent relative decline in our global standing. The only departure from this trend was the brief period between 1982 and 2003, bookended by two military skirmishes – the Falklands War and UK forces joining the US in combat in Iraq.

As it happens, this brief upward blip in the nation's relative fortunes coincided precisely with the first two decades of my adult life. Only now do I realise it was a deviation from an otherwise consistent course. Looking back, I also acknowledge that even this uptick in our standing was by no means uniformly experienced in every corner of the UK.

Britain and its people are not owed a living. Our decision to leave the European Union might, or perhaps should, have been the moment when we took full responsibility for our fate. No more blaming Brussels bureaucrats for all of our problems and life's inconveniences. Yet ever since the Covid pandemic, which helped accelerate the trend away from the previous three decades or so of relentless globalisation, the mentality of many of our fellow Britons has been to double down on that sense of entitlement. We seem to have forgotten the lessons of the past that only collective hard work, creative flair and passion for innovation will enable future generations to thrive in a highly competitive global economy.

Depressingly, in an extensive post-pandemic survey amongst developed nations, it is the British who are least likely to say work is important to them. Maybe we have also been conditioned over the years to think that whatever difficulties may arise, they will sort themselves out somehow. I worry that many of us here in the UK hold firm to a dangerously unwarranted belief that come what may, something will turn up. That it will always be 'all right on the night'.

• • •

One of the many paradoxes of the Brexit referendum in 2016 is that the outcome, which confirmed the UK's innate capacity to go it alone in the eyes of the narrow majority who supported it, has only exposed more starkly many of our national vulnerabilities. Indeed, I suspect that the most tangible of those elusive Brexit opportunities we have all been promised may turn out to be the overdue wake-up call to the realities of the nation's diminished status. Farewell to all that talk of British exceptionalism.

This reflects another aspect of the generational divide that has grown ever wider in UK society: older people still regard this nation as special and exceptional in the community of nations whilst most Britons under the age of forty are entirely relaxed that their homeland is a mid-sized European nation with a proud, imperial history and an awesome international capital city attached. This younger generation find nothing wrong with the prospect of the UK enjoying the global influence that the Netherlands or Portugal have today. We no longer punch as much above our weight in international affairs as we think. Only the continued post-war diplomatic structures that have become set in stone (for now, at least) allow us to retain institutional clout beyond our true place in the world.

Our military is still widely respected, but with an army smaller than at any time since Waterloo and naval capacity a pale shadow of its Falklands-era strength only four decades ago, we have already voluntarily relinquished our first-tier military status. A succession of political and military leaders at the Ministry of Defence have overseen an utterly dismal record in defence procurement over recent years, which makes a mockery of the clamour that yet more public money should be spent here as a matter of urgency.

The self-regard of our civil service that it runs a 'Rolls-Royce' state is fast being exposed as an illusion through its institutional inertia to reform, poor management, inadequate focus on delivery and evidence of a culture of systematic covering up of incompetence in the public sector.

The overall size of our economy and its underlying anaemic rates of growth and productivity are no longer sufficient to cater for the public services that our political class continue to tell the population, especially the elderly, they are entitled to as their right. Too much of the activity in financial and professional services – such as the law, consulting and insurance, where we retain a global competitive advantage – is prone to cyclical trends. Our over-reliance on this is a perpetual economic risk. Our expertise in many industrial sectors where we have had traditional strength, such as infrastructure, transportation and construction, has in recent years been found wanting.

More generally, there is an abiding sense that nothing works anymore – an overwhelming malaise in many public services and the overriding feeling that many working in customer service have little pride in what they do.

The NHS is no longer the 'envy of the world'. Perhaps it never was; after all, no other country of comparable size or wealth has ever sought to emulate the structure of universal healthcare that we put in place as long ago as 1948. Our universities still complacently tell themselves they are 'world beating', but before long, on current trends and with only a handful of exceptions, few will rank near the top of global league tables. The abject failure of officialdom and its immediate instinct to cover up incompetence and wrongdoing across much of the British state has become increasingly high profile, as we have seen over the contaminated blood, Post Office and Windrush scandals. They have also led to a serious undermining in trust, with countless vulnerable citizens being exposed to daily danger. This 'make do and mend' approach to life has resulted in a nation increasingly beset by an inadequate public realm; this applies both physically and metaphorically.

The ties that have traditionally bound the constituent parts of the UK are frayed as never before. Much the same applies to any remaining sense that there is, or even should be, equity and fairness between generations of Britons. Even those research-heavy sectors where the UK remains a global leader, such as life sciences, specialist technology and pharmaceuticals, face threats to their export markets as nations seek to onshore on national security grounds. Meanwhile, in politics and public life, the UK's reputation for coolness under pressure and institutional stability has taken a massive hit with the turbulence of recent years.

Needless to say, this questioning of British exceptionalism is an especially stark and unwelcome message for my own Conservative Party, whose core beliefs have been so inextricably tied up with respect for our nation's history and traditions.

Furthermore, the most recent and noticeable weakening in the UK's standing has come under coalition and Conservative governments, partly during my own time in ministerial office. So, I must take my share of collective responsibility for this decline. My party traditionally stood for sober and moderate governance, careful husbandry of the public finances and an aversion to passing on unsustainable levels of debt to future generations, and instinctive suspicion of either revolutionary upheaval or grand projects.

Arguably, conservatism's electoral success over the past two centuries implies strongly that this passion for quiet, competent governance was not just the Conservative way but the British way. Our international standing and reputation has essentially been underpinned by our steady and reliable conduct of public affairs. As I look back on my time in Parliament and public life, it is difficult not to conclude that these values have been badly shaken, if not betrayed. Instead of standing up for consistency and steady administration, the Conservative Party has been associated more with chaos, disruption and instability over the past decade.

Unusually, I have known four of the six most recent Prime Ministers when they were in their twenties. This was well before any of them came to public prominence, when their political ambitions, let alone the prospect that they might one day walk through the door of 10 Downing Street, were still something of a distant dream. In comparing and contrasting their personalities and style, in an era where performative style all too often finds favour over industrious substance, it is impossible not to conclude that the UK has been badly served by the bombastic bluster of those leaders claiming that 'our best days lie ahead'. Cheerful optimism is all well and good, but the hard daily grind of policymaking and delivery requires much more than broadbrush enthusiasm. Yet this has all too often been the blueprint of British political leadership in recent times.

• • •

The great Victorian novelist Anthony Trollope reputedly spent his first two waking hours before breakfast each and every morning writing 2,000 words of peerless prose. This inspiring level of literary output was consistently churned out at the same time as he held down a succession of demanding, serious and senior roles in the civil service. No working from home for him in those days either.

For my part, I had always rather vaguely planned to write a memoir of sorts after I had left public life for the sake of my children. Once I put my mind to the task, over a period of several months I began to haphazardly scribble down random thoughts and ideas in a magpie-like fashion. Matters accelerated and the fast-changing of personnel in Downing Street during summer and autumn 2022 also persuaded a number of old contacts in the media world that a personal memoir might be of wider interest. Eventually, after about a year of sketching out brief notes, I decided to take a more systematic approach. Suddenly, amidst all my other non-executive and advisory commitments, writing this book took on a life of its own. On some days I think the great man Trollope would have been impressed at my industry and output!

My initial thought had been to end this preface with a brief roadmap to life's journey as I have experienced it. When all is said and done, however, all the nuggets of advice and wisdom come down to this: love is everything. Especially the feelings you have for family, for blood really is thicker than water. I only became a father in my forties, and the intense and unshakeable love that you have for your children is truly life's most magnificent gift. So it is with much pride and joy that I dedicate this book to them and my wife Victoria.

The Rt Hon. Mark Field
March 2025

CHAPTER 1

AN UNWELCOME LETTER

_____

10 JULY 1975

Time and its passing have always held a deep fascination for me. Since early childhood, I have had something of an obsessive memory for dates and the marking of anniversaries and events; not simply as they impact my daily life, but in long-lasting preoccupations, such as cricket, football and pop music, where a love or slavish pursuit of statistical records often prevails. Remind me of a past event and, in all likelihood, I will instantly calculate not only how long ago it took place but will also work out what was happening at the time when an equivalent period had previously elapsed.

But I cannot claim that even as keen a memory as mine is infallible. No one fully understands what triggers our earliest recollections, but in retelling many of the anecdotes set out in these pages, I have been struck by how intimately I have been able to remember the tiniest details of encounters that sometimes took place decades ago. Yet, perversely, even on these most momentous of days, there must have been endless waking hours for which I cannot even begin to account.

The story of my political awakening starts with my eleventh birthday nearly upon me. It begins with an official-looking letter addressed to my parents arriving in the post at our then family home in Tring, the small market town lying at the far north-western tip of Hertfordshire.

Strictly speaking, my earliest political memories date back a little further still, for I was at junior school during the fabled three-day week of the winter of 1973–74. Truth be told, at the time I was far more concerned by the impact of the power cuts on school opening times, the scheduling of professional football and whether on Thursday nights we would get to watch *Top of the Pops* on TV and discover whether it would be Slade or Gary Glitter at number one (little did we know that Mr Glitter would be permanently cancelled from our screens half a century on, but that's another story entirely). I am rather ashamed to admit that all of this meant far more to me than the plight of the Heath government as it fought its battles with the National Union of Mineworkers. I do vaguely remember both general elections of 1974, but again, largely in the context of having two unexpected bonus days off school, as our classrooms were used as a polling station.

I overheard the slightly tortured discussions taking place between my parents before the February contest about which way they were going to vote. The Field household bloc, for the first and only time, fell in behind that nice Mr Thorpe's Liberal Party, as the local Conservative MP held on only by the skin of his teeth (187 votes to be precise). They switched back to their usual voting preference in the October election, but to no avail, as the seat was then lost to Labour.

Back to that letter. On 10 July 1975, I was just seven weeks away from starting secondary school education. Or that at least was the plan. My father had attended Reading School as a boarder during and after the Second World War. For him, his schooldays really were the happiest of his life. So it was quite easy to understand that he wanted me to follow in his footsteps. As a consequence of the Education Act of 1944, Reading School had evolved from a fee-paying establishment to a direct-grant grammar school. However, because of its history, around a fifth of its intake were still boarders. All was set. I had passed the entrance exam to take up a place in one of the boarding wings. My mother had already purchased industrial quantities of school kit and dutifully sewn my name tag into each and every item.

But we had reckoned without the telling intervention of the by now Labour-controlled Hertfordshire County Council. As the Field family were residents in one county and the state school I was set to attend was located in another, a netting-off process for me and the many other school pupils similarly affected was necessary between the two county councils. This was designed to take account of the modest marginal costs incurred by a local authority educating a non-resident child. The problem – and this was the bombshell set out in the momentous letter – was that the recently elected county council's anti-selective education policy meant it was refusing point blank to pay for one of its resident children to attend a grammar school. The sum of £43 per term (around £400 in today's money) lingers in the mind. To add insult to injury, those glorified pen pushers in their Hertford ivory tower would not even permit my parents to pay the disputed charge out of their own pocket.

That long summer evening turned into a fully-fledged household conference, mulling over all the options. The upshot was that, like countless other families before and since, my parents resolved to move house in order to further their children's educational opportunities. By the autumn we had arrived in Reading and, decked out in an entirely different set of sporting colours, all lovingly tagged, I commenced grammar school as a day pupil.

Unsurprisingly, this little episode galvanised me into a political partisanship, which has never really waned. The politics of envy and the casual invoking of class-war rhetoric still raises my hackles like little else. Meanwhile, that first brush with patronising local government bureaucracy instilled in me a lifelong, instinctive wariness and distrust of officialdom.

Unequivocal support for the hardy few grammar schools that had survived the 1960s and 1970s cull, alongside unwavering sympathy for parental choice in selective education, was then a benchmark of Conservative Party belief. To many of my generation, it was the issue that politicised us. Perhaps younger generations of Conservatives, besides those educated at one of the 164 surviving grammar schools, feel less passionate about this matter.

More recently, the party has toyed with watering down this commitment. Shamefully, in the early years of modernisation under David Cameron the official line was that 'grammar schools entrench social advantage' – although in fairness, like so much else, this was never followed through when we made it into government. My old friend Graham Brady sacrificed his ministerial prospects to lead the charge that even a modern Conservative Party should support aspiration, opportunity and choice, because choice is the best way to raise outcomes for all. Like him, I have always believed in promoting excellence, rather than equality, because an obsession with 'fairness' will inevitably manifest itself in the levelling down of standards and opportunities.

It is all too easy to suggest that the debate about selective education is a throwback to the ideological battles of the past. In reality, nothing could be further from the truth. Like it or not, we now live in a highly competitive global economy. The emergence in my adulthood of China, India and many Asian tiger economies as the commercial superpowers of the future will profoundly affect the prospects and prosperity of future generations of Britons. The paradox I witnessed as a constituency MP is that virtually every immigrant community making their way in this country instinctively understands this. Whilst many arrive here resigned to taking up, and remaining in, unskilled and precarious employment, they avidly want and expect so much more for their children. First-rate education lies at the heart of these hopes. The abiding memory of my final election campaign was being ushered into the living room of a rather shabby social-housing flat in Pimlico by its middle-aged British-Bangladeshi tenant. He spoke very little English, but bursting with pride, he pointed to the wall on which was hung the framed degree certificates for each of his three daughters.

• • •

Many future parliamentarians are brought up in highly political families. In my case, neither of my parents could really be described as politically active – although Peter, my father, had been a member of the Young Conservatives in the early 1950s (more of a social than a political commitment in those days). Both were traditional Tory voters. My father had served for almost twenty years as an army officer and whilst posted overseas, he did not exercise his right to vote. Like some in the armed services he took the view that being prepared to fight for queen and country necessitated being above party-political considerations. Still, there was no doubting where his political allegiances lay.

Yet it was instructive for me to see how his attitudes changed following the Conservative victory in 1979. Politics and current affairs had always been discussed avidly at the Sunday lunch table; it was crystal clear that my father was typical of many who in the late 1970s despaired of the state of the country and relished the prospect of a radical Conservative alternative to tame the power of the trade unions. However, once Margaret Thatcher arrived and started to unashamedly implement free-market economics and shake up the cosy middle-class consensus, he found the harsh reality of this unfamiliar new world a rather alarming prospect. It was for me early evidence of how Middle England all too often wants to both have its cake and eat it.

It is the normal way of things for young people to doubt whether their parents had ever really been carefree or youthful themselves. Certainly, as my brother and I were growing up there was precious little in my father's attitude, appearance or demeanour to suggest this to be so. From his late teens he had lived in a succession of drafty, spartan, unwelcoming military encampments – not even as a conscripted national serviceman but out of choice as a cadet at Sandhurst. That regimentation and his military discipline dominated our home life, so that even by the standards (a very important word in his lexicon) of the day, our upbringing was strict.

Pleasure in life or the right to freedom of thought or action had to be earned and even then, only after some combination of blood, sweat, toil and tears. By the time he resigned his commission, still only in his late thirties, the world he had known and understood was fast on its way to being transformed. He had entered Sandhurst seven years after the end of the Second World War, spending the rain-swept day of Queen Elizabeth's coronation on guard outside Westminster Abbey. When Britain still had an empire, he had served in Aden, Hong Kong, Borneo and Singapore. By the time he left the army in 1971 – funnily enough, I only recently calculated that his overall duration in military service matched my duration in Parliament to the month – overseas postings essentially meant Germany and Northern Ireland.

The ill-discipline of life beyond the warm embrace of the army – outside in Civvy Street – is something he never really came to terms with. He railed against the lack of punctuality, slovenly dress, unpolished shoes and men having either beards or long hair… especially the long hair. There was a sole occasion when we were about eight or nine years old when he was entrusted to take my brother and me for a haircut. We returned from the barber having endured a severe shearing that would have seemed excessive even for new recruits.

My mother was horrified: 'Peter, they look as though they have just come out of Belsen!'

At home we became accustomed to hearing my father refer to dark-skinned immigrants in terms that were not intrinsically unkind but would be regarded as totally unacceptable by all young and middle-aged Britons today. He had proudly served with Nepalese Gurkhas, Yemeni Arabs and Malays but had a patronising attitude towards other races and other nationalities that was commonplace for that era.

But aside from this all-pervading atmosphere of severity, my father loved his family deeply, if undemonstratively. Apart from a week's solitary vacation every year fly fishing, his entire life was devoted to the duty of providing for us all, even though this meant holding down a series of mid-level management roles that, after the excitement of military life, he found neither fulfilling nor especially enjoyable. Yet in his own way he felt he was branching out from his own austere upbringing. My paternal grandfather had been a senior RAF officer who simply refused to speak with his eldest son for almost three years after he had the audacity to sign up for the army.

On the one hand, my father wanted his sons to have a very different life from the one he had been forced to lead. But then on the other, he felt let down somehow when we turned into different kinds of people. Not totally – my values are probably more similar to my father's than I would care to admit. Nevertheless, my brother probably hit the nail on the head when the two of us met up in Westminster for lunch with our families on the day of the Queen's Platinum Jubilee and toasted his memory: 'What would Daddy have made of his country seventy years on since lining the route for the coronation?'

Needless to say, like so many teenagers trying to work out their parents' relationship, we wondered what on earth our mother saw in our father. My mother, Ulrike, had an altogether more exotic background. She was German, although having a German mother in those days was not unusual amongst families in the armed services. Indeed, intermarriage between the British and Germans was one of the lasting legacies of the huge post-war British military presence in West Germany. What was perhaps more unusual is the enormous pride I have always had in the country of my birth (I was born in October 1964 at the British Military Hospital, Hannover) and my half-German ancestry.

My mother had been a refugee twice by the age of fifteen. Born in November 1939, just outside Breslau in Silesia (now Wrocław in modern-day Poland), her family, along with much of the civilian ethnic German population, were displaced in the first few weeks of 1945, ending up with relatives near Leipzig. This part of Saxony had initially been liberated by the Americans but was eventually incorporated into Soviet-administered East Germany. Nine years later, my maternal grandfather, a doctor in general practice, was tipped off by a patient in the Stasi that he was about to be arrested. Travelling to Berlin – this was still seven years before the Berlin Wall was built – the family walked across from east to west and into a refugee camp. They went from there to Bielefeld, which lay in the heart of British Army territory in Rhine country. There, whilst working as a translator for NATO in the early months of 1961, my mother met a dashing young captain in the Royal Corps of Transport.

I suspect my mother was able to take advantage of the absence of clearly defined benchmarks that often arises when different cultures come into contact. A haziness, bordering on mystery, has always surrounded the precise background of her wider family in Silesia. My grandfather's status as a Heidelberg-educated medical professional and Burschenschaft member was never in question. Like post-war West German Chancellor Konrad Adenauer, he bore the tell-tale facial scar of the student duelling ritual. But his precise movements during the Second World War were less clear.

My mother was bright, strikingly attractive as a young woman and in her late teens had more than a slightly wilful streak. Within four years of leaving the drab, grey conformism of East Germany and only months after her eighteenth birthday, she had arrived in north London – in Hodford Road, Golders Green, to be precise – to work as an au pair with a view to improving her English. She spent the next eighteen months there and so began her love affair with the country she would make her home for almost the entirety of her adult life.

After her death, I discovered amongst her papers, in pristine blue ink, a handwritten letter of recommendation from her employer. In due course, I was able to piece together a rather intriguing but touching story. It transpired that my mother had worked for a

9

Jewish couple who had escaped Nazi Germany as children in 1938. Forever grateful to the UK for providing them with sanctuary, they also longed for the land of their birth. Above all, they wanted their children to learn the mother tongue of their own childhood and also to understand that not all Germans should be tainted by the calamity of the Hitler era. My mother was treated as family and would often observe the Friday evening Shabbat rituals. Whilst not unique, this was still rare in the late 1950s when the lived experience of the Holocaust was still so raw.

In later years, my mother would always have my undivided attention whenever she reminisced about her childhood and her tales of strife and fear as a refugee were brought to life. She spoke movingly of her flight at the age of five from Silesia, in a rickety family car packed with her mother, three siblings, nanny and whatever heirlooms and items of sentimental value could be squeezed in. On the way, they passed tens of thousands of fellow expellees (the term ethnic cleansing was not then in vogue) trudging westwards on the roadside.

But above all there would be endless stories about food – or more accurately, its scarcity – during wartime and especially the post-war period. Her first taste of chocolate, courtesy of the kind-hearted American GIs who had been billeted in her grandparents' Leipzig home in the spring of 1945; the heartbreaking insistence every lunchtime from her painfully malnourished grandparents that the children should eat 'as we have had such an enormous breakfast earlier'; and the constant, aching hunger of her childhood years.

As a mother, she would compensate for this privation by constantly baking. Friends would remark that there always seemed to be a cake or homemade biscuits on the go at our house. For my part, a lifelong sweet tooth was cultivated from an early age, but even the finest London patisseries fail to match up to my mother's warm Streusselkuchen, Pflaumentorte and Kugelhopf.

On the matter of politics, she was always more circumspect. Her first vote, at the age of fourteen, had come at East German elections, in which her father taught her how to spoil her ballot paper. No matter; Walter Ulbricht was still safely re-elected. It amused her that once they were safely in the west, it still took many months for her parents to get used to the idea that politics need not be discussed in hushed tones when out in public.

But my mother instinctively knew of the disruption and sacrifice that politics had entailed for so many of her generation of Germans. I shall never forget her congratulating me at my 2001 count, at the very moment of my first election to Parliament. She hugged me close and whispered, 'I am so thrilled, darling, as I know it is what you have always wanted.' The sad, almost wistful expression in her eyes told a different story.

In his deeply moving memoir about his parents' odyssey to north-west London, *Hitler, Stalin, Mum and Dad*, Daniel Finkelstein perfectly captures the innate insecurity all of us have begun to feel about political stability as children of refugees. It is something that in our hearts we have been able to spend most of our lives taking for granted. Yet watching the unpredictable global political tides of recent years, with some reaching even our shores, my generation has been forced to remember with a deepening sense of unease the lessons of family history that were passed down to us.

I had always felt confident that building up capital, owning a home and accumulating possessions here in the UK was providing me with the ultimate security against the grasp of arbitrary power. But that small voice of doubt has become just a little louder this past decade. I suspect that my grandfather must also have felt himself fortunate to have been only a student in 1923 when hyperinflation destroyed the savings of countless millions of his fellow country-men in Germany. Yet in time, the impact of political upheaval and a desire to live in freedom twice wiped out everything he had worked for, in his mid-forties and again in his mid-fifties.

• • •

The main upheaval of my childhood existence was the almost con-stant moving around that is part and parcel of military life. By the time the family had finally settled in Reading, I had lived in eight homes and attended six different schools. All this by the ripe old age of eleven. One constant was my brother, Dominic, who had been born only twelve-and-a-half months after me. Our sister, Antonia, arrived a decade later. Now approaching her fiftieth birthday and even with her eldest child in her twenties, in the eyes of her two brothers she will always be the baby of the family.

Despite – or perhaps because of – our being so close in age, Dom and I were never especially friendly as we were growing up. Later on, we placed much of the blame for this on our mother. She had two older sisters, and the rivalry and sense of competition between the three daughters, often over trivial matters, was a running sore throughout their lives. This was then played out between her two sons, with a near constant pitting of one against the other as we were growing up. The simple truth was that we had very different boyhood characters. Perhaps it is inevitable that all of us parents who pride ourselves on treating each child equally are unable to understand why, when our input has been identical, the outcomes seem so very different.

Dom has always been far more intrepid than me. As my seventh decade approaches, I have never had any trouble declining what I regard as the dubious potential pleasures that come, for example, with abseiling, sky diving, mountaineering or potholing. Dom, by contrast, is much more of a thrill seeker. Of the two of us, he alone enjoys country sports – he is never happier than when he is out on the golf course, fishing for trout or on a shoot with his beloved black Labrador Retriever, Badger. My only contribution to the pursuit of field sports has been in the voting lobby. Whilst I have no desire to engage in such activities, nor have I ever wanted to ban others from doing so.

In middle age, we have grown much closer. Death and divorce have played their part. Our first marriages ended in our early forties and for both of us, unquestioning fraternal support was the best antidote to the attendant stress and misery. Around this time we also became orphans, so to speak. When the moment eventually arrives that you become part of your family's oldest living generation, there is real comfort in strong sibling ties, if only to chat about early life as well as reminiscing about a uniquely shared past. All those childhood irritations and rivalries can now be laughed off; we frequently catch up by text, WhatsApp or phone and regularly enjoy long lunches together.

The gradual realisation that blood really is thicker than water has been one of the great joys of middle age. For me, it culminated a few years ago when Dom asked me to be best man at his second wedding, which is genuinely the greatest personal honour to have been bestowed on me. We have also become the ideal sounding board to each other in later life, not least when we can both indulge and find some crumbs of comfort in our mutual hypochondria.

Ours was a solid and unspectacular middle-class upbringing, albeit one with a traditionally English approach to openly intellectual pursuits. I cannot make the claim that there were *no* books in our house, but the sum total was many years' worth of rather dog-eared copies of *Reader's Digest*, a fairly pristine set of *Encyclopaedia Britannica* and a few dozen novels by Barbara Taylor Bradford or her German equivalents. In fairness, the *Daily Telegraph* and the *Sunday Times* were invariably present, albeit with especially well-thumbed back pages.

My father's prowess and enthusiasm for team sports rubbed off on me – or at least the latter did. My only claim to sporting fame came as the opening batsman one summer for the Berkshire County under-12s. This owed more to my having a determined and effective defensive technique than any great flair; the shortcomings in my game were quickly exposed as I got older, not least as the cricket season clashed with school examinations term. But I still love watching the game, and as well as Test and county matches, I have finally been won round to the T20 format.

Football has always been an abiding passion of mine. My father supported Reading, the home town of his youth, and it was as a direct result of this – or rather, two results – that at the age of six my unlikely loyalty to Bury Football Club was sealed. I had absolutely no connection to that former mill town and have only ever visited it to watch football matches. However, during the 1970–71 season, when I was just getting interested in sport, Reading was thrashed by Bury both home and away by 5–1 in the space of a month. So, in a tribute of sorts to my father, I settled on this rather unfashionable team when sensible boys of my age were striking up allegiances for the Leeds Uniteds, Liverpools or Manchester Uniteds of this world.

It has been a labour of love, but once you are a genuine supporter, you follow your team through thick and thin – or, in Bury's case, thin and thinner. Until they had the singular misfortune of going into liquidation and being expelled from the Football League in 2019, I would endeavour to watch them whenever they were playing in or around London. A low moment came when I witnessed the biggest ever league defeat in the club's history (8–0 at Swindon Town in 1979). But I was also there in person eighteen years later when they were promoted for the first time in three decades to what is now the Championship by holding out for a nervy goalless draw at Watford. As it happened, this match took place on the Saturday before the general election that brought Tony Blair to office. I was a candidate in nearby Enfield and raced down the M25 after a morning's campaigning activity, arriving outside Watford's Vicarage Road moments before the afternoon kick-off. Leaving the car on a double yellow line, I rushed into the stadium and returned two hours later, exhilarated after a dismal spectacle of a match but a triumphant result. Expecting at least a parking ticket, if not a clamped front wheel or even abject evidence that my car had been towed away, I sprinted back to find my vehicle standing absolutely untouched. God bless Watford District Council parking enforcement!

Through most of my time supporting Bury, there was an uncanny inverse correlation between the club's fortunes and that of the Conservative Party nationally. Bury were promoted in 1974, when the Tories crashed to defeat – twice. In 1979–80, the club were relegated but the Conservatives won the general election. In 1992, bad news and relegation once more for Bury was cancelled out by John Major's victory and so on. This theory all went a bit haywire in the 2010s with promotions in 2015 and 2019, but by then the club's finances had gone similarly awry. The bankruptcy of the club has been devastating for its loyal band of supporters and a sizeable blow for the town itself. In all honesty, it has also taken the edge off my once near-obsessional interest in the game. I suspect only fellow football fanatics will fully understand, but even as a grown man in my fifties, there was nowhere I would rather be on a Saturday afternoon than watching the football scores unfold. But with the demise of the club that has meant so much to me for so long, that lifelong intensity has been lost.

Nowadays, all politicians are expected to display an avid attachment to the national game, even if their professed favourite team may seem something of a public relations contrivance. This is only a fairly recent development. The notion that Anthony Eden or Harold Macmillan would have been expected to have the remotest interest in the game is frankly laughable. Even as recently as the summer of 1983, when filling in my university application form, one well-meaning piece of advice from my father was to remove any reference to football from my list of interests. The reputation of the game was then at an all-time low. Beset by hooliganism, racism, corruption and appalling facilities, few self-respecting university admissions officers would be much impressed by a potential undergraduate claiming any association with the sport. Or so we both thought. Some years later, I discovered that my tutor was in fact a passionate Stoke City fan; in the year below me was another law student who had apparently clinched his place at interview not by any evidence of great jurisprudential insight but by asking plaintively whether he really needed to hang around overnight waiting for further questioning because he had tickets the following afternoon for Tottenham Hotspur's home match.

One affection that my father proved unable to pass on to me, however, was his love of classical music and opera. This would have been even more disconcerting had he known then that one day in the future, I would become the constituency representative for the Royal Albert Hall, the Royal Opera House and the English National

Opera. I would always dutifully attend events when invited, and in all fairness, I came to enjoy the spectacle and sense of occasion of the proms and set-piece operatic performances. But nothing I saw or heard even in these wonderful settings has induced me to play classical music at home or on the car radio.

My musical tastes have always been unashamedly mainstream. Not for me the achingly trendy contrivance of an apparent passion for obscure indie music, reggae or the like. Through childhood and until well into my thirties, I would attentively follow the weekly pop music charts. After all, there is a good reason why bestselling pop and rock music is played relentlessly on commercial radio stations. It has widespread appeal. The classic American soft rock of the Eagles and Daryl Hall & John Oates will always be the sort of stuff I shall automatically turn to.

My teens began in 1977, the year when punk rock was all the rage. I guess by then I was already too conformist to be much interested in the rise of this cynical and derisive commercial movement that tapped into the bad-tempered mood of the time. Beyond the school gates, within which strict rules about permitted uniform were demanded and observed, I watched with a wry cynicism of my own as classmates desperately tried to reinvent themselves away from their middle-class roots. Some dressed like down-and-outs, others hung around with unsavoury local characters. Virtually all of them eventually knuckled down to their studies and made it to university. Looking and listening back on the entire punk rock farrago, it is remarkable how tame it all now seems.

The revelatory musical epiphany of 1977 for me was first listening to Donna Summer's 'I Feel Love'. Legendary producer Giorgio Moroder introduced the world to the Moog synthesizer, and in the near half century since, it has been its derivatives, from disco to mainstream electronic dance music, that have been the soundtrack to my life.

• • •

It is so strange how snippets of memory linger in the mind for us all – relatively mundane encounters that seize your attention and stay with you for life. Around about the time that Donna Summer was topping the charts, I had a first major economic awakening in the unlikely surroundings of a Tesco supermarket. This all took place in the unlamented Butts Shopping Centre, a brutalist concrete monstrosity in central Reading mercifully long since demolished and rebranded. I must have been about thirteen years old, looking to invest my weekly pocket money on cut-price sweets and biscuits. There, in one of the aisles, stood a short, fairly well-dressed elderly man, desperately counting the coins in his outstretched hand, muttering away angrily at the rising cost of items on the shelves before him. And weeping. I don't think I had ever seen a grown man crying before. It was a truly shocking experience. Presumably he, like many others, survived on a fixed income and inflation – then running at over 20 per cent a year – was fast eating away at his meagre savings.

This was the economic story for many as the 1970s played out: the Nixon administration had torn up the Bretton Woods settlement that had underpinned the economies of the free western world since 1944 by taking the US off the gold standard. This momentous decision, coupled with the oil shock of 1973–74, ushered in an era of inflation after decades of price stability. Control of inflation became the overriding economic and political imperative of the second half of the 1970s. As we have seen recently, the most debilitating impact of endemic inflation is psychological. If each and every time you go to the shops to buy staple foodstuffs you do so not knowing the price but assuming it will be higher than it was previously, trust in money, trust in the government and, before long, confidence in the entire economic system is badly shaken. Politicians of all parties have much to answer for in their mismanagement of the UK economy since the turn of the century, but once it was clear that inflation was returning with a vengeance, I believe it was absolutely right for the Sunak government to make taming it the number-one political priority.

I am about as young as it is possible to be to still remember using pre-decimalised currency. Schooling began for me in autumn 1969 and weekly dinner money then was the princely sum of seven shillings and sixpence. Reluctantly, even I have to confess that this represented pretty good value, even on the days when the much-hated cheese pie, liver or butter beans were on the menu. I am sure some of my generation blame the inherent confusion that arises from grappling with two parallel money systems for any arrested mathematical development they may have experienced. To be honest, I reckon having to deal with this from my earliest school days has been a lifelong boon to my powers of mental arithmetic, a skill all but unknown to my children. Needless to say, they are bewildered to hear that I grew up in an age before universal pocket calculators. They are horrified to learn that there were only three TV channels, none of which started broadcasting until midday and wound down programming well before midnight. And let's not get started on the internet and digital era that they take for granted.

I remember that my mother's calls to German relatives required the help of an operator until well into the 1970s. Mobile phones were unknown, and the red telephone boxes that proliferated contained dialling equipment rather than defibrillators. As a pedestrian in those days, you could walk in a straight line along any urban or suburban pavement for more than ten yards without the risk of bumping into someone gawping at some screen or other... or being obstructed by a backpack-wearing music lover whose state-of-the-art earphones have made them blissfully oblivious to the world beyond.

One of the pluses of the modern era is that the endless electronic and digital distraction has all but banished boredom. It is difficult to recall now just how stultifyingly dull Sundays were as I was growing up. Middle-class folk, even those who were non-church goers like my parents, respected the idea that Sunday was special, so my brother and I were expected to play together at home and were not permitted to see other friends or even play at the local recreation ground. No shops other than newsagents (which normally closed by noon) were open; there was no live sport to be shown on TV. It was almost always a joy to return to school the following day.

There were no health clubs, gyms or joggers; yet obesity was virtually unknown. We were all less sedentary and ate far, far less. Eating in the street was strictly frowned upon. There were no fast-food outlets with all their resultant packaging littering the pavements. Trainers were only worn on the sports field rather than as universal footwear. The consumer society had yet to take off, and every two or three days, come rain or shine, my mother, being a housewife, would shop at local stores, including specialist butchers and fishmongers that were on every high street. Only later in the 1970s did self-service supermarkets and the ubiquitous weekly shop come into vogue. Fruit and vegetables were only available 'in season'. No one questioned this or assumed that every variety of food should be universally on sale throughout the year, even if that required transportation from the other side of the world.

Electronic surveillance was barely in its infancy and the mass security and civil liberties industry unknown. Even in large cities, white faces predominated and the monochrome nature of life extended to general, rather than celebrity, fashion. Dull colours, sober dress, shirt and tie, clean-shaven men and certainly none of today's virtually universal designer stubble for anyone under the age of forty.

During my childhood, the only tattoos on show were on middle-aged men, invariably extending no further than their forearm and almost always borne by someone who had served in a non-commissioned role in the armed forces. Earrings, meanwhile, were almost always worn as a solitary pair. The modern fad for assorted face furniture, ranging from nose rings to studs and multiple clips, was unknown. A man sporting an earring was widely assumed to be making a statement about his sexual orientation.

My children are amazed by the tales of the universal pall of cigarette smoke that hung over every enclosed space. Smokers seemed to be everywhere, and their habit was tolerated on Tube trains, in shops, offices and, memorably, even on hospital wards. I voted the libertarian line when, early in my time as an MP, smoking was eventually outlawed in one of its last redoubts, the public house. Whilst I cannot claim to regret my decision to take that principled line, equally I recognise that there is, probably rightly, no going back.

The routine of an annual overseas holiday, let alone several per year, was still undeveloped other than for the wealthy, international jet setters. Of the four overseas vacations during my childhood, two were to Germany (the second of which even exotically extended to a few days in Switzerland and France) and the other two to Guernsey. All involved my family driving to the coast, taking a car ferry and, on arrival, staying with relatives. As a result, I did not step onto an aeroplane until a post-A levels trip with a group of friends to Rhodes at the age of nineteen. The sum total of my childhood hotel-staying experience was a five-day break at the Royal Beacon Hotel in Exmouth (where even at the age of nine I was able to detect the all-pervading sense of faded grandeur) visiting a relatively recently widowed great-aunt.

With a half century of hindsight this all sounds quaint, but it was by no means unusual. To my teenage children, this level of deprivation, as they see it, is a cause of hilarity and some sympathy, as if my childhood had been endured in almost neo-Dickensian genteel poverty. For them, holidays abroad have already included hotel stays in New York, on three Caribbean islands and two Gulf states, not to mention having a second home in Mallorca for over a decade. By contrast, my first venture beyond European shores did not happen until after my thirtieth birthday.

• • •

All of this lay well into the future as my secondary education commenced at Reading School. If I skate relatively briefly across my seven years there, it is not because I had painful memories of my schooldays that I now prefer to gloss over – rather the opposite as a matter of fact. It was – and has consistently been for many decades – one of the top-performing state schools in the country. I thrived academically and I owe the institution and several inspirational masters there more than I shall ever be able to repay. In my first year, I was subjected to one small episode of bullying; I fought back and received a bloodied nose but thereby won the respect of my tormentor, a notorious aggressor in the year above. The only contact I had with him during the rest of our time at the school came in occasional corridor encounters when he asked after me and offered to 'sort out' anyone causing me trouble. I never had any cause or inclination to take him up on his kind offer.

Although it was nominally a direct-grant grammar, Reading School was run more in the manner of a minor public school, albeit with considerably superior academic results. It was an all-boys institution with three boarding houses, Saturday morning school, pupils addressed by their surname and sporting fixtures against the top public schools in the locality, which included Eton, Harrow, Radley and Wellington. In short, the best education that no amount of money could buy.

I have never been one to suffer from imposter syndrome, save I think for that daunting first day at Reading School. I can remember as if it were yesterday the sense of awe and rising panic as I walked up the steps of its somewhat austere late-Victorian main building (still occasionally used in filming for period murder-mystery dramas). Long wooden honours boards listed in gilded lettering the names of past pupils who had served as school captain and had won scholarships to Oxford or Cambridge University. I gulped at the sense of expectation now on my shoulders – seven years on, as vice-captain and a mere Oxbridge commoner, I contrived on both counts narrowly to miss out on my little piece of immortality.

We then settled down in alphabetical order in class. Directly behind me sat the one fellow pupil who has since become a lifelong friend. How strange it is that so much hangs on such seemingly small coincidences. Or perhaps we are all so amazingly adaptable that countless other boys in class could easily have become my best buddy if only we had by chance been seated next to each other? Anyway, John Cullen and I still see each other regularly and are godparents to each other's eldest child. Funnily enough, our friendship ebbed and flowed a little at school as we hung out in different groups, but the mutual admiration we had from each other's mother meant we always stayed close. In fact, there were times as teenagers when we were convinced that domestic life would be a lot less tense for us both if we simply swapped homes.

When I reveal that John trained as an accountant with Price Waterhouse and has recently retired after almost thirty years working in financial roles with global insurance giant Aon, where he ended up as the chief financial officer of one of its main operating arms, it would be very easy to form a misleading impression of the man. He is the absolute antithesis of the staid, risk-averse bean counter that one might reasonably expect from that thumbnail CV. John is a charismatic, work-hard, play-hard force of nature, never happier than glamping at an outdoor rock festival or watching international rugby at Twickenham or his beloved Chelsea at Stamford Bridge. Several times in recent years he tried to wind down his career, but his employer invariably fought back, offering new responsibilities. Now finally in semi-retirement, he has served as deputy chair on the council of Imperial College London. Meanwhile, having generously used his share options to set up and fund a trust, he devotes much of his time and energy working alongside his wife, Cathy, on charitable endeavours for the homeless in Brighton. I reckon his career mirrors our friendship as a clear lesson in the virtues of consistency. He has always known where his talents lie, and it has been a pleasure to have shared his friendship over so many years.

At school, I studied consistently in the classroom and became something of an academic all-rounder. But it is not undue modesty when I claim that my performance was 10 per cent inspiration and 90 per cent perspiration. Reading School set me up well for life beyond. I was able to help persuade the headmaster that the school should offer economics at A level – back in 1981, this caused no end of complaints from some in the staff room who feared that in doing so, the school was dumbing down its fine academic standards. But it was only this – and finding a school subject in which I genuinely excelled – that opened up the opportunities that lay ahead for me.

A few well-selected words at an impressionable age count for everything. At thirteen, as I perused that year's Oxbridge results on the school notice board, the then headmaster Anthony Davis caught sight of me: 'Ah, Field, that will be you in five years' time.'

Later still, after sitting our O level exams, all ninety boys in my year assembled in the school lecture theatre. It was customary for former RAF Officer, John Oakes, who ran the Combined Cadet Force and taught biology at the school, to give his communal pep talk immediately before the summer vacation. As ever, he cut an inspirational figure, admired by many but feared by others. Standing before us, he uttered words that stuck in my mind even if the ambition they inspired remained unspoken for many years to come: 'Sitting in front of me today are future captains of industry, senior officers in the armed forces and Members of Parliament.'

If I have one criticism of the teaching I received at school, it is this: everything was geared to the exam curriculum and this instilled in me an overly utilitarian spirit towards education and learning. As a result, poetry and fiction, for example, are largely strangers to me. I have absolutely no ear for verse and whilst I became an avid book reader, especially in adulthood, it has been almost exclusively to sate a hunger for history, biography and factual content.

One of the quirks of timetabling meant that in order to study

German, I had to give up history and geography from the age of thirteen. Mercifully, this did nothing to impair my interest in constitutional issues. Perhaps even the opposite. Appreciating and interpreting the ties that have historically bound our nation and, more importantly for a Conservative, realising that these are in flux played a key part in my political development. Whilst few pulses are set racing by speculation over constitutional settlements outside the world of politics and public policy, they have always been central to my thinking. Rather absurdly, discussion on the floor of the House of Commons about the monarchy has always been ruled out of order. Surely this, like so much else, will have to change.

• • •

It is perhaps still too early to judge, but the drawing to a close of Queen Elizabeth II's long reign will, I believe, herald a colossal shift in attitudes in the fundamentally conservative country over which she reigned for seven decades. Elements of modernisation were already evident in King Charles III's coronation service. Nowhere will this impact more than upon the Commonwealth.

Before long, I reckon that Australia, New Zealand and Canada, notwithstanding substantial pro-monarchist movements, will conclude that they had only persisted with the head of state being located in a foreign country out of lasting personal respect for the Queen herself. These three substantial internationally minded nations (two of which are in the G20) will in time 'regularise' their constitutional arrangements; it is highly unlikely that these three dominions will persist with a constitutional settlement whereby their head of state resides in London.

I also suspect that India will soon cut formal ties with the

Commonwealth. It is evident that Prime Minister Narendra Modi regards the organisation as little more than a colonial throwback and has reluctantly retained membership out of a genuine high personal regard for the Queen. India's departure may herald a flood of other Asian nations, such as Sri Lanka, Malaysia and Singapore, to do likewise.

Here in the UK, we have witnessed from the Brexit vote that age and educational attainment, rather than traditional class distinctions, have become the clear dividing line in UK politics. As I have already observed, it seems to me that most Britons under the age of forty are entirely comfortable with the prospect of living in a country that is a middle-sized European nation. The overwhelming majority of this upcoming cohort will actively support a constitutional modernisation that will leave the UK shorn of its historic sense of exceptionalism on the international stage. I suspect this will also lead to a slew of radical political changes and progressive policymaking in a state best known for its passion for tradition and incremental adaptation. This questioning of the UK's delusions of historic uniqueness will come as a great shock to many of my generation.

My maiden speech in Parliament back in 2001 focused on constitutional issues even closer to hand – namely the future shape of the UK. My time in Edinburgh shaped my earliest recollections of Scotland. My father was posted there and between the ages of two and four, we lived on the outskirts of the city; tiny fragments of disjointed memory survive, but in an era when few military homes had central heating, I recall most vividly two freezing cold Scottish winters!

Few realise that the relationship between England and Scotland has never been one of equals. The respective imbalance between the two nations' populations and wealth has been a running sore in relations since the Act of Union in 1707. Moreover, the absence of a unified and common system of law, established church or educational system runs counter to the generally understood definition of a unitary state. Indeed, the treaty that brought the countries together came about as a rushed result of a calamitous financial overreach by Scotland as it sought, in modern-day Panama, to create an overseas empire of its own to match the then fledgling English colonial march.

In short, a little over 300 years ago, Scotland was forced to seek a financial bailout by England, and it was on this basis that a political union between the two was forged, 104 years *after* the two countries' monarchies had been united following Queen Elizabeth I's childless death.

Fast forward to the late 1990s, when to pacify the demands of an increasingly vocal Scottish National Party (SNP) – albeit one that until 2015 had never managed better than fourth place in a UK general election – a devolution settlement was agreed, giving Scotland the autonomy of a parliament with extensive powers, though excluding strategic economic, foreign affairs or defence autonomy.

By the turn of the century, the political map, in UK general elections at least, was dominated by the Labour Party with a handful of SNP and Liberal Democrat MPs making up the numbers. This all changed with the Scottish independence referendum in 2014. Although the outcome was 55 per cent to 45 per cent in favour of the status quo, the vigorous campaign by the SNP brought thousands of enthusiastic new activists into their ranks. It also exposed the moribund state of Labour's organisation in a part of the UK it had taken for granted for decades. That pendulum has recently begun to swing back quite sharply. Despite its ongoing internal dramas, the SNP still has the potential for a widely spread appeal, sweeping up the votes not only of nationalists but also the sizeable number of perennially disaffected Scots who see the SNP alone as sticking up for Scotland against Westminster rule. Today, many confidently assume that the debate about Scottish independence is closed for a generation or longer, but I suspect it will return with a vengeance the moment the UK Labour government becomes electorally unpopular.

Ultimately, Scotland remains an evenly divided nation on the issue of independence. Opinion polls ebb and flow but rarely show a decisive trend, save that younger voters are more inclined to see Scotland go its own way, with few minds seeming to change much on this issue as they get older. In the medium term, time will probably be on Scottish nationalism's side, regardless of the fortunes of the SNP.

But what of the economic consequences of Scottish independence? In 2014, the picture was more straightforward. By leaving the UK and remaining in the European Union in a single leap, trade and border control would have been unaffected. Since Brexit, this easy option has lapsed. Scotland now has to choose – echoes of the furious and fruitless Westminster debates we all became used to between 2016 and 2019. The choice is between a customs union with the rest of the UK (which accounts for almost two-thirds of its imports and exports) or taking up single market membership with the EU, where only a fifth of its exports currently end up.

More fundamentally, striking right to the heart of the sovereignty issue, would an independent Scotland align itself to the pound, create a Scottish currency or seek to join the Euro? As we have seen from the UK's painful post-Brexit manoeuvrings, goodwill would likely be in short supply and a hard border with England would be inescapable, adding potentially unsustainable costs to Scottish exports in their largest captive market. Using the pound would tie Scotland to UK policy with no say in the matter, a move entirely at odds with national sovereignty. Interest rates would be higher if Scotland were to borrow in the international capital markets without the backstop of a central bank servicing the fifth-largest global economy.

And borrow it most certainly would need to. The pre-pandemic budget deficit in Scotland was 8.6 per cent, which has been historically masked by fiscal transfers from the rest of the UK. Public spending per head in Scotland is 30 per cent higher than in England, whose taxes fund the disparity courtesy of the Barnett formula. This was created as a temporary measure in the late 1970s but no UK government since has had the courage to reverse it. Independence would also crystallise Scottish responsibility for its share of the fast-rising UK national debt, which would almost certainly be ever more expensive to service if Scotland were to go it alone and issue its own currency.

Surely these political economic pitfalls will help persuade the Scottish people that independence is not such a good idea after all? Well, the outcome of the Brexit referendum is a clear indication that detailed arguments about economics fare badly against the emotional pull of identity politics. Nothing in the interim suggests that such instincts are being tamed – indeed, the spirit of the age surely points in the opposite direction.

The nationalist grievances pile up, and this is increasingly now matched by English resentment at the Scots' financial featherbedding within the UK. Nowhere is this more evident than amongst the so-called Red Wall seats, who watch with dismay as 'our money' is spent north of the border rather than being devoted to urgent 'levelling up' projects closer to home. Remember, these are the voters whose allegiances are being most fiercely fought over by the UK's two main political parties.

The only recent example of a successful breakaway is the 'Velvet Divorce' of Slovakia from the Czech Republic in 1992, unravelling the artificial central European state that had been created at Versailles after the First World War. In the short term, Slovakia, as the junior partner, struggled with a 10 per cent contraction in its economy between 1992 and 1994 as household savings from its citizens migrated to the stronger Czech financial institutions. The value of the Slovak currency also depreciated by almost one tenth and has remained the weaker of the two. After a bumpy start, both countries prospered but only by tying their futures together. To protect internal trade, they formed an immediate customs union with a common external tariff, maintaining this by becoming members of the European Union together in 2004.

However, the separation owed its success in no small part to good fortune. There was strong global economic growth in the 1990s and clear political will between the two independent nations to stand together even as they pulled apart. If this history lesson were to be followed, Scotland's best chance of making an economic success of independence is to take the path of tying itself more closely to the rest of the UK, rather than the EU.

The price of national sovereignty in this interconnected world may prove illusory for the Scots – a weaker currency, higher taxes and ongoing dependence upon its much larger neighbour. But do not bet against this happening – after all, isn't this exactly how Brexit is playing out? Changes in technology, culture and economics have brought with them an almost overwhelming emotional pull that political decision-making must be brought closer to home. At any cost. And virtually regardless of that cost.

• • •

The even more highly charged 'Irish question' has never been far from the headlines during my lifetime, although regrettably the grand total of my time there comprises a week's holiday on the west Irish coast two decades ago and a parliamentary day trip to Belfast to oversee security arrangements. History, and its partisan interpretation, is inevitably at the heart of the debate, but patient understanding and impartial perspective has been in short and diminishing supply from most in the UK Parliament. This makes for a dangerous road ahead.

The Act of Union of 1801 between Great Britain and Ireland came about as an essentially defensive move by the British establishment following the uprising and independence secured by the colonialists across the Atlantic a couple of decades earlier. As such, this union also was never really one of equals and throughout the nineteenth century, there was unrest over the constitutional settlement.

Religion lay at the heart of this conflict. Irish landowners were invariably Protestant and often absentee landlords; their impoverished, overcrowded tenants were Catholic. Ireland is the only European country whose population today is smaller than it was in 1840, and it was during that tragic decade that potato crop failure, famine and a mixture of incompetence and indifference from the UK government (then wedded to protectionism on agricultural produce) resulted in widespread starvation or desperate migration to the US.

In 1867 and again in 1885, electoral reform in the UK vastly expanded the franchise. Consequently, Ireland's importance to the outcome of a succession of close-run UK general elections in the 1880s and 1890s increased. The centre-left Liberals under Gladstone offered Irish Home Rule, designed to enable Ireland to have parliamentary autonomy within the UK, in return for this crucial electoral support. By the eve of the First World War, Ireland stood on the brink of civil war as the practical implications of Home Rule galvanised paramilitary participants on both sides of the loyalist and nationalist divide. The Easter Rising of 1916 in Dublin and its brutal suppression by the British authorities irreversibly polarised the debate about the nature of Ireland's future relationship with the rest of the UK.

Once the First World War had come to an end, the majority of the Irish political class demanded not simply devolution but fully fledged independence. Eventually, in May 1921, a partition was agreed. Northern Ireland was carved from six of the historic nine counties of Ulster in such a way as to ensure a comfortable Protestant majority. The south, meanwhile, was plunged into a civil war during 1922–23, the outcome of which was defeat of the faction led by Michael Collins, which had negotiated a compromise of dominion status within the British Empire (similar to that obtained by Australia and Canada). Instead, the path taken was one of an independent republic led by another surviving alumnus of the Easter uprising, Éamon de Valera.

During the four decades immediately after independence had been achieved, violence was more sporadic as the two Irish states became constitutionally established and diversified. Many of the (12 per cent) minority Protestant population in the Republic of Ireland left for the UK, whilst others from the one quarter Catholic population in Northern Ireland relocated to the Republic. Those who

stayed often found their employment, housing and education opportunities restricted as a bunker mentality took hold in Northern
Ireland, whose Parliament reflected the majority Protestant vote.
The unsustainability of these arrangements became apparent in
the late 1960s as the US civil rights movement received global publicity. Violence erupted on the streets of Belfast and Londonderry;
the British Army was brought in to restore order and protect the
Catholic minority and the Northern Ireland Parliament was, for the
first of many occasions, suspended and direct rule from Westminster imposed. These were the Troubles, in which over 3,500 people
were killed. Half were civilians and one third were members of the
British security forces.

Paradoxically, it was at the height of this carnage that in 1973, the
UK and the Republic of Ireland simultaneously became part of the
second wave of countries to join the EEC. This reflected the strong
economic and trading connections between the two countries, which
would have been adversely impacted by the imposition of tariffs. A
series of political initiatives in the 1980s and beyond, aimed at providing a lasting, sustainable peace on the island of Ireland, culminated in
the Good Friday Agreement, which, for the first time, established acceptance by all parties that the future constitutional status of Northern Ireland would be subject to change only if agreed in a referendum
held amongst residents of the province. This commitment to peaceful co-existence enabled the 'hard' (i.e. supervised by the military)
border to be lifted and free movement of people, goods and trade
within the entire landmass to become commonplace.

This fragile framework has been seriously threatened by the implications of Brexit. Some of us foresaw this before the referendum
and watched with dismay as the leading unionist party in Northern
Ireland, the Democratic Unionist Party (DUP), supported the UK

leaving the European Union. I always assumed that the DUP's per-verse reasoning came about as a consequence of fervent nationalist and Sinn Féin support for Remain on the 'if they say white, I must support black' principle. The DUP then doubled down on this by re-peatedly voting against the proposed exit treaty in 2018 and 2019. In order to break the political impasse at Westminster, Boris Johnson's incoming government in late 2019 agreed to the Northern Ireland Protocol, which kept the province within the EU's customs union.

On the plus side, this has eventually ensured that there is no need to reinstate a hard border between the Republic and Northern Ire-land. However, its effect has been to drive a massive economic and constitutional wedge between Northern Ireland and the rest of the UK. The resulting disruption and delays in movement of goods be-tween Northern Ireland and the rest of the UK was financially ruin-ous to many businesses. The Windsor Framework adaptation to the protocol has eased matters, but at the cost of integrating the Northern Irish economy ever more closely to that of the Republic. Brexit is now recognised by many, either wishing such an outcome or fearful of it, as an important step towards a reunified Ireland. A telling straw in the wind is that in every year since 2022, more citizens of Northern Ireland have applied for Irish rather than British passports.

Paradoxically, these days some of the most persistent opposition to the prospect of a united Ireland comes from those in the south who are horrified at the financial burden of taking on a Northern Ireland economy virtually entirely dependent upon government subsidy of one form or another. I suspect that salvation will likely come to a large degree from investment initiatives, underpinned by the financial backing of the UK and Irish governments, from the affluent Irish diaspora in the US.

As we all know, the seething constitutional fires that have been stoked up over many years by extremist loyalist and nationalist politicians alike may prove difficult to tame once all the people of the island are expected to coexist, and the uncertainty that continues to hang over the future of the UK has a deeply debilitating impact on both our international reputation and institutional self-confidence.

As if this cauldron of constitutional activism boiling over in the near future is not enough, reform of the House of Lords is already in train under the recently elected Labour government. Predictably, the government has initially had its sights set firmly on removal of the small remaining hereditary element, but in truth, the presence in our legislature of appointed peers and bishops is no less 'outdated and indefensible'.

Debates about the future of the House of Lords during my time in the House of Commons were always incredibly narrowly focused. Invariably, far less attention was paid to its prospective powers than to its unsustainable membership. In indicative votes held back in 2003, I was the only Tory MP then to support a unicameral system; more recently, several dozen Conservatives have indicated they would prefer abolition to tinkering with the composition of a largely unelected second chamber. Evidently, change is afoot, but ideally all these constitutional issues should be considered together – perhaps having the House of Lords as a Senate of the Regions or perhaps as the Parliament of the UK alongside English, Welsh, Scottish and Northern Irish Parliaments with identical powers.

Supporters of the status quo swoon that the sheer number of amendments to legislation made in the House of Lords is irrefutable evidence of its capacity to provide effective scrutiny and an independent outlook. The truth, as so often in the world of politics, is a little less romantic. As bills make their way through the parliamentary process, a charade is all too often played out; government whips are unwilling to lose face – or votes – in the House of Commons, so they collude to ensure that a huge number of acceptable, sensible changes are only allowed to go through 'in the other place'. Small wonder that nowadays lobbyists, who are invariably responsible for drafting amending clauses, barely waste their time with elected representatives. Instead, the bulk of their influencing efforts are concentrated on biddable members of the House of Lords, safe in the knowledge that the register of interests there is also far less revealing or rigorous. The extra-curricular activities and outside earnings of our unelected legislators is set to be the subject of the next big financial scandal in UK politics.

So when eventual wholesale reform of the House of Lords comes, we shall look back in disbelief that we tolerated for so long such a constitutional and democratic outrage. Hereditary landed gentry, patronage and cronyism lie at the heart of the system of UK governance that we laughably and misguidedly pride ourselves as being universally admired across the globe.

• • •

My childhood was spent under the threat of imminent nuclear war. Countless TV documentaries and radio programmes of the time explored what political miscalculation leading to catastrophe would look like. From the time of the first Aldermaston Marches in the late 1950s, the Campaign for Nuclear Disarmament enjoyed a stranglehold on public debate that never reflected its level of support with the public at large. As children, many of my generation were genuinely fearful that their lives would be curtailed by a nuclear attack. Only with the collapse of Soviet communism at the end of the 1980s did this anxiety begin to wane.

It was surely no coincidence that the decline in that brand of 'the end of the world is nigh' political activism heralded the birth of environmentalism as a mass movement. It was largely the self-same campaigners whose allegiances were transferred from one form of judgemental, prescriptive and censorious preaching to another. In the mid-1970s, expert opinion had been almost united in warning of an impending ice age. Within a decade or so, it was global warming that was all the rage before the well-funded academic community settled on catastrophising that the catch-all 'climate change' was going to be responsible for the imminent destruction of the planet. Now, of course, we are in the midst of an apocalyptic 'climate emergency'.

None of the conventional wisdom or political narrative on this subject takes account of historical fluctuations in global temperatures. There have been centuries-long periods, well before fossil fuel industrialisation, when recorded temperatures in the oceans and on land were higher than today. That is not to deny that we are living through a period when something substantial is happening to our planet's climate and in all likelihood this has, at least in part, been brought about by human behaviour. Greater rainfall in many parts of the world during this century has brought flooding in some areas, but it has also ensured that global crop yields are at an all-time high.

Nevertheless, we should support a wider range of views on climate change policy and promote the efficacy of adaptation as well as mitigation measures. Back in 1989, the head of the UN's Environment Programme claimed that we had 'three years to win or lose the climate struggle'. At about the same time, the UN was predicting planetary devastation 'as irreversible as any nuclear holocaust' by the year 2000. Habitually, political leaders and climate activists have told the population that we are in the last-chance saloon with no more than 'three or five years' to avoid catastrophe. Then, when we reach that point, the clock is stopped and a new countdown to global doom begins.

Like snake-oil salesmen, many politicians in the west seek and gain plaudits by making superficially visionary pledges about renewables, net zero and the like. Nearly all target dates are well beyond normal political cycles and those making these promises know they will not be in the public arena when the reckoning comes. There certainly seems to be minimal evidence, in most cases, of any immediate urgency in making the tough changes to lifestyle that will be required. This leaves the millions who genuinely worry about the planet that we will pass on to future generations without guidance or leadership when it comes to those tangible changes in everyday habits and behaviour that will make this all achievable.

The rest of a bewildered general public are entitled to be a little sceptical about some of the more outlandish claims that have been persistently made over the years. It was that healthy sense of scepticism that I have always reckoned to be the single most important quality of my typically British school education.

CHAPTER 2

A WELCOME LETTER

19 DECEMBER 1983

It is often said that you can reliably tell within ten minutes of meeting an Oxbridge graduate where they have attended university.

This has little to do with evidence of incisive intellectual brilliance or even their possessing a general air of effortless superiority. No, the truth is that it normally only takes about this long for them to crowbar into conversation – any conversation – the fact that they have, often in the dim and distant past, studied at one or other of England's two ancient universities.

As ever, I should like to think of myself as an exception to this rule; my close friends assure me that it usually takes at least a quarter of an hour of animated discussion before the tell-tale phrase 'when I was at Oxford' passes my lips.

My dreams of becoming an irritatingly conceited Oxford alumnus had begun in my early teens with that headmasterly encouragement; they came to fruition on the Monday before Christmas 1983. At the time, admission to Oxford and Cambridge relied less on A level scores and more on performance in their own bespoke examinations. This often involved continued study for the best part of a term after A levels (the so-called 'seventh-term entry') culminating in the sitting of three or four papers in late November. If all went to plan, you would expect to be invited to your chosen college for the dreaded entrance interview within a further two or three weeks.

That at least is how autumn 1983 played out for me. Any post-A level results euphoria was short lived. In truth, it turned out to be a rather unsettling and lonely time. Almost all of my school contemporaries had headed off to university and were reporting back with great enthusiasm about their newfound first-term freedoms. Needless to say, these breathless accounts only served to compound my doubts and increase the sense of isolation I was enduring whilst still living at home, attending lessons at school for only one morning a week to brush up on my economics and achingly fearful that I would have wasted a year if I failed to get into Oxford.

Although the Oxbridge papers I was studying were the classic route for prospective philosophy, politics and economics students, I had decided instead to apply for law (or, strictly speaking, the Honour School of Jurisprudence), which at the time was statistically the toughest of all subjects to get into at Oxford.

Never one for making life easy for the sake of it, I guess there were three reasons I chose this path. First, out of respect to my parents, who felt law was a 'proper' subject leading to a professional qualification, which they believed was the only real purpose for attending university at all. Second, my own view that it was one of the most prestigious degree courses that would likely set me up well for life beyond. Finally, and with rather more mercenary intent, I remembered well the words of Bob Brough, my economics master at school, who reflected on the career choices of his own undergraduate contemporaries and concluded that the most financially comfortable were those who had ended up as solicitors.

The exams came and went in a blur, and a few weeks later, I travelled by coach the twenty-five miles between Reading and Oxford with an almost ambivalent fatalism about my prospects. Arriving, as instructed, late in the morning at the porter's lodge of my first-choice college, St Edmund Hall, I scrolled down the long list of law interviewees. Butterflies were rising in my stomach as I finally located my name almost at the bottom of the typed page. My interview was not until late the following afternoon, which meant a lot of hanging around, nervously chatting with other candidates. We all tried to make sense of the interview order – it was not alphabetical and there seemed no other rhyme nor reason to it. Only much later I was to discover that being late on the list was in fact a positive sign. The earliest interviews went to the most borderline candidates so that those who remained touch and go could be passed on to other colleges. Those being interviewed last were typically those nearly certain to be offered a place.

I must confess that I also avidly picked up as much information as possible about likely lines of questioning after listening to snippets of conversation from those who had already gone through their ordeal. There seemed to be a fairly standard set of four or five scenarios, on which candidates were expected to unleash their legal potential. By the time my turn came, I reckoned on being able to talk a good game whatever the line of interrogation. Even so, there was only so much eavesdropping that I could bear, so in an attempt to clear my head, I headed out of this nervy and claustrophobic atmosphere and went for a couple of long walks around Oxford's famous parks and meadows.

This decision, of course, turned out to be a major mistake. Within a few hours, the casual indifference with which I had arrived at the interview had been replaced by an absolute, passionate yearning to live and study in the city of dreaming spires. The architecture, the ambience of the place, the beautiful open spaces (greatly inferior to Cambridge, but it would naturally take me at least a couple of decades to openly admit that). How could the admissions tutors be so wantonly cruel as to offer a sampler of this life to so many interviewees and then so brutally snatch it away?

Finally, my time came. The defensiveness of more than a few of my answers was reminiscent of playing a game of Russian roulette with an automatic weapon – one false move and I ran the risk of being totally wiped out. But all things considered, the 25-minute grilling went well enough. I returned home to Reading and then the waiting game began.

Ten days passed. Still no news and not a waking hour had gone by without replaying in my mind some aspect of the interview ordeal. Then on the morning of 19 December, the letter from Oxford finally arrived. Grasping it in my hand, for a split second my reaction was one of indignation and disbelief. The franked envelope was second class... dated no less than four days previously. My instinctive support, even back then, for penny-pinching on the part of public sector institutions was momentarily forgotten – for heaven's sake, I had been living through hell waiting to find out my fate.

My parents hovered over me expectantly as I opened the precious cargo with all the careful precision of a bomb-disposal officer. My eyes alighted on the first line: 'I am very glad to be able to tell you...'

It may have been down to some midwinter bout of hay fever, but I could swear that there was a tear even in my father's eye as the news sunk in. Here I was, first in my family – well, strictly speaking, first in my *English* family – to win a place at university. As my dear brother has ever since pointed out, he was in fact the first in this branch of the Field clan to *attend* university (he started his degree course, no gap year needed or taken, at the University of Bradford the following October, with his first term starting a few days before mine).

The remainder of the academic year was not spent, as might be the case today, on some extensive international backpacking tour. I have always been immune to slumming it, excessively cheap travel or being more than a single night away from access to a warm bath. The mere prospect of a camping holiday ranks lower than unanaesthetised root canal surgery in my book. Instead, for the next seven months, I took a clerical job with what was then one of the largest international computer companies, IBM. I was based in its West End office on London's Wigmore Street, just behind Selfridges.

I should like to report that this extended work placement turned me into a technology expert, but sadly my role was entirely administrative. But it was enjoyable and broadened the mind, especially as our little department, Delivery Systems Centre, was manned mainly by business degree students on secondment. By the end of my time there, I had learned how to use a stencil machine without getting ink everywhere (photocopiers were not universal at the time even at IBM), acquired a lifelong aversion to commuting any substantial distance to work and developed a lasting taste for real ale. I had also squirrelled away enough savings to ensure that from that day to this, I have never needed to go overdrawn. This admirable Germanic distaste towards debt was, or at least was always supposed to be, a cornerstone of Conservative belief.

• • •

Political thinking began to play a more important part in my life.

My first vote had come at the age of eighteen at the general election of 1983, which fell in the middle of my A level examinations. Even before the Falklands War, which made the outcome of that election a formality, I had become a firm and fervent admirer of Margaret Thatcher's determination and resolution. Her avowed support for sustainable wealth creation, the lowest reasonable level of taxation and aversion to inflation or passing on debt to future generations chimed with my own instincts. So too her abiding passion for the promotion of freedom and individual responsibility. Just how those inclinations and feelings developed remains something of a mystery, but I reckon I was a Conservative before I knew the Conservative Party existed.

I also began to think more deeply about the lifetime experiences of my relatives, my German forefathers in particular. In my heart, I have always believed that politics is too important to simply be left to someone else. The root causes of political extremism in 1930s Germany are a complicated matter. This is still the subject of fierce debate in academic circles. However, amidst the economic upheaval that came with hyperinflation and the never-ending succession of short-lived governments and dramatic political disruption that scarred the Weimar Republic, moderate, middle-class professionals – people like my grandparents – had avoided active involvement in the entire political process. To their dying day, my maternal grandparents deeply regretted this collective renouncing of what they came to regard as their civic duty.

So it was that I arrived at Oxford with a clear plan to involve myself in student politics and a range of other extracurricular activities. I am afraid that my studies never really stood much of a chance. In fairness, an overwhelmingly strong commitment to academic study is a rarer phenomenon amongst Oxford undergraduates than many might imagine. I had worked relentlessly over many years to secure my place there but was equally determined to spend the eight-week terms making the most of everything else on offer. This meant that most of the university vacation turned into a mad scramble to catch up on coursework that I had skated over in the preceding term, as well as preparing cases or written assignments in advance for the academic term that lay ahead. But university life was surely about so much more than essay writing, lectures and tutorials?

That was not quite how my tutors regarded things. Although I did not always see it that way at the time, I was fortunate to have the guidance of two highly gifted academics who were more tolerant of my lax approach to study than I deserved. Both were young – in their early to mid-thirties – and left-leaning politically. Derrick Wyatt was an expert in European Economic Community law (as it then was) and public international law; he guided me painlessly through finals in both of his specialisms. The only time he came close to displaying any irritation with me was when he had a quiet word in the front quad as my penultimate term, packed with the usual high-profile, non-academic activity, was drawing to a close. 'Come on, Mark! You are one of life's winners; don't end up with a third [class degree] for heaven's sake!'. For the record, and the avoidance of doubt, I didn't.

Adrian Briggs was inclined to give me a lot more grief, but I should like to think it was because he had seen glimpses of my academic potential, which clearly were not being fulfilled. He realised I was keeping myself busy with other activities rather than frittering my time away entirely (although knowing him, he would put special emphasis on the word 'entirely'). When first elected to Parliament, one of the earliest letters I received came in a tell-tale St Edmund Hall envelope. It contained only an unsigned note in familiar handwriting: 'I suppose all that hacking has finally come to fruition.' A few years later, when I was in some political difficulties, I received a supportive email from him unexpectedly, which cheered me up immensely. Later still, just as I was leaving Parliament, he took the trouble to contact me from Myanmar – he is the global authority in the study of Myanmar's law – to reassure me how highly regarded I was by our high commission there.

I loved my three years at Oxford. It was the first time I had lived away from home, so for me it represented a sense of freedom that many who had been through boarding school had already experienced. With few real responsibilities, the happiness and joy of making new discoveries and friendships was never far away. Despite this rose-tinted view of my charmed and privileged life there, this never extends to false memories of endless sunshine. The weather in the Thames Valley can get bitterly cold in winter and it was relentlessly so during the mid-1980s. Early summers were always beset by showery weather – and term was over by late June. Whenever I think of my carefree days at Oxford, it is forever autumn. Walking back down St Giles', past Martyrs' Memorial, in the early hours of the morning amidst the crunch of brown leaves or wandering through Christ Church Meadow, sometimes alone, more often in company, and putting the world to rights.

I played plenty of college football and cricket, had a very active social life and, at the end of my second and third terms, was elected to senior office in the Oxford University Conservative Association (OUCA). It was there that I first came across the person who would become my closest friend and trusted adviser. Matthew Davidge has now lived in the US for the past thirty years, so we get to see each other only intermittently. But the wonders of modern digital communication mean we never feel that far apart. He was in the

academic year above me at another college and had been seriously active in Conservative student politics before my arrival. We
became political allies, then the very firmest of friends. Put simply,
over almost four decades and counting, he is the most reliable and
wholehearted confidant, whom I would trust with my life.

Somewhat less conventional has been the career path – or rather,
paths – he has taken: two spells in management consultancy, four
years trying in vain to scale a start-up, almost six years in Hollywood as a wannabe screen and script writer and now based in
Manhattan as a serial entrepreneur in healthcare and local TV and
radio. But for him there is a perennial sense of unfulfilled ambition.
In the same way as both G. K. Chesterton and Evelyn Waugh described Catholicism as a 'twitch upon the thread', so has the intense
longing for engagement in politics been to Matthew. Our friendship has provided him with a ready-made outlet for that youthful
passion. He up-ends his busy New York diary in order to return to
London in advance of every general election to eat and breathe the
campaign. Even in my political retirement, I suspect this tradition
is set to continue.

Back in Oxford, there was one election where Matthew was on
hand to mastermind my campaign and produce my manifesto.
Even after all these years, it is still the political contest where the
outcome has provided me with most pride and satisfaction.

Each Oxbridge college has its own undergraduate student union,
known as the Junior Common Room (JCR). Some are a hotbed of
partisan politics; others are more social and pastoral in what they
do for the student body. When I was there, St Edmund Hall (Teddy
Hall as it is more affectionately and colloquially known) definitely
fell into the latter category. The college still has a strong sporting
reputation, but during my time it was regarded as *the* pre-eminent

Oxford sporting college, especially for rugby. When I went up to Oxford, five years had passed since the hall had first started taking female students, so the highly vocal rugby club had an influence on college affairs that far outweighed its relatively limited numbers. One aspect of that influence was the tacit understanding that the presidency of the JCR would continue to be passed down from year to year to one of its number.

There was also some unease that party politics had begun to play a part in JCR affairs. In fairness, beyond the rarefied world of St Edmund Hall the nation was going through some turbulent upheaval. The year-long miners' strike had polarised opinion as nightly scenes of violence were broadcast into living rooms across the country. A motion put before the JCR to send money normally earmarked for sporting clubs to striking miners was fiercely debated and only narrowly defeated.

So, it was in an attempt to both counter the boorish influence of the rugby club and the perceived slide towards politicisation of the student body that early in my second year, I was approached by several undergraduates to be their standard bearer for what was shaping up to be a fiercely contested JCR presidency election in December. Everyone knew my politics. Perhaps in that more innocent age being a Tory was regarded by some as being above – or maybe beneath – party politics.

Naturally, I didn't need much persuading, but my dedicated team of supporters agreed that the element of surprise was key. So, the plan was to declare formally only at the close of nominations, a week ahead of the vote. We had quickly identified that the most important electoral group to cultivate were the freshers who had only been at the hall since October. Living in college, they were also the most likely to vote, but as all the candidates were second year students living out, we were likely to be something of an unknown quantity to this large section of the electorate.

It was a stroke of luck that the annual college room ballot to determine accommodation for the following academic year was to take place five days before the close of nominations. This provided a ready-made excuse to introduce myself to all these unsuspecting voters. I spent those next few days systematically visiting one fresher's room after another, all on the pretext of checking out student accommodation. This gave me a priceless opportunity to engage in a series of friendly five-minute chats with these vital voters. Naturally, not a word about the forthcoming election was spoken – this was definitely the undergraduate equivalent of kissing babies. By the end of the week, I was probably the only candidate most of the first years had ever met.

The landslide victory duly followed. Then, an intense but enjoyable year in office that probably did more than anything to confirm my parliamentary aspirations. Most student politics is about the process of getting nominated and fighting elections, often on a termly basis. That is why it has such a terrible reputation amongst 'normal' students. By contrast, the role of JCR president involves – even more so nowadays – a year-long practical commitment to pastoral care, representation and working together with college authorities.

The law students at Teddy Hall were a close-knit bunch. I suspect our cliquiness owed something to the notoriously heavy workload of our course. Law students the world over moan incessantly about how hard they are expected to work, but on reflection, I reckon it was not a patch on what medical and most other science undergraduates had to go through with their relentless schedule of practicals. Many of my oldest friends from the hall were my fellow law students. Tim Fallowfield and Alison McCormick ended up getting married and having distinguished careers as company secretary at Sainsbury's and a coroner respectively. Richard Fleetwood was a corporate partner for twenty years with a leading national law firm before his entrepreneurial instincts won through. I still also regularly cross paths with Stephen Ferguson, a barrister whose high-profile international clients often make the news, whilst Alison Cooke, my girlfriend at the time and beyond, is a private client partner in Hertfordshire.

The college library was located in a charmingly deconsecrated church that stands adjacent to the seventeenth- and eighteenth-century front quad. One far-flung corner contained endless shelves of law reports and was always monopolised by law students studiously poring over their books.

It was on one of my infrequent visits there shortly after becoming JCR president that I first caught sight of a new face – a smartly dressed, slightly ruddy-faced guy with neatly combed hair. We made our introductions and started up conversation without either of us having the slightest inkling that almost exactly thirty years later, the two of us would end up as MPs for neighbouring parliamentary constituencies. He was a Bachelor of Civil Law student. This was the tough-as-nails postgraduate course that was open only to top Oxbridge and starred first-class law graduates from other universities. I remember that he told me a little about his background – he hailed from Reigate and then the University of Leeds – and he evidently knew that I was the JCR president and something about my politics. He confessed that he was a Labour Party supporter: 'Mind you, with a name like mine, I couldn't be much else.'

Such was my first encounter with Keir Starmer. To be honest, we had relatively little to do with each other from then on, but he did become involved in JCR politics. In fairness, I should point out that the level of apathy at Teddy Hall was such that in the eyes of many students, simply turning up to the thrice termly general meetings would give rise to suspicions of near fanatical political activity.

I recall a couple of issues where he made calm and reasoned interventions. On the first, that the JCR disaffiliate from the Oxford University Student Union, we disagreed (in the end, the proposal was narrowly defeated in a referendum). But on the other, a motion by some of the sporting clubs to divert consolidated funds money in their direction and away from local charitable causes to which the student body made modest contributions, we were in blissful agreement and firmly opposed. Our cross-party coalition, such as it was, won the day.

Unlike many involved in left-wing politics at Oxford, Starmer was always smartly and conventionally dressed; he invariably spoke with a quiet, uncharismatic determination rather than the flamboyant rabble-rousing more usually associated with student politicians. Then, as now, his political outlook was difficult to categorise. Whilst there has always been a suspicion that his instincts are more radically left wing than he lets on, his style and demeanour from that day to this have been unthreatening and low key.

Many years later, even though we represented adjacent constituencies, most of the collaborative work over cross-border issues, such as the activities of the Covent Garden Community Association or developments at University College Hospital, was handled by our private offices. I always found Keir to be dutiful and diligent on local matters – and no one reaches the high legal office of Director of Public Prosecutions without a steely sense of purpose and a keen understanding of the workings, failings and limitations of the Whitehall and Westminster systems.

Above all, in an era when performative politics and attention-seeking antics have been the quickest way to develop a reputation, Keir has benefited from being widely underestimated. Even as he stood on the cusp of pulling off a remarkable victory at the July 2024 general election, many Westminster village insiders put his success primarily down to luck and 'being in the right place at the right time' when the Conservatives imploded. Yet unlike Tony Blair and David Cameron, the only other party leaders of the past forty-five years to enter Downing Street at a general election, Starmer was forced to refashion his party from the ashes of an almost existential and catastrophic defeat. The other two were able to build on solid foundations of electoral progress made by their immediate predecessor – by contrast, Starmer first had to banish into exile the previous incumbent. Even after a much more turbulent baptism during his early months in office than anyone had predicted, it would be unwise to write off Starmer and his party too soon. He still has firmly in his grasp those most precious of political gifts, time and a huge parliamentary majority; over the next four years, his supporters will be hopeful that his reputation for quiet, if unexciting, competence can be restored. Exuding utter self-belief in his mission, Sir Keir Starmer may still be the man best suited to take our nation forwards in a world where Britain finally shakes off its sense of self-regard and exceptionalism.

• • •

Meanwhile, beyond the walls and gates of St Edmund Hall, I met several other people for the first time whose lives and mine have continued to overlap. Take the two most prominent student politicians of my time at Oxford, who were both in the year above me.

A remarkable symmetry in their professional trajectories has taken place in the four decades since those undergraduate days.

One was an active Conservative student politician, winning election to the presidency of OUCA by the largest majority in decades and at the same time building a national powerbase in the Young Conservatives movement, which he chaired the year after his graduation. Yet almost from the moment he left Oxford, he has sought to play down this partisan activism. It has been airbrushed out almost entirely from his autobiography. Instead, he has pursued a high-profile and successful career in the media, which has culminated in his serving as political editor of the BBC and as one of the longest-serving presenters of its flagship Radio 4 programme, *Today*.

The other became president of the Oxford Union and adopted a distinctive persona and speaking style, which divided opinion then as strongly as it does to this day. Overt Conservative connection was regarded as the kiss of death to many an Oxford Union prospect in the mid-1980s, when the Social Democratic Party was in its heyday. Despite his father serving as a Conservative MEP, he ostentatiously – some might say opportunistically – remained above the party-political fray, bar some maverick words of support for animal rights and the environmental movement, then very much in its infancy. Strangely enough, whilst little of his subsequent career has suggested a strong sense of conviction or undying principle to any political position, the golden thread of his passion for the environment has been constant. Only in his *Daily Telegraph* columns in the early 1990s did his political affiliation become crystal clear. He and I became MPs together in 2001. He subsequently became the most influential (and that word is not necessarily synonymous with being successful or worthy) Prime Minister since Tony Blair. He is the lodestar – or dead weight, according to your tastes – around which the Conservative Party's fortunes will be forged for the foreseeable future, even in his political retirement.

I refer respectively, of course, to Nick Robinson and Boris Johnson.

My first encounter with Nick Robinson came on my second full day at Oxford. The freshers' fair introduces first year undergraduates to the vast array of student societies and activities on offer – sporting, musical, international, gastronomical… and political. Wandering through the wood-panelled, seventeenth-century rooms hosting the event, I was struck by the bustling enthusiasm surrounding the stands promoting offerings as diverse as the OU Sherlock Holmes and OU Ballroom Dancing societies. By contrast, amidst all this feverish activity, a rather forlorn stall stood empty. Perhaps the anticipated stampede of interest had already happened before my arrival? Thus began my involvement with the Oxford University Conservative Association.

To be fair, its booth was not *entirely* deserted. A senior OUCA officer was on duty, and it was this apparently friendly and articulate chap who struck up conversation in a distinctive voice that would become a familiar backdrop to me and millions of others in the decades to come.

It did not require herculean powers of persuasion for Nick to sign me up as a party member that day. From that fateful moment to this, I have discovered the sad truth in The Eagles' sage observations about the Hotel California – I can check out any time I like, but I have never been able to leave. Only my affiliation as an account holder with Lloyds Bank – another institution that by its high-handedness and wilful incompetence has periodically driven me to fury and baseless threats to withdraw my custom – has lasted longer.

In those days, state school pupils were in the minority at Oxford. Learning of my grammar school background, Nick attempted to put me at ease with the memorable claim, 'I come from near Liverpool.' Strictly speaking, this was true – in the same way as I would later gently provoke Labour MPs by referring to my Mayfair and Belgravia constituents as being 'inner-city residents'. In point of fact, Nick, despite his carefully cultivated northern vowels, had been brought up in Prestbury, which even then was a wealthy north Cheshire village, more recently made famous as the location of choice for an array of super-rich Manchester City and United footballers.

The reference to Liverpool, which in the early 1980s was a watchword for riots, poverty and far-left municipal politics, reflected Robinson's brand of one nation Conservatism. Presiding over speaker meetings addressed by Cabinet ministers of the time, he rarely missed the opportunity to rail against the heartlessness of the Thatcher government's social policies. Needless to say, this infuriated the right and their abiding nickname for him, Red Robbo, reflected not only their interpretation of his politics but was also a tribute to his namesake, Derek Robinson, the Marxist trade union agitator who had made life a misery for bosses at British Leyland's Longbridge factory for many years.

It also struck me, and a fair few others, as bad form that the leading student Tory was not only reluctant to publicly defend government policy but so clearly relished putting the boot in. As this was all happening at Oxford, Nick's interventions quickly reaped national press coverage. In due course, I worked out that this was the whole point – there is nothing like a little contrived controversy to establish a reputation and raise one's profile.

So, a little mutual wariness has hung over our relationship ever since those days. Our paths would occasionally cross after I had entered Parliament, although probably more often at Oxford political hacks' reunions than on pressing matters of state. Most recently, however, he interviewed me down the line at some unearthly early hour when I was staying at our high commission in Bangladesh. For only the third (and I strongly suspect final) time, I had secured the coveted 8.10 a.m. slot on the *Today* programme to reflect on my visit to the Rohingya refugee camps near Chittagong and meetings across the border with the then Burmese premier, Aung San Suu Kyi. Our discussion ran smoothly without technical or any other hitch, but it still sounded strange coming from that source when Nick signed off our ten-minute interview with the words, 'Thank you, minister.'

I had less to do with Boris Johnson at Oxford. Other than seeing his blond mane sweep past at Oxford Union debates, we moved in very different circles. The Gridiron and Bullingdon Clubs held no interest for me – a feeling that was, I am quite certain, entirely mutual. But he did once seek me out and as I recall, we ended up chatting away for a few minutes in the insalubrious surroundings of the workman's cafe at Gloucester Green coach station. He needed a favour. By this time, I was news editor on the student newspaper, *Cherwell*, and given my political connections, it was widely presumed that I also had a hand in writing its notorious gossip column. The union's presidential election was now only two weeks away and there was some rumour doing the rounds – the details of which I have entirely forgotten in the mists of time – that Johnson and his team felt would be very damaging if published. I assured him that it would not see the light of day and we parted on good terms. The salacious gossip never made public attention, Boris won his election by a landslide and once again (for this was his second stab at the presidency), I voted for his opponent.

Naturally, we had a little more to do with each other after we both entered Parliament. Not much more though. In our first year, we were assigned as the two new boys to sit on the standing committee of the Proceeds of Crime Bill. This meant over forty half-day sessions poring through its 462 clauses – nowadays, with the routine guillotining of legislation, it would be nothing like as onerous. With some background in money laundering legislation and an interest in civil rights, I had volunteered to serve on this committee; Johnson had evidently been press-ganged into it by the whips as a punishment of sorts, given how thinly spread his commitments as editor of *The Spectator* had left him. He also had trouble being taken seriously by MPs across the House whenever he ventured to speak. This reflected what I have always regarded as one of the more unsavoury aspects of Parliament – a desire by many of the longer-standing MPs to belittle any achievements made beyond the vanishingly narrow Palace of Westminster grounds on which they had made their name.

David Cameron's rapid rise to party leadership seemed to have blocked his path, so Johnson took the opportunity to reinvent himself as Mayor of London. Any credible Conservative candidate should have won in 2008, as New Labour was fast running out of steam and a financial crisis loomed, but Boris Johnson's re-election in 2012 was a remarkable personal achievement, as we were in government by then and London's demographic change was continuing apace. It was at around about this time that I attended a small dinner party at the Mayfair home of Stephen and Kimberly Quinn, who had become friends of ours at the school gate. Kimberly had previously served as publisher of *The Spectator* and one of the other guests was her former colleague, the journalist Matthew d'Ancona, who had succeeded Boris as editor. Inevitably, the conversation turned to politics and then, given the imminence of the mayoral contest which many expected him to lose, to Johnson's career prospects.

'I really wouldn't rule out Boris becoming Prime Minister once Cameron has gone,' I suggested. Kimberly was utterly incredulous at the prospect. She had seen his notoriously disorganised working patterns first-hand at *The Spectator*; like many in the world of politics, she also doubted whether he was competent enough to run a national government. Matthew kept his own counsel, but I remember all too well his knowing and wry smile.

So eventually the agonisingly inevitable came to pass – first, the Johnson intervention in the Brexit referendum had been absolutely key to getting Leave over the line. Then when the Tory vote was eviscerated at the European Parliament elections of 2019 in the dog days of Theresa May's premiership, the sole criteria in the minds of many ambitious young Tory ministers – the people who had most to lose by the party going back into opposition – was who was best placed to win back all those Tories who had supported the Brexit Party. The rest, as they say, is history.

Where now? Well, no one ever got rich by betting against Boris Johnson. Nevertheless, the ignominious circumstances of his departure from the premiership in September 2022 – and from Parliament altogether nine months later – have left him without a conventional political platform. Now that Nigel Farage has finally secured his own House of Commons pulpit, I suspect Johnson will find it even more difficult to position himself as the Conservative Party's only 'prince across the water' as the party seeks to find its voice again after its recent calamitous removal from office. I also suspect the hard grind of rebuilding from opposition holds little appeal for someone as self-centred as Johnson; the very idea of sacrificing a decade of hard graft rebuilding the Conservative brand with no guarantee of personally reaping the rewards has never been his style.

But as always with Alexander Boris de Pfeffel Johnson, one should never say never...

An Oxford contemporary about as far removed from Boris Johnson in temperament, seriousness of intent and personality is David Miliband, with whom I probably spent more time during my undergraduate days than I did with many Tories. Throughout 1986 we served as JCR presidents at our respective colleges. I liked David immensely. He was engaging company, had a self-deprecating humour and, even then, was clearly set on a high-profile life in public office. Those JCR presidents who wished to would meet up as a group every week to exchange ideas and notes. In the eyes of most of us, David was seen as the leader of this pack. The role was certainly becoming more professionalised as student representation was being taken more seriously by college authorities and undergraduates alike. Nowadays I am sure the year-long commitment is far more burdensome than it was even for us, and I notice that some Oxbridge colleges have made it a sabbatical role.

David also entered Parliament in 2001 and as a close confidant to Tony Blair, he was very quickly on the ministerial fast track. This probably worked against his building the broad base of parliamentary support essential to winning the Labour Party leadership. He also began to gain a reputation for being rather aloof with backbench colleagues. In time, this was to matter.

We would often quickly pass the time of day in our early years as MPs, but I best remember a conversation we had shortly after Labour had gone into opposition and he was preparing to launch his leadership campaign in June 2010. To my mind, he seemed excessively gloomy about Labour's electoral prospects and this diffidence reminded me of Michael Portillo's reluctance to give every ounce of energy to his leadership campaign nine years earlier. There were probably other similarities between the two men. Crown princes for a time within their parties, excessively cool and distant to colleagues, and reluctant, despite being well-placed whilst their party was struggling in government, to grasp the prize. Party leadership and the Prime Ministership, albeit after a bloody, brutal, and unpredictable fight, was there for the taking for Michael Portillo in 1995 – ditto David Miliband between 2008 and 2010.

What surprised me even more was that the most impressive of Labour's 2010 intake, whom I had already started coming across as we did radio and TV panels together, were all backing Ed Miliband rather than his brother. Rachel Reeves, Emma Reynolds and Chuka Umunna had all seemed to me natural David Miliband supporters. But then again what did I, as a Tory, know?

The next time we spoke at length, David was in a far happier place. It was in New York in 2018 at the UN General Assembly, which I was attending as an Foreign Office Minister. We both bemoaned the geopolitical price of Brexit and he looked mightily relieved to be well out of Labour Party politics as the Jeremy Corbyn era continued its path to its eventual *Götterdämmerung*. He was massively enjoying his role as CEO of the International Rescue Committee, and it was like turning back the clock to Oxford when he enthusiastically explained some of his ground-breaking policy initiatives.

Simon Stevens was regarded at the time by our contemporaries as the person most likely to succeed in politics. Our paths have intermittently crossed over the years. However, as is sometimes the way, I probably spent more time in his company in my first couple of terms in Oxford than I have in the entire period since. We first met through a mutual friend well before he began his run in student politics that led to the presidency of the Oxford Union.

There are two incidents that I have never forgotten. The first was bumping into Simon one freezing cold spring morning in Balliol College front quad, looking ashen faced at the news that a college friend's mother had suddenly died after a routine operation. That friend, whom I had first met the previous week, was James Brooke and sixteen years later I would succeed his father as MP for Cities of London & Westminster.

The second was unexpectedly meeting up during our first vacation in the Reading University library. Simon lived near Newbury and, like me, was taking advantage of the generosity that Reading University extended to students from other universities in allowing them to use their facilities outside term time. We had a coffee together and, being blissfully unaware of his politics (the fact that he was at Balliol should probably have been something of a clue), it became clear to him from what I was saying that I had assumed he was a Tory. Presumably, in my rather cosseted world, I had worked on the basis that anyone smartly dressed and sensible could not have much truck with the party of Michael Foot and early Neil Kinnock. 'Mark, you do know that I am a supporter and member of the Labour Party?'

At first, Stevens followed the well-trodden path as a departmental and No. 10 special adviser. Then he narrowly missed out on selection in several safe Labour seats – perhaps those hardline Labour Party activists were as confused as me by such a clean-cut, well-spoken prospective candidate. Afterwards, he spent a decade at the helm of a US healthcare provider. In 2014, he became chief executive of NHS England and now sits in the House of Lords, where the Labour government will surely make use of his expertise.

What can one write about Michael Gove that has not already been written? He was in the year below me and very quickly made his reputation as a brilliant public speaker, equally effective in serious and humorous debates and invariably attired in a kilt. Then came the classic dilemma between career and principle. By now an officer of the Oxford Union and with his sights firmly set on the presidency, a massive controversy loomed as Sinn Féin president Gerry Adams was invited to speak at the union. Remember, this was still a decade or so before the Belfast Agreement and a time when the terms IRA and Sinn Féin were regarded as virtually interchangeable. Terrorist murders on the mainland and in Ulster were being committed with heartbreaking regularity.

So, was the Adams invitation simply a matter of free speech or was it justifiable that he should be no platformed? Neither the right nor left in student politics had a consistent line here – most Tories were usually fervent supporters of free speech but vehemently opposed Adams being allowed to speak. Meanwhile, the self-same left-wing activists defending his invitation to the hilt had only weeks before disrupted and forced the abandonment of a speaker meeting where a notorious but uninfluential backbench Tory MP with robust views on immigration had been due to appear.

Essentially, Gove took the pragmatic path designed to keep as many of his potential voters as possible happy. He sided with those who had issued the disputed invitation; the meeting duly went ahead amidst rowdy protests outside, but Michael also achieved his electoral goal and won the presidency. But his actions also sowed the seeds of mistrust that all too many Conservatives continue to have for someone of such undoubted political talent.

All too often we risk reading too much into small incidents from early life, but whenever I listened to Michael Gove as a Cabinet minister defending the United Kingdom and unionism with such articulacy and vehemence, I used to think back to our university days. Perhaps some of this intensity reflected his lingering guilt at his undergraduate expedience.

Michael was a force of nature as a minister, albeit one who had a tendency to leave awkward post-dated cheques for his departmental successors. In that respect he had much in common with Kenneth Baker, another hyperactive visionary who was always happiest painting broad brush policy strokes and of whom it was said in the 1980s that the worst job in government was the one he had most recently vacated. However, I had the privilege of seeing Gove in action during the brief time when our ministerial service overlapped. He had just returned to government in 2017 in the apparent backwater of the Department for Environment, Food and Rural Affairs. I watched with wonder as he injected energy and urgency into everything he and his department did.

A former journalist, Gove typically received rave reviews for his ministerial activities from many in the fourth estate. But amongst his Tory colleagues, it was widely assumed that this relentlessly favourable treatment was at least partly earned by Gove's propensity to leak like a sieve the details of supposedly private meetings and conversations to his favoured press contacts.

So, finally, to the Oxford contemporary who went into politics that I have spent most time with since our university days. Funnily enough, although he was only in the year below me, we barely knew each other as undergraduates. It was only in the last few weeks before my finals that our paths first crossed, naturally enough at a Conservative Association event. We immediately hit it off and as I prepared to leave Oxford, a charming note arrived in my pigeonhole in the college porters' lodge. This, of course, was in a pre-digital age, so he provided me with home contact details in his trademark neat and diminutive handwriting, signed off, presciently as it turned out, with the message, 'See you in Westminster!'

Jeremy Hunt and I both yearned to put some of that Thatcherite theory into practice by starting up businesses. After graduation, we each endured only short spells in more conventional employment before branching out on our own. At around the turn of the decade, I remember our having supper together in one of those small, family-run restaurants in an alleyway just off the Covent Garden piazza. He had already had enough of working long hours as an analyst with a global management consultancy firm and was determined to head off to Tokyo. At the time, Japan boasted the world's second-largest economy and Jerry spoke excitedly of learning the language (which he soon did) and setting up in business to export UK speciality produce to the Japanese. That venture was somewhat ahead of its time, but two years later, on returning to London, he quickly linked up with his oldest school friend, Mike Elms, and they soon began to develop the market leader in educational listings.

As well as keeping in regular touch with our political circle, Jerry and I would also get together every so often to provide each other with an invaluable sounding board as we both grappled with the day-to-day challenges of personnel management in our start-up businesses. His wise counsel spared me many a sleepless night of worry and, I suspect, countless thousands of pounds in legal fees. The tremendous success he and Mike achieved with Hotcourses came only at the end of a long and winding road, as I knew only too well.

Jerry's steady and unflappable determination in the face of adversity set him up well for what was to lie ahead in politics. Never was this sheer grit more in evidence than at the 2024 election. Like several other prominent Conservatives, he might easily have taken the expedient path of announcing his retirement from the House of Commons rather than leaving himself open to the humiliation of electoral defeat in his home town constituency. On election night, the television media could hardly contain their excitement at the prospect of the sitting – and Conservative – Chancellor of the Exchequer losing his seat, but for Jeremy Hunt this battle was personal and he alone survived of the fifty or so Liberal Democrat Tory targets that were swept away in the tsunami of defeat that night. This was a tribute to his often underestimated political appeal.

•   •   •

Involvement in student politics is an addictive and time-consuming activity. So too student journalism, where, if anything, the future career path of its active participants was more clearly set out. The more recent contraction in conventional newspaper journalism opportunities has been balanced out by the emergence of endless online publications and careers in the ever-expanding communications industry.

For my part, despite being actively engaged on the news desk on what was then the university's only weekly newspaper, *Cherwell*, for almost half my time at Oxford, I never seriously contemplated a career in journalism or the media. I didn't really get a kick out of writing for its own sake. I remain in awe of those journalists who can turn around a dozen paragraphs or more to order in double-quick time. But I was never so in love with the thought of journalism or becoming a writer that I would have willingly started out in provincial obscurity or subsume everything else in my life in pursuit of a new angle on someone else's urgent story.

I spent two terms as one of the news editors on *Cherwell*, just before the era of desktop publishing, which transformed the entire newspaper production process. When I recall what we had to go through, it seems almost antediluvian. Publication was on a Friday and that meant finalising the news stories and laying out the news pages until very late on the Wednesday evening. Normally, our ordeal would only end with the editor and a couple of us news editors staying beyond midnight, devising headlines and trying to estimate precisely the number of words of text to fit the space on mocked-up pages. Heaven knows how long it would all have taken if there hadn't been an unofficial ban on alcohol in the *Cherwell* offices. Clearly our ambitions to emulate Fleet Street's finest had some limits.

The next morning, one of us would have to make the trip to the printers in Bicester, hanging around whilst the text was set and, most vitally, being there to make last minute additions or subtractions if the previous evening's estimation efforts had been off beam.

We tended to do this by rota, so two or three times a term, I would either catch a bus to and from Bicester or else persuade a car-owning friend to give me a lift there, take them out for a pub lunch whilst the printers did their typesetting magic and then head back.

I suspect the whole shooting match is fully online nowadays, with stories being updated in real time from laptops out of student journalists' rooms. All a world away from our joyful amateurism in the mid-1980s, though it turned out to be the breeding ground for many a top-flight journalistic career. As fate would have it, I ended up remaining in contact later in life with all four of the *Cherwell* editors I worked with.

Christina Lamb has an often well-disguised resilience and

bravery that has served her well, especially in her beloved Pakistan and Afghanistan. Chris has worked on international newspapers since leaving Oxford; we would link up in Washington where she was bureau chief for the *Sunday Times* and I was the beneficiary of her invaluable insights before my ministerial visits to Afghanistan and Pakistan. Anne McElvoy was more openly ambitious in those days and over the years we have stayed in contact, more often than not in the same TV or radio studio discussing the ebb and flow of UK politics. I regard her as one of the most insightful UK political commentators and have often reread the perceptive book she wrote in her twenties, *The Saddled Cow*, about East German life and politics. Philip Sherwell has made his career as a long-serving foreign correspondent in Asia and it was an unexpected pleasure to meet up with him again professionally in 2018 when I was in Bangkok on a ministerial visit. Judith Higgin spent only a couple of years in the regional press, but we came across each other throughout most of my time as an MP when she held senior press relations and communications roles at the London School of Economics and later with the homelessness charity, St Mungo's, both based in my constituency.

•   •   •

The most far-reaching and lucrative of all my extra-curricular activity began in the unlikely surroundings of the Oxford University Careers' Service. It was early October 1986 and I was beginning to realise that the sands of time were draining away. My halcyon undergraduate days would soon be a thing of the past. Life beyond beckoned. A career. And for us law students, the path of least resistance was to become a solicitor or barrister. One more year of study and one final set of exams. You sign up for law school in your very first term at university, and so the conveyer belt turns.

Careers advice, if it can really be called that, was delightfully quaint. Just before the end of the previous summer term, Adrian Briggs had all twelve law students in my year in for an early evening sherry. For the majority of us who were contemplating training as a solicitor in London, we were reassured of the 'strong college links' with three or four firms, to which most of us duly applied and were promptly taken on.

It was almost out of curiosity one afternoon early in the following term that Richard Fleetwood, my friend and tutorial partner, and I wandered up the Banbury Road. It was shortly after the large City of London law firms had come to Oxford to snap up our cohort of articled clerks (the term trainee solicitor was only slowly coming into vogue). With offers in hand, we both wanted to discover more from the careers' service about comparative salaries, bursaries at law school and overseas offices.

The assistant sitting on reception handed us a sheaf of indifferently copied A4 papers containing only the sketchiest information about London law firms, none of which seemed to be anything less than a year or two out of date. It was Richard who then had the eureka moment – surely there must be a better way to collate and distribute this vital information? It was our good fortune that, as recently as the previous year, the Law Society had lifted its historic ban on advertising by solicitors' firms.

So, there was now a gaping hole in the market for a publication providing just the sort of information we had been lacking. It was also an oven-ready route for the two of us to show off some entrepreneurial flair. For a split second I worried about loading yet another time commitment into my already busy diary, but I knew I would have kicked myself if I had passed on such a golden opportunity.

In a flurry of activity, Richard and I designed some headed note-paper and got it printed at one of the many stationers' shops in the centre of Oxford. We then spent the early hours of every morning for the next week uploading data and addresses of 100 of London's largest law firms and their recruitment partners on one of the two Apple Macs in the college computer room. Next, we devised and typed up marketing letters, designed forms to be completed and returned, printed off labels, stuck them and stamps on smart brown envelopes… and then we waited.

To our relief and surprise, a steady trickle of responses started to arrive virtually by return of post, containing £100 deposit cheques and often more. Picking up the morning mail became the highlight of the day and the trickle turned into a small flood of lucrative re-plies. Within a couple of weeks, we had over forty firms signed up and had banked almost £10,000.

This was when the college authorities got wind that something was going on. Identical notes from our tutor appeared one morning in our pigeonholes, summoning us to a late afternoon meeting. By this stage, I had become fairly blasé about these little tutorial pep talks, but Richard had been a model student so was far more anx-ious at what might be in store.

At the appointed hour, we clambered up the narrow and worn wooden staircase to the eaves of the traditional front quad room that Adrian Briggs had made his own. He played it beautifully. He started by warning us that this sort of venture, a plausible-sounding business with an Oxford college address requesting up front depos-its, could easily be a classic financial scam. And, by the way, it was strictly in breach of college statutes and university regulations for undergraduates to run a commercial enterprise from their college rooms.

All's well that ends well, however. The powers that be decided our commercial venture was not going to embarrass the good name of the college, and as we were both final year undergraduates and therefore not long for this world, a diplomatic blind eye was turned. In his own valedictory the following year, the hugely popular and long-serving domestic bursar, Rear Admiral George Cunningham Leslie, reflected how in his twenty years at the hall the student body had turned from 'indolent young gentlemen to prototype Thatcherites'. I think he had us in mind and I certainly took it as a compliment.

Our venture turned out to be a triumph. We got our little handbook published, had it distributed to over 5,000 law students at Russell Group universities, turned over almost £25,000 and made a tidy profit of virtually half that.

This was only the beginning. The following year, Richard and I shared a flat in Chester whilst studying at law school. We set up a second publication, focusing on training opportunities outside London. Our reputation having preceded us, we had the rather blissful experience of several law firms contacting us unsolicited and plaintively requesting to be included in the new edition. We doubled the print run, our turnover quadrupled and profits rose sixfold, to the extent that we were subjected to a very friendly inspection by the local Customs and Excise who were amused at this cottage business in their midst.

In essence the business only really required active involvement for four or five months of the year and most of that work was done by correspondence. So, by the time we got to year three of the business, now in London and about to start our training contracts, Richard and I felt able to run it by earmarking a couple of weekday evenings and every Sunday in the autumn and early winter to catch up on all the administrative tasks. This arrangement just about worked, and as we were still earning multiples of our trainee solicitors' salary, we decided to put everything on a slightly more sustainable and professional footing by taking on an employee for the busy period. Keeping it in the family, this was Richard's sister, Hilary, who did a great job.

But inevitably, the best days were now behind us. Competition had emerged, as it always does when super-profits are being made. For us, this came in the form of established publishing houses who muscled in on this new-found market. Over time, our first mover advantage, client base and turnover gradually declined, but we kept going until the millennium when, after fourteen annual editions, we shut up shop. By this time, Richard had moved up to Manchester and become a partner with Addleshaw Goddard and I was on the cusp of going into politics, having established my second entrepreneurial venture.

Nothing has ever matched the thrill and excitement that came with the hopes, fears and graft associated with setting up and properly establishing that first enterprise. Recalling the dreams and frenetic activity of those early weeks and months in business never fails to hasten my heart rate, even with the passing of the decades. At a time when it is fashionable to berate and criticise voracious business practice, it is always worth remembering that behind each and every start-up are creative dreamers, for whom profits are merely an incidental aspect of their romantic vision and ideals.

• • •

All good things must come to an end, and I reckon the intense stress of sitting eight finals papers inside a week or so is probably as good a way as any to manage the transition to life beyond university. When I graduated in 1987, it was as one of around 14 per cent of my age-group cohort in the UK at the time; admittedly this was up from only 8 per cent at the beginning of the 1970s. Nowadays around four in ten young British adults enrol into the UK higher education system. This almost exponential increase in numbers has brought fundamental change to a set of institutions once universally regarded as a jewel in the crown of British educational excellence.

Almost as soon as he became Prime Minister, Rishi Sunak initiated a national debate about 'rip-off' degrees, identifying that one fifth of graduates (some 70,000 a year) would have been better off not attending university at all according to the Institute for Fiscal Studies. Sadly, the challenges facing our self-styled world-beating higher education sector are much more deep rooted than that.

In reality, despite all the persistent protestations to the contrary from vice-chancellors and education ministers alike, the quality of a British degree has been devalued and, in many cases, quite literally degraded as a result of the expansion of recent decades, which was carried out for largely ideological reasons to promote egalitarianism in UK higher education.

'Ah, yes, but look at all the international students we continue to attract,' is a familiar counterblast to any criticism about falling academic standards. This is true – for now. There is no doubt that the vast influx of students from abroad has made for a handy contribution to the UK's invisible earnings and has boosted many a university town's local economy. Over one fifth of the income received by UK universities comes from international students, with their numbers having doubled in the five years up until 2022.

More skewed towards postgraduate research disciplines, this overseas cohort pay on average almost three times the level of fees compared to the £9,250 annual fixed cap for domestic students in England. Worryingly, this has made many institutions highly (some would say, overly) dependent upon continuing to attract ever more international students for their financial well-being. It has also led to a widespread complacency that this flood of foreign students arriving on our shores will continue indefinitely.

By 2023–24, there were clear indications that this apparently endless boon to UK higher education finances was coming to a juddering halt. The numbers arriving from Nigeria, the fastest-growing cohort of recent times, has collapsed by two thirds alongside a commensurate fall in the value of its currency. The numbers of postgraduate Indian students have dried up as a result of a stricter visa regime around accompanying family members, and in the meantime, political tensions have brought to an end the seemingly inexorable year-on-year rise of Chinese students studying here.

Perhaps more worrying still, our single biggest unique selling point, namely the fact that we offer native English language courses, is fast coming to an end – fluent written and spoken English is now virtually universal amongst the up-and-coming global ruling and professional classes. This was brought home to me time and again in my travels to Asia. Whenever I met a ministerial counterpart in their fifties, we would invariably need an interpreter to translate our exchanges. This was rarely necessary with the younger generation of politicians or businessfolk in their thirties or early forties.

Once the current generation of high-paying Chinese and Indian students (who between them have typically made up over two fifths of the entire international student population in recent years) have rinsed all the benefit they can from our institutions, who would necessarily bet on their relatives or offspring coming to study here? Asian universities are rapidly stepping up the quality of their home-grown degrees and colleges, often in partnership with international providers; other European institutions are increasingly offering all their courses in English and, as protectionist geopolitical clouds darken, in future fewer overseas students may be tempted or even allowed to study abroad.

Before long, I fear the entire UK university sector faces a potentially ruinous financial crunch. We swept away the polytechnics in the early 1990s and since then have further marginalised non-graduate further education both in esteem and funding. Arguably, this has left industry so short of skills that despite producing record numbers of home-grown graduates, the UK economy these past two decades has been characterised by low-growth, stagnant productivity and static real-terms earnings. It is estimated, even at a time of virtually full employment, that well over a third of UK graduates have ended up in jobs for which they are over-qualified.

The real missed opportunity of recent times was when the controversial coalition government decision to allow universities to triple tuition fees did not open up a much more diverse and competitive higher education landscape. To all intents and purposes, the permitted maximum fee level became a market minimum. University finance departments across the land essentially banked the increase, knowing that future generations of students would sign up to the loans aware that they would never pay them back in full. Meanwhile, an array of government departments have massively underestimated the cost to the taxpayer of defaults on the student loan book.

By a sleight of hand that has spirited university funding out of conventional public expenditure, the true cost will only become evident in future years. In the end, much of this mountain of debt, already running into hundreds of billions of pounds, will be borne neither by universities nor students. The current calls for bailouts have been isolated to a small number of troubled institutions, but financial overstretch in the sector is endemic. In addition, there is clearly no political appetite to raise the levels of fees paid by domestic students, which have now been frozen for over a decade, apart from the very small increase that will come into place in 2025, despite university operating costs (not least the obscene and absurd salaries of many vice-chancellors and their ever-expanding cast of deputies) having soared with inflation. So, in all likelihood, this debt burden will fall upon the general taxpayer in the decades ahead.

As with so much else, the prolonged ultra-low interest rates in place since the 2007–08 financial crisis have also dangerously disguised our ability to manage the cumulative debt being built up. Rising rates and becalmed levels of graduate earnings have suddenly exposed the real costs of the student loan book. The original assumption in 2011 that the government would pick up 30 per cent of the tab have been revised almost every other year and are now estimated at nearly twice that original figure.

What should have happened was the creation of a dynamic marketplace at the outset, offering students two-year degrees in more practical vocational degree subjects. These courses might have been priced at a level well below what quickly became the market norm of £9,000 a year.

Time for a declaration of interest. Back in 2005, I joined the advisory board of the London School of Commerce (LSC). This was a private college with an array of international offices, offering two-year BA and MBA courses in business studies and technology at highly competitive fee levels. We had several UK university partners whose degree-awarding powers meant that, with proper verification, the LSC's courses were offered under that umbrella, and our stream of overseas students and their fees were similarly shared.

Our CEO, Tim Andradi, originally hailed from Sri Lanka and had made a highly successful career in accountancy in London before turning his hand to training and education. Over the next decade, I would help oil the wheels of those international university relationships. It also gave me a ring-side seat to many of the developments that have taken place during recent times in UK higher education. To my regret, it has not always made for the prettiest of pictures.

Grade inflation has become a perennial concern of those seeking to uphold our system of public examinations. This starts with GCSEs and A levels, where the vast increase in those being awarded top grades over recent decades has undermined one of the basic functions of the tests – namely, to differentiate between candidates for university entry. This has been more than replicated by UK universities themselves, where the proportion of first-class degrees awarded has risen from a consistent 7–8 per cent of graduating students in the first half of the 1990s to a high of 33 per cent in 2021. Given the near fivefold expansion in university numbers over this period, this means that for every student achieving a first thirty years ago, no fewer than twenty-two are doing so now.

No doubt some senior figures within the school and university teaching unions, assuming they can be prised away from the picket line, will try to persuade a credulous general public that this is down to their members producing higher-calibre students and much more capable graduates than in the past. Common sense – not to mention Organisation for Economic Co-operation and Development (OECD) international school attainment comparisons and ever more woeful employment and productivity levels amongst young British adults – suggests the reality is somewhat different.

There has been a scandalous spiral of silence, in public at least, as to what has been going on. Partly, this is down to a climate of fear amongst academics, who are all too aware that much of this has come about as a result of universities relentlessly gaming a system that successive governments have put into place. None of the incentives they work towards involve maintaining or enhancing the quality of education offered. Little thought is given to breaking away from the centuries-old tradition of three-year courses.

It is also as if the revolution afforded by technology and online learning has played little part in strategic thought about the structure of courses offered, other than as a means of keeping costs to a minimum whilst continuing to charge students as much as possible. Then there is the ubiquity of league tables and the need for institutions to rank highly in them in order to attract future generations of students, as grades awarded play an important role in employability metrics. Only by attracting more students can future funding be guaranteed. The commitment to the highest-quality teaching has also been sacrificed at the altar of ever greater pressure by government on university departments to produce and publish research.

A blind eye has been turned by every government over the past thirty years to the consequences of the rapid expansion that has taken place since the fateful decision to turn colleges and polytechnics into universities at a stroke. But this was well understood as long ago as 1960, at a time when a little over 4 per cent of Britons went to universities. It was a young Swansea University academic, Kingsley Amis, on his way to greater fame and fortune, who railed even then against 'the delusion that there are thousands of young people about, who are capable of benefiting from university training but have somehow failed to find their way there'. No one today, in an era where widening access is regarded as totemic, would conclude – as Amis did all those years ago – that more means worse, but when a quarter of the massively inflated number of students being handed a first in 2023 got A level scores of DDD or worse, he surely had a point.

Even the safeguard provided by the Quality Assurance Agency (QAA) is more superficial than it seems. I know this all too well. I was out in Bangladesh and Malaysia in the late 2000s visiting two of the LSC's overseas colleges when they were subject to a QAA inspection on behalf of our degree-awarding partners. I was struck, perhaps somewhat naively, by the extent to which process was being scrutinised and checked rather than the academic content or rigour of what was being taught, let alone the vocational standards of the courses. A tick-box process was completed over several days by assessors in an admirably systematic way, but it was my first encounter with the truism that applies to every publicly funded organisation – if you fail to quantify a target to be achieved, then the target defaults to nil.

The whole system is in a mess. Ever larger numbers of students are racking up ever larger piles of debt, much of which will eventually fall on future generations of taxpayers; they are studying courses that are less academically rigorous, less internationally renowned and poor value for money. Before long, the public outcry about all this will become deafening, but by intervening, government risks further diminishing the autonomy of our universities, which are becoming increasingly desperate to secure guarantees about fee income.

In a nutshell, this is why universities continue to scramble to take on so many foreign students. They simply cannot afford to teach only British students. At the same time, the inflated income they receive from abroad helps to maintain the substandard courses they continue to offer to large numbers of UK school leavers, who would be far better advised to sign up for vocational training. Worse still, as a result, the UK economy is denuding itself of the home-grown skills it requires and as a result, the pressure from employers for immigrant labour to boost economic growth becomes irresistible. Rather than tackle these deeply controversial public policy dilemmas, it suits governments of all colours simply to continue lauding our 'world-class university sector'. I fear the end game for many in the world of UK higher education may soon be upon us all and it is going to be painful.

• • •

The transition from full-time education into the world of work is always an important one. So too the other rite of passage into adulthood – namely, saying goodbye to your parents. First figuratively, as you leave the family home to make your own way in life, and then more definitively when they pass away.

Looking back on it, I reckon my father spent his entire adult life under a cloud of clinical depression and tobacco smoke. He lived on his nerves, habitually smoking two packets of cigarettes a day. Whilst this unquestionably led to his early death – he contracted terminal lung cancer in his late fifties – I don't think he would have ever countenanced taking anti-depressants. He snorted with contempt at the very idea of counselling and took the conventional view of most Britons of his generation that mental health issues were best dealt with by 'pulling oneself together'. I suspect he was at times overwhelmed by a sense that he was duty-bound to quietly provide for his family, and money was probably far tighter at home when growing up than I ever realised at the time. He kept his own counsel about his feelings and certainly had no close male friends of his age in whom to regularly confide.

Only when I reached adulthood myself did I finally realise just how proud he was of me. During those last few years of his life (he died at fifty-eight, when I was twenty-six) we were able to talk together a little more openly. I remember fondly how in my first couple of terms at Oxford he would appear every few weeks and take me out for a pint or two in the early evening. It was only decades later that I realised that his excuse for travelling the twenty or so miles from home in Reading, namely that he was 'visiting a work contact', was entirely fictitious. He simply wanted to spend some quality time with his eldest son whilst he still could.

So, after all she had already been through, my poor mother, who had lost both her parents in her twenties, was widowed at the age of fifty-one. Although still glamorous and attractive, she never showed the slightest interest in sharing her life with anyone else. For her, male companionship was tied up with memories of my father and the bringing up of their three beloved children.

I would write her short letters or postcards to mark each anniversary of my father's death. To my surprise, I discovered every single one of these nineteen personal messages neatly packaged up in her bedside table after she passed away. Ill health plagued the last decade of her life, culminating in a serious fall, a broken hip and three months' hospitalisation. It was during this time in confinement that her consultant surgeon called me and my siblings into the hospital and warned us that she might never leave, but if she did, we should brace ourselves that her life expectancy would be no more than 'two or three years'. It turned out to be virtually two-and-a-half years to the day that, in September 2010, she died peacefully at home, having lived long enough to meet all bar one of her seven grandchildren.

CHAPTER 3

A FATEFUL MEETING

---

25 FEBRUARY 1994

As recently as the early to mid-1990s, life as a City of London professional remained decidedly low tech. There was no internet to speak of, social media was a blessing or curse yet to be foisted upon us all and even having a computer on one's desk or possessing a mobile phone were still far from universal. Meanwhile, the dress code (or at least that below the forehead) had more in common with office workers of the 1950s than their present-day successors.

Other habits have changed more slowly. Sufficient numbers of wine bars and pubs survive to this day in the Square Mile to suggest that the tradition of the City lunch has not quite expired. It was during the course of a late winter's congenial Friday lunch in early 1994 that I was made an intriguing and unexpected offer. As is so often the case with life-changing opportunities, timing is everything and this one came at exactly the right moment.

But I am getting slightly ahead of myself. I had finally started work as a trainee solicitor in the City of London in autumn 1988. But this was only after the mind-numbing, ten-month grind of law school, which essentially involved parrot learning, and then regurgitating over an intense week of exams, the contents of a four-foot-tall mound of paperwork, unaffectionately known as the core material. There was probably some method in the Law Society's madness – if this unpleasant experience didn't put you off becoming a solicitor, then it was likely that nothing would.

When we commanded an empire, the City of London had sat at the heart of global finance. That all changed with the outbreak of war in August 1914. From that day forward, financial power shifted westwards – to the US and Wall Street. The costs of fighting two world wars and our brief attempt in the interim to re-establish sterling as a global reserve currency were financially and reputationally ruinous.

Then, slowly but surely, the City began to re-establish its international credentials. Excessive US regulation and withholding taxes triggered the development of the Eurodollar market from the late 1950s. The Thatcher government rapidly abolished currency controls and deregulated financial services with its 'Big Bang' reforms in 1986. As luck would have it, this meant that the UK was almost uniquely well placed to benefit from the era of globalisation that began with the fall of communism and the opening up of Chinese and other Asian markets.

Until only a few years before I started working there, the City was regarded as something of a private club to its non-participants. That sense of being part of a closed shop applied equally to its leading law firms. Only with legislation implemented in 1967 were solicitors permitted to practise in firms with more than twenty partners, a far cry from the scores of law firm factories today boasting over 1,000 qualified lawyers. Although the term 'Magic Circle' had not yet been coined (that would happen in the 1990s), the rapid domestic growth of London's top law firms and their international expansion opened the way for a new generation of graduates to take up the mantle.

No longer did a lack of connections to the world of professional services imply an incapability in mediating the demands of corporate clients and the requirements of the market. Rather the opposite, in fact. The world of graduate recruitment was fast being transformed. In my time, Freshfields, the law firm I ended up working for, largely restricted themselves to a milk round consisting of two days of concerted interviewing at Oxford and Cambridge. A very friendly and discursive 45-minute-long interview at the Randolph Hotel with two partners was followed by an offer letter after I returned to college.

By contrast, and to great fanfare, in 2023 Slaughter and May (use an ampersand at your peril), arguably the bluest of blue-blood City practice, announced that in future, one quarter of its trainee recruits would be selected on the basis of social mobility targets in order to 'increase the number of individuals from lower socio-economic backgrounds'. Whenever I suggest that nowadays I wouldn't get a look-in if I applied to join one of the top international law firms, I am not being falsely modest.

For me, life as a trainee solicitor was essentially an extension of my comfortable undergraduate existence – featuring many of the same people. In fairness, the highest quality academic and professional legal training I was fortunate enough to pick up in my twenties also gave me a lifelong ability to marshal effectively my thoughts both orally and in writing. I took it as praise of a sort when decades later the Permanent Secretary at the Foreign Office once noted in a meeting that 'you think just like a lawyer, minister'.

Older partners at the firm seemed, at least to my fresh-faced graduate eyes, to be over the hill. They were probably only in their early or, at a push, mid-fifties. However, in the late 1980s, there was a general expectation in City professional circles, with a few notable exceptions, that retirement should take place within a year or two of one's fifty-fifth birthday. Only with hindsight is it clear that the pace of change during the thirty or so years of their working lives was as nothing compared to the transformation that has taken place in the period since. Yet I, at age sixty, still regard myself as young(ish) at heart, culturally with it and having my finger on the pulse of the modern world. How deluded we all become as we are lost to the sands of time!

The tasks I undertook as a trainee were suitably mundane – proof-reading, paginating sets of documents, writing up formal minutes, drafting verification notes and the like. Much of which nowadays, with the advent of artificial intelligence, has probably been taken firmly out of human hands.

Then, all of a sudden, as qualified lawyers (we were designated as managers at Freshfields, although we didn't manage anything or anybody) we were let loose on clients. At times you felt some kin-ship with those stories that occasionally appear in the newspapers of an imposter passing himself off undetected for years on end as a hospital doctor despite lacking any semblance of medical capacity. Reading through the many hundreds of pages that make up aircraft financing contracts, my eyes would often glaze over. I would often get to the bottom of the page of the clauses on security provisions and realise I hadn't taken in, yet alone understood, a single word of what had been written.

There were some exceptions. I took to the cut and thrust of insol-vency and restructuring. For over a year, I acted for an ailing public company property developer. We had several false dawns, and for a while a financial rescue from Hong Kong investors was tantalisingly close before the client finally sank into liquidation. Competition law – or what in the US is called anti-trust law – was a specialism where I was able to contribute to a political understanding that often lies

at the heart of decision-making. I had been assigned to an intellectually brilliant female partner, who had the reputation of being
a very tough taskmaster. Indeed, my fellow junior managers felt I
had drawn an especially short straw in joining her team. However,
we not only got on well, but our paths unexpectedly and happily
crossed again over thirty years later in my post-political life.

But these were straws in the wind. Drowning under the paperwork, I was painfully aware that I was struggling as never before. I
had been desperately searching for the right niche, but gradually
realised to my dismay that I was simply not cut out for top-flight
corporate law.

Part of the problem was something that has recurred time and
again in my life – a reluctance to put all my eggs in one basket. I
have always enjoyed the challenge and absence of monotony that
comes with variety, but often this has provided a useful alibi against
failure or disappointment in what should be my primary purpose
at any one time. Telling myself that my legal career was only really
a stepping stone to my ambition of a future in politics became
self-fulfilling. So too did refusing to take entirely seriously those
lawyer colleagues who displayed total commitment to their work.
I was well on the road to becoming a semi-detached observer of
events, rather than being properly focused.

• • •

So, in summer 1992, I left Freshfields without really knowing what
I was going to do next. The publishing business we had set up at
Oxford continued to provide me with a handy financial safety net,
but its day-to-day administration was now safely in Hilary's hands.
Even my dabbling in it here and there was hardly time-consuming.

With hindsight, I had a lucky escape from the clutches of a public affairs agency, which was keen to take me on. Lobbying, as an industry, was then a relatively new import from the US and very much in its infancy in the UK. The subject matter naturally appealed, but I was concerned about being typecast as a political insider at such an early stage of my working life. Little did I realise that before long it would be professional politicians who would be dominating the parliamentary and ministerial ranks. As it transpired, the agency who were so keen to employ me went through some high-profile difficulties and by the end of the decade the firm had collapsed.

I even tried my hand at a little freelance political journalism. My *Cherwell* exploits had led to me winning one of the inaugural Philip Geddes Student Journalism awards, which were run by the *Daily Express* in honour of their young journalist who had been killed when the IRA detonated a bomb at Harrods. As a previous winner, I was usually invited to the annual awards lecture and dinner. Sitting near the then editor, Sir Nicholas Lloyd, we avidly chatted about UK politics – the *Express* and *The Sun* both took credit for John Major's surprise general election triumph earlier that year – and when he learned that I was at something of a loose end, he suggested that I do some writing for them.

At the time, the circulation of the *Daily Express* was virtually on a par with its great rival the *Daily Mail*, albeit on definitively opposing trajectories. I ended up helping to write a few leader columns, assisted with research on several political articles, attended some momentous House of Commons debates from the press gallery as the Tories' Maastricht Treaty civil war kicked off and, amongst others, first came across Jon Craig, the newspaper's newly appointed political editor. He is truly one of the great survivors in political broadcasting. Later in life he interviewed me frequently on the BBC and Sky News, and I am thoroughly impressed that his Westminster career outlived mine.

But this was only really an exercise in treading water. I was now twenty-seven, that notoriously ominous age for rock star demises. On the plus side, I felt neither suicidal tendencies nor any inclination to overdose on drugs, but I was more than a little bewildered. This experience has made me instinctively sympathetic for graduates who leave university either in the teeth of a recession or genuinely unsure of what to do next. Others quickly regret their first step on the career ladder or realise that their dream occupation is not quite what it was cracked up to be. With hindsight, two or three years of post-graduation finding oneself is never quite the CV disaster that well-meaning parents or mentors might think. Later, as an employer and especially in my private offices, I made a beeline for candidates who had been through this particular mill.

Spending my days at home watching ball-by-ball Test match cricket on the TV or reading voraciously, I felt a rising sense of panic as the seasons moved on. At the time, the apartment where I lived was a stone's throw from a small primary school and I well remember hearing the excited chatter of school children as term ended, then the weeks of relative calm over the summer holidays, to be replaced once again with noise and bustle as September arrived. Yet here I was, stuck at home and feeling that the world was passing me by. I was something of a lost soul and sank back into my shell. Despite having all this time on my hands, I even avoided meeting up with friends as frequently as in the past. After all they were, or so I convinced myself, all moving relentlessly forward in highly fulfilling and successful careers.

I even recall devoting one afternoon during this debilitating period to a walk through leafy west London across to the perennially up-and-coming district of Shepherd's Bush in order to spend an hour with a fortune teller. I made my way up to a small top-floor flat by way of a rickety staircase, stepping over piles of mail and glossy pizza delivery fliers that were sprawled across a woefully threadbare carpet. To say that it had seen better days does not do justice to its soiled, stained and generally desolate state. At the top of the stairs the astrologist and tarot reader appeared before me, sporting, as if out of central casting, a goatee beard and ponytail, which was then a much more unusual combo than it has become today. Typically, I have had a healthy scepticism for clairvoyancy and much of the new age industry without dismissing all of its insights out of hand, but at the time I really just wanted some reassurance that all would be well. I still have a copy of the birth chart that he drew up for me but more memorable still were his words of assurance about destiny and family.

'I see you in some high-profile public position, travelling extensively and having two children,' he pronounced confidently and then, as I recall, somewhat more disapprovingly, 'Hmm… your chart is remarkably similar to that of Margaret Thatcher.' We are both Librans with Scorpio rising, apparently. Needless to say, I returned home with a renewed spring in my step and reassured by these unmitigated snippets of good news ringing in my ears.

• • •

It was equally evident that I needed to get back into stable employment. An in-house legal job that sounded intriguing was advertised in *The Times* and I responded to the market-leading recruitment agency handling the assignment. To my surprise, the agency's managing director, Gareth Quarry, called me directly and we arranged a meeting then and there, which took place within a few days. It soon became clear that he had an agenda and that agenda was me. My entrepreneurial foray in recruitment publishing meant that my CV had been noticed when it landed on his desk. Gareth believed, correctly as it turned out, that I would be ideally suited to working in legal recruitment. So, rather than being a gamekeeper, I was to become a legal poacher.

Gareth was only six years older than me. He has been a consistently successful lawyer-cum-businessman who has built up and sold two recruitment groups for awe-inspiring sums over the past thirty-five years. If his name sounds a little familiar, it is because he came to public prominence towards the end of 2022. At that year's Labour Party Conference, it was announced with great fanfare that Quarry had defected from the Conservatives, for whom he had been a lifelong voter and, until Brexit, a reasonably generous donor. Rather worryingly, when I read his reasons for making this dramatic gesture, there was not much in his economic and fiscal analysis with which I would honestly disagree.

I have no idea if Gareth has any other plans afoot and I am sure Sir Keir Starmer does not need my unsolicited human resources advice, but a struggling Labour government could do a lot worse than bringing someone like him on board in an economic ministry or department. There has been a tendency for all governments to promote so-called captains of industry to the House of Lords, with backgrounds in senior roles in the Confederation of British Industry and large multinational companies. But the UK economy's productivity and supply-side challenges require expertise drawn from small- and medium-sized enterprises (SMEs) too, and I have long believed that we need far more people in government who have hands-on experience of running a payroll and embody an entrepreneurial spirit.

I should point out that Gareth and I have not been in contact for well over twenty years and even when a party vice-chairman, I was, quite correctly, unaware of his financial support for the Tories. Nor, as we shall see, were we ever that close. My comments are drawn from my belief that, especially at this time, the nation requires uncommon talent in political office.

Even in the most meritocratic organisations and especially in a small start-up business, a trusted employee's length of service counts for more than it should. That was the problem I faced when I arrived as the ninth most senior fee earner at Quarry Dougall. With the best will in the world, there is not much that anyone can do about this and no disrespect is intended to any of my then colleagues. There is always some friction generated by recruitment consultants battling to claim credit about 'ownership' of clients and candidates when money is made. Mostly this was a relatively healthy competitive tension, but sometimes things could spill over. I always thought life in a recruitment agency would have made excellent fodder for either a TV sitcom or a fly-on-the-wall documentary.

Things came to a head for me after I had worked there for about a year. I had been developing business well and bringing in fairly substantial fees. I considered myself financially under-rewarded but was not inclined to make too much of a fuss – as they say in any performance business, you are only as good as your next quarter. It was at this point that Gareth misjudged things rather badly. Unbeknownst to all other members of staff, his fellow director had indicated his intention to leave the business. Understandably, Gareth set about quietly shoring up his key team, which he considered me a member of, but crucially never let on, even obliquely, why he was doing so.

Out of the blue, I was called into a meeting and offered a three-year rolling contract on slightly improved terms. When I asked about how my role would develop, he told me we could discuss all that detail in due course but only after I had signed up to this long-term commitment. I am afraid I have always been resistant to blatant pressurising of this sort. Matters quickly deteriorated; the updated contract was plonked on my desk one morning with instructions to sign within the next week and more compliant colleagues were deputed to take me out for coffee and sometimes something stronger to tell me in no uncertain terms that this was a 'once-in-a-lifetime offer'.

Coincidentally, it was precisely as this stand-off was playing out in late February 1994 that the two-bottle City lunch referred to earlier took place. My host was the head of personnel at City solicitors Ashurst Morris Crisp, Hugh Kelly. Although I hardly knew him at the time, within months he would become my business partner.

These days, by all accounts, working from home means the City of London is something of a ghost town on the final day of the working week. Back then, client lunches on a Friday were regarded as a popular way to start the weekend. Hugh walked me the short distance from a packed and noisy wine bar in the sparklingly modern Broadgate development to his firm's plush offices. I was introduced briefly to his assistant and secretary, and only as he closed the glass door to his cramped office and shifted files to the floor from the only vacant chair did I suspect for the first time that something was up.

Having sat me down, he came straight to the point. He had had enough of working for a law firm. He now wanted to run his own business. As a client in the recruitment process, he reckoned there was a huge gap in the market for a professional, ethical recruitment firm focusing on large City law firms. He had a financial backer willing and able to fund the start-up costs of such a venture. All he now needed was someone who understood this market from the candidate side. He had seen me in action and I was his man.

This all sounded positively liberating compared with the claus-trophobic atmosphere back in my office. But inevitably, nailing down and finalising plans of this sort takes time. There are people to meet, assurances to be given and received – and all of this has to happen under an atmosphere of cloak and dagger deception. It made for an unsettling few months.

Meanwhile, back at Quarry Dougall, the time finally came to hand in my notice. It cannot really have come as much of a surprise to Gareth as we sat in the boardroom at the end of one working day. He went through the 'I think you're making a big mistake that you will regret' motions, but the only time he came close to losing his cool was when we jousted over finances. I felt I had nothing to lose in telling him that there was a fundamental mismatch between the fees his employees were bringing in and what they were taking home in salary and bonus. He responded by claiming that he only took out drawings marginally higher than the rest of us. 'Hang on a minute,' I spluttered back. 'It is thanks to all of our efforts this company now has reserves of over £1 million. If we close up shop tomorrow, you get 57 per cent of that, but I get nothing.'

I had always admired Gareth's self-control under pressure, but I could see at this point that even he was tightly gripping the table edge in front of him. Anyway, by the time I had repeated a variant of this exchange several times over with different colleagues in the staff kitchen the following morning, knowing full well that it would rapidly be reported back, my three months' notice period had miraculously been transformed into immediate gardening leave. Needless to say, when my turn came to manage truculent staff and their demands in the years ahead, I began to have a lot more sympathy for Gareth's position. But for now, I was finally free.

• • •

In the starkest of contrasts to the bleak outlook only a couple of years earlier, by late 1994 I was enjoying a perfect coming together of opportunity with all the necessary support behind me. I had nothing to lose and everything to gain. A legal services market in flux meant no end of possibilities, and bolstered by an investor and partner giving me free rein based on my proven track record, it was the greatest of liberations to strike out on my own.

Hugh and I formally set up shop as Kellyfield Consulting in January 1995. My business motto has always been to make hay whilst the sun shines. For a short time, around the turn of the century, our legal recruitment business made lots of it, but I never fooled myself that luck and good timing were not by far the most important ingredients of this success. Still, it is sobering to reflect that the highest-earning years of my professional life, by some considerable margin, were resolutely behind me by my mid-thirties. From my experience, most people running start-up businesses are either poorer than you think (albeit desperately trying to keep up appearances to the contrary) or richer than you could possibly imagine. You could hazard a guess as to the fee income being earned, but the likelihood was that you would be out by a factor of five either way.

A number of factors contributed to a hefty spike in work and fees for those in legal recruitment during this time. First, the ties of loyalty that bound people into partnerships had begun to fray as law firms became larger and ever more corporate in approach. Second, a variety of specialist publications opened up earnings transparency firm by firm. Third, in a legal market deregulation equivalent to the Big Bang, the Law Society allowed US firms in particular to open offices and practise UK law here. Finally, there was far more legal work around, so higher salaries chased the available pool of qualified associates as the 1990s wore on.

Hugh and I were reluctant to dilute our brand and niche quality reputation by taking on additional staff to work alongside us in solicitor recruitment. Instead, we decided to expand by developing a wholly owned subsidiary that recruited for law firm support staff roles, including IT, HR and executive PAs working for senior and managing partners.

These were happy days as we developed a fierce loyalty amongst a select group of UK and US law firms in London. On the other side of the coin, many lawyers remained in touch after we had acted for them, recommending friends and colleagues and sometimes coming back on our books for second and subsequent moves. There was nothing especially intellectually stimulating about any of this, although dealing with people meant there was always the risk of witnessing some of the worst (and occasionally best) aspects of human nature. Motto number two, which applies to politics as much as business, is, 'What goes around, comes around.' So, it never ceased to amuse me when I met lawyers who told me they wanted to go into recruitment because they 'liked people'. Recruitment is not for the faint-hearted and it teaches you some timely lessons about resilience.

I was never able to take entirely seriously the concept that there was much intrinsic value tied up in any recruitment company. Surely the barriers to entry being so very low, with employees and their past books of business eminently portable, made this line of work virtually the very definition of ephemeral? Yet at the height of each successive economic boom, there always seemed to be hard-headed investors queueing up to pay millions of pounds for the rights to exploit future, highly contingent streams of income.

One of the occupational hazards of working in recruitment in those days was that during salary review season you did virtually nothing other than field speculative telephone calls from long-forgotten former candidates asking for information about 'the going rate'. Nowadays I suspect there are websites that provide instantaneous data to ensure the frenzy around comparative salary levels is updated in real time. Needless to say, this is not the only way in which technology has cut out the middleman – not that professional services themselves will be immune from further commoditisation as the brave new world of AI takes hold.

Over those years, I acted on key early career moves for many who have ended up in senior positions in leading international law firms. At the other end of the scale, Chris Watson was already a well-known partner when we moved him on, although he assured me when we first met that his little-known actress daughter, Emma, would soon become far more famous. We also ensured that my old friend, Martin Winter, became senior partner at two different firms, whilst Simon Levine's dual claim to fame is that he was until recently CEO of DLA Piper, the world's largest firm, and that his wife, Jane, had sat next to me throughout that gruelling law school year. Then there was Vincent Keaveny, successfully placed twice by us and subsequently a Lord Mayor of the City of London.

But one person whose hour-long meeting with me in late 1998 has always stuck in the mind was not a lawyer at all. His then girlfriend and future first wife, Melinda, was a tax law specialist who asked if I could spare her would-be entrepreneur boyfriend some time to pass on a few tips about the challenges of managing a start-up. That is how I came across Richard Reed, whose passion and enthusiasm about life and business was infectious. He spoke with energy about the new venture he was setting up with two friends from the world of management consulting. Confident of getting the final piece of pre-launch funding in place, he confided that they had settled on the name Innocent Smoothies. Even then, I was fairly sure there was probably more he could teach me about business than the other way round.

• • •

These professional upheavals and excitements were all well and good, but my eye was never long deflected from the ultimate goal. Political activity was a constant from the moment I turned up in London. One of the first things I did was to join and become active in my local Conservative Party branch, Islington North Conservatives. Given that over twenty years had passed since any Tory candidate had last been elected to the local council, my reaching the dizzy heights of deputy chairman of that local constituency association within a year was not quite as difficult an accomplishment as it might seem.

Even estate agents would think twice about calling Finsbury Park fashionable or upmarket, but neither was it the cesspit of criminality and disorder that some of my friends who had never set foot in London N4 would have me believe. True, refuse collection and street sweeping was apparently regarded as an optional extra by the Labour-run Islington Council, but I guess they relied on a popular mandate to focus on more important priorities, such as the avid promotion of its nuclear-free zone policy and a full assortment of minority rights.

In a fit of nostalgia, every few years I return to walk around the streets where I bought my first flat, and every time I do so I am always struck by how much more affluent the place looks. Trendy restaurants and shops now proliferate, muggings, graffiti and burglary rates have plummeted and the drab monochrome of yesteryear has been replaced by smart new buildings, tasteful pedestrianisation and greenery on virtually every street corner. The long-promised gentrification has finally taken place, albeit three decades or so too late for me.

I was not to know it at the time, but London was where my entire political career would play out. Each of the three local government and six parliamentary elections that I was to contest took place within the M25. Not bad for someone who had very deliberately avoided applying to study in the capital either for university or law school. Whenever I gave it any thought – and there was plenty of daydreaming in my twenties – I guess my assumption was that I would end up with a Home Counties or market town constituency and a life, or at least half a life, spent near open countryside, rural walks and village pubs.

What was also far from clear back then was that the late 1980s represented a very high water mark for Conservative political fortunes in London, which we have never since come close to emulating. Just to hold our own, London's Conservatives have had to sprint relentlessly up a downward escalator over recent decades. Arguably, in electoral terms, Brexit represents for us the mirror-image equivalent of the damage done to Labour's fortunes by the 'loony left' in 1980s London.

Take two sets of election results that demonstrate both general demographic change in the capital and the contrast between London and the rest of England. The 1992 and 2015 general elections had very similar outcomes – a narrow overall Conservative majority and a vote share lead over Labour of around seven percentage points. In London in 1992, the Conservatives almost exactly mirrored the national result with a 8 per cent lead over Labour (winning forty-eight seats to Labour's thirty-five). Only twenty-three years later, however, Labour 'won' London by 9 per cent securing forty-five seats to our twenty-seven. The comparison between 1987 and 2019 is starker still. Again, there were comparable national outcomes, with a Conservative majority of 102 and eighty seats respectively and a vote share lead of around 12 per cent. But whilst in 1987 the Tories were fifteen percentage points ahead in London (and won fifty-seven seats to twenty-three), only thirty-two years later, in 2019, it was Labour, even under Jeremy Corbyn, who had a 16 per cent lead in London, winning the seat count forty-nine to twenty-one.

The relentless advance of Reform UK was markedly less pronounced in London than anywhere else in Britain at the 2024 election, and the Labour vote in parts of the capital came under sustained attack from the Green Party and from pro-Gaza independents. Nevertheless, the Conservatives still slumped to an all-time low of just nine seats in London, all of which lie on the capital's outer fringes. For the first time in 150 years, the famously wealthy districts of central London have become a Tory-free zone. Belgravia, Chelsea, the City, Marylebone, Mayfair and South Kensington are all now represented by Labour MPs for the first time.

Apologies for the rather tortuous psephological lecture, but this is the backdrop to my entire political life as a Conservative in London. These political changes reflect the hypermobility and hyperdiversity of the UK's capital city and its rapid demographic change, with only 37 per cent of Londoners in 2021 self-describing as 'White British'. The failure of the Conservatives to extend their appeal to more non-white electors is perhaps unsurprising when our apparent obsession with reducing immigration has persuaded many Londoners of colour (with the notable exception of the Hindu community) that the party regards them as second-class citizens. There has also been a substantial increase in the proportion of graduates and younger voters living in London, the two categories of elector least likely to have supported leaving the European Union. As has become painfully clear over the years, particularly since the turn of the century, London, in its values, culture and outlook, seems increasingly like an island off the coast of the UK rather than an integral part of the nation.

Over the years, the Islington North Conservative Association has proved a remarkably fertile training ground for future MPs. Sadly, it has not been able to match this with as plentiful a supply of activists on the ground. In a strange inversion of the principles that lay behind the Katyn massacre, it was almost as if the Islington North Tory officer class have been spared at the expense of all its foot soldiers. When I was involved there, far too much time was spent attending internal meetings and haggling with the most bitter of local opponents, namely the officers of the Islington South & Finsbury Conservatives. However, I also learned some useful rudiments of campaigning and began to enjoy taking the fight to the real enemy on behalf of residents over a range of genuine local grievances.

As local elections approached in 1990, one of the most thankless tasks was getting candidates formally nominated. The ward where I lived, Labour's safest in Islington, had a paid-up Conservative membership of one. Me. That meant it was my job to find another nine local residents to sign the nomination papers of those candidates willing to stand under the Conservative banner here. Never mind that these hardy souls had poorer electoral prospects than Kim Jong Un's opponents in North Korea – it was deemed important to fly the flag everywhere and not allow Labour to take voters for granted any more than they already did.

Sensibly, I gave myself a whole weekend to complete this task because we had absolutely no idea where our admittedly miniscule support might lie. Now you might think, as I did for the first few minutes of that momentous Saturday morning, that the best place to start trying to locate Conservative sympathisers would be in the largest and most expensive houses in the locality. Think again. Even the curiosity value of actually meeting a self-confessed Conservative in the flesh did little to ward off the sneeringly dismissive unpleasantness of many of Islington North's wealthier folk – such a shame I was unable to share their strongly professed liberalism.

Eventually, after knocking on countless doors, by early on Sunday afternoon I was getting close to completing the forms. I shall be forever grateful to a middle-aged couple, both teachers, who took pity on me but also despaired that their teenage children had no interest in politics. So, a deal was struck – if I joined them all in their cosy kitchen for a mug of tea and talked about my political involvement to their apathetic offspring, they would sign the wretched nomination papers. I did the honours and the nominations were duly completed. On election day I smiled to myself as I walked towards their house, recalling their kind deed. It was only then that I saw the large Labour Party poster in their front window.

Five miles or thereabouts separate Kensington & Chelsea from Islington North, but the two were poles apart politically. Any remote possibility that I might not become actively involved in the local Tories when I moved to Chelsea in 1991 was snuffed out on the day my brother and I shipped my belongings over to my new apartment and realised that the local Conservative Association offices were located less than 100 yards away.

Almost immediately we were on red alert for an imminent general election, which was eventually called for April 1992. Meanwhile, I quickly became chairman of my local branch. If that sounds like a bit of a come down from my previous exulted position in Islington, it was not. What was then called Cheyne Ward in Chelsea, where I lived, had four times the Conservative membership of the entire Islington North Association. Granted, the foot soldiers here could hardly be described as crack storm troopers. Most were old enough to be my grandmother. Nevertheless, they all thought I was 'a very nice young man', baked some wonderful cakes and biscuits to reward helpers and were fantastically efficient at folding leaflets, stuffing them into labelled envelopes and delivering them to the electors. To my eternal shame, I ranked these attributes in descending order of importance.

Election day arrived. It had been a strange campaign. Virtually all the national opinion polls pointed to a Labour victory, but it didn't seem like that as I canvassed night after night in Chelsea. Admittedly this was a super safe Tory seat, but whilst there was certainly not much love for us, there was genuine, heartfelt fear of Neil Kinnock and his party. To spare my band of elderly ladies the rigours of an early morning start, I volunteered to man the polling station from its 7 a.m. opening and take electors' poll card numbers so that we could 'knock up' (I appreciate that to any US reader this phrase has somewhat different connotations) those of our known supporters later if they had not already voted.

I could not believe my eyes as I arrived a few minutes before the appointed hour. A queue of about thirty people had already assembled waiting to vote. Several of them, seeing my blue Conservative rosette, grabbed me by the arm, desperately seeking reassurance that despite everything we were going to win. Much as I wanted a

Tory victory, even I didn't think that 'this country will be finished if Labour gets in' as many of those hapless Chelsea folk said to me. All was well, however – the Conservatives won a famous, unexpected and narrow victory in 1992. And thereby laid the foundations for our most crushing defeat in 150 years at the following election.

• • •

The prospect of my using up a valuable week of annual holiday leave from work in order to attend the Conservative Party Conference was always met by office colleagues with a reaction that varied from disbelief to pity. I tried hard to explain that sitting in the conference hall and listening to speeches was by no means all that went on – in fact, within a few years I would spend the entire week at conference without ever even venturing into the main auditorium. It was all about the socialising, the gossip, the parties, the bars remaining open all night. Almost like reliving your first week at university with an endless freshers week – in my case uncannily similar, as Nick Robinson was also there. I fear the more I protested, the greater the suspicion from my non-political friends that I had got myself caught up in some kind of crazed cult.

If this were so, the shadowy figures at its helm were doing a good job at exerting their manipulative control. After an assessment board at the Marriott Hotel in Slough (every bit as dire as it sounds), I found myself on the party's approved list of parliamentary candidates. Then, in May 1994, I was elected as a councillor in the Royal Borough of Kensington and Chelsea. By this time, the reputation and opinion poll standing of the Conservatives was at rock bottom nationally. Even so, getting the nomination to be a candidate in a plum district like Abingdon Ward (the area between

Kensington High Street and Cromwell Road) was highly competitive. No risk of paper candidates being needed in this plush corner of central London. I was one of seventeen applicants put through their paces and my victory was a triumph of diplomacy… and some mild deception.

The power in Abingdon Ward lay in the hands of its delightful, universally admired, long-standing councillor Elizabeth Christmas, who had lived in the ward all her life and had forgotten more about it than most of its residents would ever know. She had been on the council since 1952 and was equally devoted both to the council and her omnipresent Border Collie dog. I must admit that I have never by nature been an instinctive lover of our canine brethren, but this was a confession I felt it wise not to share with Councillor Christmas. So too my German heritage – Liz had been orphaned as a child when a V1 missile destroyed her family home, and as a result she harboured a heartfelt hatred of all Germans and of British membership of the European Union. It was only her other passions – chain-smoking untipped Craven A cigarettes and a taste for the strongest gin and tonics I have ever sampled – that ensured she was not around to celebrate Brexit in person.

As the old saying goes, they really only needed to weigh rather than count the Tory votes in Kensington. Even in 1994. As stories of electoral carnage piled up across the country, the Conservative vote share in Abingdon Ward plummeted from 65 per cent to a mere 62 per cent. Now an elected councillor, I set to work. The excessively deferential approach towards the views of council officers by many well-established Tory councillors in Kensington & Chelsea and their overly paternalistic attitude when it came to running social services and housing swiftly put me at odds with the then council leadership. Many years later in the aftermath of the Grenfell Fire tragedy, this would cause serious problems for the council – rather unfairly in my view, it was portrayed as being heartless and unresponsive to local opinion when, if anything, it was the lack of political leadership that had got them into trouble in the first place.

All of this meant that I was happier busying myself with some of the less politically partisan matters. Planning is quasi-judicial but lies at the very heart of the concerns of many Kensington & Chelsea residents. Being on the planning committee meant lots of reading to be done before its meetings, and before long I had worked out that the really contentious issues would invariably be placed by the officers about three quarters of the way down the 300-page agenda. This was in the hope that the relevant papers would either not be read properly or that in a rush to reach the end of the meeting, the officers' verdict on the matter in hand would be approved on the nod. Five times in my years on the planning committee, the public gallery was cleared and we were warned gravely by the legal director that our refusal to accept a particular recommendation would lay the council open to ruinous legal costs if we were challenged by developers. On three of these occasions, the developers threw in the towel before going to appeal. On the other two, it was the committee's decision that was upheld in the courts and the council was awarded its costs. Expert opinion is all well and good, but effective democracy requires politicians with good judgement and the courage of their convictions.

Until I joined the ministerial ranks, I would often remark that I had never wielded as much political power as I did when chairing two small council committees. There, working with fellow councillors and interest groups, I was able to exercise discretion, have control over a budget and genuinely make things happen. I was chairman of the Housing Benefits Review Board and we were able to make a real difference to the lives of an admittedly small number of vulnerable families whose situation would otherwise have fallen just outside the parameters of inflexible rules. Applicants would sit across the table from us, clutching a few scraps of paper, and nervously try to explain their plight. Sometimes, as we coaxed their story out of them, it would become apparent that some minor apparently insignificant fact had been lost in the ether and this would allow us to act.

Whatever the outcome, these local residents would almost always be pathetically grateful just to be given a hearing. Never far from my mind were thoughts of my proud maternal grandparents, who presumably during the post-war chaos had also needed to throw themselves at the mercy of faceless officialdom. What I found especially gratifying was the opportunity this gave me to work cooperatively on these heartrending cases with Labour councillors, whose default position at main council meetings was to be hostile to virtually everything that the Tory council did.

Less life changing but no less contentious to those who deeply cared, the Friends of Holland Park committee was charged with strategic overview of the fifty-four acres of green space that had been bequeathed to the local authority in perpetuity. Even now, whenever I walk through the park, I am proud of our decisions to rewild and not over-manicure its more wooded areas.

In reality, I always saw my stint in local government as something of a stepping stone towards getting into Parliament. I never desired a senior chairmanship position on the council, which was just as well since I was regarded by some as rather forthright for a young councillor. Many of my fellow councillors had several decades of service under their belts – in six cases they had first joined the council before I had been born. They had grown up with an expectation that new councillors were there to be seen, to vote and, for a few years at least, not be heard. I never intended to upset or offend, but nor would I happily be steamrollered into silence, especially at our monthly party meetings, which were, notionally at least, the policy forum for the majority Tory group.

• • •

In any event, parliamentary selections were soon occupying my mind. With an election due no later than May 1997 and with parliamentary boundary changes now settled, from autumn 1995 a steady flow of seats began to be advertised. Just about to turn thirty-one, I assumed that I would be fighting a safe Labour seat this time around, with a view to securing a better prospect for the election after next. Only later would it become apparent to me that one of the great charms of politics is its unpredictability. Naturally, that is very much a double-edged sword. But when you appear to be on the outside and have few reasonable expectations, events can suddenly transform your situation for the better.

So, I started to apply for seats that on paper were good Conservative prospects, although in the event, I lost each of the three where I made the final round. I was pipped to the post in Colchester by Stephan Shakespeare, who I am sure was more than happy to forego a parliamentary career for the untold fortune he has made as one of the founders of the polling company, YouGov.

Next up, in my home town seat of Reading East the Transport Minister John Watts stole the nomination from under my nose, having made the 'chicken run' from Slough (presumably he was as keen as me to escape from the orbit of his local Marriott Hotel). What I remember most about that selection process was that on the night before the final meeting, Watts had appeared on *Newsnight* and this evidently impressed the selectors in Reading. Conservative Central Office were quite understandably keen to help sitting MPs needing timely publicity, but what made it all the more galling was that the rather contrived transport initiative that he had promoted with such ministerial fanfare was being launched right in the heart of the ward I represented in Kensington. Sadly for Watts, there was a painful sting in the tail. Not only did the Conservatives lose Reading East but his getting selected meant he had to pull out of the final selection later in the week at Bury St Edmunds, where he had been the favourite. It was a constituency he and his wife would have preferred – and we hung onto it at the following year's general election by 368 votes.

Then, just as I was thinking of dusting down my South Yorkshire and Greater Manchester atlases and vowels ready to fight a Labour stronghold in one of those regions, I received a letter calling me to interview in Enfield North. The most northerly constituency in Greater London and only twelve miles or so from the City and West End, I had never visited nor even travelled through Enfield. Discretion being the better part of valour, I thought it best not to advertise this fact too widely. In any event, by the time of the first interview a couple of weeks after receiving my invitation, I had spent two full days driving and walking around the patch as well as an afternoon in the library swotting up on the local issues described in the last six months of local newspapers. Nowadays, of course, this level of research and more can be done online and instantaneously from the comfort of home. As recently as 1996, these efforts were regarded as well beyond the normal call of duty.

The candidate rumour mill suggested that there were two very strong local candidates up for the seat and, especially this close to the last possible date for the election, one or other would get the nomination. A noticeable development in recent years has been the tendency even for safe Conservative seats (if such things exist) to select local activists. Previously, and certainly in the 1990s, the mentality of parliamentary selection committees in strongly Tory areas was that they were selecting national politicians and potential future ministers. More often than not, even impressive local candidates would fall by the wayside on the basis that it is always difficult to be a prophet in your own land. That is duly what happened to the two local hot favourites and I ended up as the beneficiary.

The first couple of rounds of interviews went very well and I could see I was building a strong rapport with some of what turned out to be the key local activists. The stage was set for the final three, which is when nerves suddenly began to grip me. Enfield North was a seat that had been Conservative since 1979 and where we had had five-figure majorities in the 1980s. Although that had been pared down to 9,430 in 1992 (a more ominous sign than I gave credit for at the time) even five years later it just failed to qualify as one of Labour's list of 100 target seats.

In a break from the usual format, the local Conservatives decided that in advance of the standard final selection, where each candidate separately gives a ten-minute speech and then takes fifteen minutes of questions, there would be a brief social event. This would normally have come earlier in the process, but when local candidates were still in the running it was felt to give an unfair advantage to them. Anyway, I was chaperoned smartly around the membership by the wonderfully efficient local organising secretary, Audrey Thacker, and it became blindingly obvious to me that a vast number of the people present had been specifically called to attend with clear instructions to vote for me.

By rights, this should have given me a supreme sense of confidence. Of course, it had the opposite effect. I fluffed the punchline of my set-piece joke to such an extent that absolute silence greeted even the scripted pause I had left to await laughter. In answer to a question about the economy, usually my strongest suit, I got into such a terrible tangle with statistics that by the end of my reply I had totally forgotten what I had been asked. Yet the selection gods were finally shining on me and I won handsomely on the first ballot. Intriguingly for a political party that sets itself so firmly against any form of proportional representation, Conservative candidate selection works on exhaustive ballots rather than anything as grubby as first past the post.

Naturally I was thrilled. The selection had taken place on the Friday before the early May bank holiday and the long weekend was spent taking congratulatory calls from political contacts, friends and even a few enterprising journalists who had got hold of my number. The assumption was that I was going to be elected. After all, in each of the last three parliaments, the opinion polls had narrowed significantly in the year up to election day. Few thought there was any chance of the Tories actually winning a fifth term, but on a uniform swing the Tories would have to be down to 204 seats and our worst result in almost a century for Enfield North to be lost. Things were looking grim for the Tories, but the outcome of the next election would not be that bad, would it?

Part of the skill set that any candidate needs if they are to retain their sanity is the ability to suspend disbelief. I never took for granted that I would win in Enfield North. On the night I was selected, I reckoned there was a 30 per cent chance that the recovery in the opinion polls we all assumed was as automatic as night following day would not happen. Not a day passed without thinking through the implications of the 9.1 per cent swing that Labour needed to pick up the seat and extrapolating every new opinion poll to my own circumstances. But if you spend every waking hour worrying incessantly about the outcome, you will drive yourself to an early grave. There is an enormous amount of campaigning work to be done and you simply have to get on with it. You have to trust that all that hard work has some virtue in its own right and that is what I did.

Every weekday night I would be up in Enfield, meeting residents' associations, amenity groups and knocking on door after door after door or delivering literature, rain or shine. Every single night. My usual social life was eviscerated. I missed two sets of friends' wedding receptions because I had promised some Enfield group or other that I would turn up to some inconsequential event. Having made the promise, I needed to stick to it. When I think of my itinerary that year, it exhausts me. I never worked harder on a campaign. Some political activists and even long-standing MPs claim to love spending hour after hour canvassing, meeting and exchanging conversation with random constituents. I don't doubt their integrity, but by the time I left Parliament I knew that on that score I had nothing left in the tank to give.

Even in my single year in Enfield North I could see some of the early signs of the demographic change that has engulfed much of outer London ever since. There were many conversations with elderly, Conservative-voting couples in the more working-class eastern area of Enfield who told me proudly of the successes of their children, all of whom had moved further out into Hertfordshire or Essex. There was the sudden proliferation of starter homes and commuter flats close to railway stations. There was a marked increase in Turkish, Somali and West African families moving in from further down the Lea Valley.

Finally, it was mayday for the Conservatives – 1 May 1997. We assembled for the count at a large sports hall in the south-east of the borough, where all three London Borough of Enfield constituency counts were taking place. Everyone remarked on how well I looked. The weather over the previous six weeks had been glorious; all the outdoor campaigning had given me a tan and I had lost half a stone in weight. A tremendous, small team of perennial Enfield Tory stalwarts had helped keep my spirits up during our frantic local campaign, including Frank Thacker and John Boast, who have both since passed on, whilst Andrew Young and Andrew Nicholas continue to lead the Enfield Tory charge. But defeat was coming. In the event, I took it all very calmly – indeed, I spent most of the evening commiserating with and boosting the spirits of my team, who seemed considerably more upset by the crushing defeat than me.

It must be much more devastating to lose a seat you have held, and at least I was spared that indignity. By contrast, the two fellow Conservative candidates in the other local constituencies had both been elected three times. Ian Twinn had perhaps been living on borrowed time in Edmonton, which he had first won against the odds in 1983 and clung on to ever since, but there must have been tens of thousands of residents he had personally assisted. The other Enfield seat, Southgate, had formed part of a safely Conservative constituency at every election since 1885. It had been held for the previous thirteen years by Michael Portillo; his sensational defeat and the gracious way he accepted it became the story of election night. 'Were you still up for Portillo?' became the famous question that summed up the election, but for me it was worse than that – I was actually there to witness the event.

His well-chosen words rang firmly in my ears as I finally went to sleep in the middle of the following morning. Portillo had expressed deep regret that he would not be able to play a full role in the Conservative recovery outside Parliament. But what part would there now be for me as a candidate? I had been entrusted with a seat where our lead had been 9,430 and I had contrived to turn it into a Labour majority of 6,822.

To be honest, I never doubted for a single moment that my day would come. Though never afflicted by the slightest notion of being born to lead or destined to greatness, even on the morning of 2 May 1997 I was quietly confident that I simply needed to bide my time and a political future beckoned. In the meantime it was back to running my business, which, along with the London property market, was thriving.

• • •

The extent of home ownership had blossomed in successive decades as I was growing up, from a dream to a goal to an expectation for most Britons. Getting onto the housing ladder was seen as a natural rite of passage for young people, certainly before the age of thirty and usually in advance of marriage or starting a family. It also had a distinctive political twist, as the single strongest correlation with likelihood of supporting the Conservative Party was ownership of your own home. By extension, capitalism is most likely to be supported full-throatedly only by those possessing capital. It is one of the reasons that housing and house building remains such a contentious issue in the current political debate. All these apparent certainties have broken down in one form or another, with social and political consequences that are only slowly beginning to play out.

My experience was entirely conventional, but it is also worth pointing out that even for my age group the path was not entirely smooth. I made that initial Finsbury Park flat purchase at the age of twenty-three on starting work, bolstered by the savings from my first entrepreneurial foray. I paid almost three times the price it had changed hands for a little over six years earlier. Indeed, those of us who first entered the property market in late 1988 feared for many years that we had missed out on the boom. Rising interest rates, a deep economic recession and negative equity cast a long shadow over property prices for some time. More than a few who were badly burned by the experience during this period were wary about ever owning property again. Only in 1995 did prices return to the peak they had reached seven years earlier. It is worth recalling that the benefits of 'getting on the property ladder' has never been a sure-fire, guaranteed, one-way bet, whatever estate agents and mortgage lenders might have you believe.

When it came to selling that first flat two-and-a-half years later, I did so at a price 15 per cent less than I had paid for it. Admittedly, I was trading up by buying a larger apartment in ultra-desirable Chelsea at a recession-driven, deeply discounted asking price, so was willing to take something of a hit when it came to getting the deal over the line. Curiously for someone who will tarry endlessly over minor purchasing decisions in clothes stores or supermarkets, I have always been remarkably decisive on major financial decisions. I guess it must be a variation on the theme that looking after the pennies enables the pounds to look after themselves.

Four years later it was off to a mews house in Kensington, but it was only from about that time on that house prices continued their stratospheric progress. We sold that home a further four-and-a-half years later, just before I became an MP, to a tax partner in a leading City law firm who was amassing a buy-to-let empire, at well over double what we had paid for it. He was willing to purchase at what I regarded as a ludicrous asking price after a cursory visit to the property. Some years later we bumped into each other again at an Institute of Taxation lunch held in one of the parliamentary dining rooms. Somewhat sheepishly I approached him, fearing that I might get an earful of resentment that he had paid massively over the odds. I need not have worried. 'Your old house has been the best investment I have ever made,' he boomed delightedly. 'Fantastically reliable tenants and three-fold increase in capital value.' It almost put me off my prawn cocktail starter.

Just after the turn of the century I moved to Elizabeth Street, buying a house from a developer who I suspect had either run out of patience or money. Slightly incongruously, the ground floor was between two shops in the heart of the retail section of that well-known street in Belgravia. This meant one of our neighbours was the celebrated milliner, Philip Treacy. He and his partner, Stefan Bartlett, were not just lovely neighbours but invited us to some great celebrity parties in their shop and back garden.

It was shortly before one of these glamorous events that I first almost literally stumbled across the fashion icon Isabella Blow, who was standing outside our house and peering through the ground-floor window like some sort of crazed stalker. It transpired that she and her great friend Alexander McQueen used to live in our house before its extensive renovation, when it was little more than a squat. She regaled me with tales of hosting raucous parties that lasted for several days and involved industrial quantities of drugs and alcohol. Little did I realise the distinguished pedigree of my latest home – meanwhile, poor Isabella was rather disappointed to learn it was now in the hands of such a sober and respectable pillar of the establishment.

This type of canter up the housing ladder was quite common for the baby boomer and early Generation X cohort. With a bit of luck, anyone consistently on that ladder will have seen the value of their home – in London, at least – rise six to tenfold over the past thirty years. Almost everyone of my generation has accumulated far more wealth courtesy of rising house prices than through saving or other forms of investment. We all know this is not sustainable. In our hearts, we all know it is not really that desirable. And for those of us with children, we worry intensely that they will not have the opportunities that we have been able to take for granted. For the first time in living memory, outside of wartime conflict, the next generation are much more likely than not to be worse off than their parents.

The dynamics of housing supply and demand remain as skewed as ever. They have been made worse by Conservatives pandering to our core vote and support by insisting that top-down housing targets be scrapped. You do not need to be Hayekian to have concerns that the ordering of the building of 300,000 homes alongside a presumption of sustainable development is a statist imposition, but it provided some form of incentive to cash-strapped local councils whose instinct would otherwise be to block any proposed schemes.

A succession of initiatives during the coalition years designed to prop up the housing market in the aftermath of the financial crisis have also proved calamitous for young would-be homeowners. Cheap credit was pumped into the financial markets, making house prices ever more unaffordable. The votes of existing homeowners were pursued remorselessly. Planning regulations remained as strict as ever on the green belt and beyond. This led to the bubbling up of a genuine sense of cross-generational economic injustice. The excessive stimulation of an already overheating residential property market (further pumped up by quantitative easing and Help to

Buy loan products) was all well and good for those already on the housing ladder. But it has given capitalism a bad name for many of the Millennial and Gen-Z age cohort, who no longer feel they have any stake in the nation's economic success. It should have come as little surprise that the percentage of Conservative votes at the 2024 election amongst electors under the age of thirty languished in the single digits.

A decade or more of ultra-low interest rates has distorted so many economic priorities. It has also meant the woeful mispricing of risk. Now that some normalcy is returning to the cost of borrowing, many of the most recent folk clambering onto the property-owning democracy bandwagon are likely to be most exposed. When those of my generation retort that we repaid mortgages when interest rates were 15 per cent, we neglect to point out that the sums we borrowed also reflected the likely servicing costs. Affordability was nothing like as stretched back then. More recently, many young mortgagors have borrowed huge sums, which seemed eminently manageable when interest rates remained at rock-bottom levels but now appear terrifyingly tough to service.

But reducing economic dependency on the housing market will be difficult for a nation that has come to regard home ownership as an almost inalienable right. Given the reliance of so many people on constantly increasing house prices for future income, which might have been more sensibly tied up in conventional pensions schemes, this is a tricky subject for any government to tackle with honesty.

Our tax system encourages all bar the super wealthy to tie up their savings in housing assets rather than investing in innovation, highlighted by the fact that no capital gains tax is currently payable on the sale of a main residence. There is also the all-pervasive sense that home ownership is the only reliable route for the aspirational. At the risk of being accused of selfishly pulling up the ladder after an adult lifetime benefiting from a generally buoyant property market, perhaps we should encourage different aspirations for future generations? The German model of renting a variety of properties during a lifetime to reflect changing family circumstances makes more sense, perhaps. Then spare capital could be invested instead in businesses large and small or other more liquid assets than bricks and mortar.

• • •

All of these concerns are closely tied up with the potential that inter-generational conflict may boil over into something more dangerous for UK democracy. A steady and increasing stream of constituents' concerns during most of my tenure in Parliament were tied into the increasing division of UK politics along the lines of age, rather than the more traditional class or public/private sector divides.

There is some evidence that the steady rise in life expectancy is now plateauing, but with ever more Britons retiring in their fifties, the proportion of retirees to those in the working population continues to rise. This places an ever-heavier burden upon the younger generation, who realise all too well that the private and state pension benefits that current retirees enjoy are unlikely to be there – to the same level, at least – when their time comes. The same is likely to apply to both health and social care costs, the funding model for which will, before the world is that much older, simply have to adapt to changed conditions, however much the current generation of politicians vehemently deny the fact.

Naturally, no one can reasonably expect those who have already retired and are reliant upon accepted levels of support to see a hair-cut in their post-retirement entitlements. Nor can anyone already beyond retirement age be expected to return to the workplace, but this will only increase the burden of sacrifice to be made by the current generation of workers, who are already having to make up the deficits and shortfalls in private pension schemes that they have been disbarred from joining.

In the scheme of things, the triple lock on state pensions, which ensures they rise annually by whichever of inflation, average wage increases and 2.5 per cent is highest, probably matters less to elderly voters than the other vital coalition government decision – to ring-fence healthcare spending. However, its retention has become symbolic of Conservative support for its core voting bloc. It is also corrosive in the debate over perceived intergenerational unfairness. Not least because the redistribution between young and old has become an increasingly one-way street in the UK since the turn of the century. Education, which is most consumed by the young, has seen its share of government spending drop from 12 to 9 per cent during this time. The share eaten-up by healthcare, by contrast, has risen from 14 per cent to over a fifth of public expenditure. That gap is rising fast.

Nowhere is the starkness more pronounced than within the graduate generation, where the recent sharp rises in inflation and interest rates threaten to burden students with far higher marginal tax rates than many of the population properly understand. Many students assume they will never have to pay off their student loans and if history is a good guide, it is likely that the government's modelling will once again prove massively out of kilter. Nevertheless, the wave of strikes by junior doctors, teachers and barristers has come about largely as a result of the additional cost of living burden that student debt has imposed. This has only worsened damage to the already threadbare state of public services.

Perhaps it is inevitable that the main political parties look at these matters primarily through the prism of their core vote. My Conservative Party has traditionally relied upon disproportionate support from older electors. The assumption that is breaking down fast, however, is that as people become more middle-aged, their political allegiances move rightwards. The neglect, as younger generations see it, of political support for a level intergenerational playing field on house building, pensions spending and the relative costs of health and education may well be storing up serious problems for the Conservatives – and for democracy as a whole.

CHAPTER 4

A KEY TO THE KINGDOM

5 DECEMBER 1999

There are so many walks of life where the margins between success and failure are painfully thin. Narrowly missing out on early opportunities has helped put paid to countless apparently promising sporting, acting and musical careers. On the other hand, lucky breaks in mid-life have propelled seemingly steady but unspectacular executives and commanders into acclaimed business and military leaders.

It was on a cold Sunday evening a few weeks before the end of the last millennium that my own political fate was decided on the hinge of a mere three votes out of almost 400. For that, as I later discovered, was the extent of my victory at the final selection meeting to become the Conservative candidate in the Cities of London & Westminster constituency.

The path from defeat in Enfield North to being entrusted for a second time with a 'safe' Conservative seat involved two by-elections and a funeral. My relationship with the local Tories in Enfield North had always been excellent. I could not have asked for a more supportive team of activists and no one blamed me in the slightest for losing the seat. It turned out to be perversely fortunate for me that the party's crushing national defeat positioned my own local setback in the middle of the tidal wave rather than as a notably poor outlier result.

That might have been different if John Major had called an election in autumn 1996. Given the state of the opinion polls, few blamed him for hanging on to the bitter end in the hope that Labour might falter or simply that something would turn up. But in doing so, the Conservatives won no more credit for the improved state of the economy and instead the argument that it was time for a change became ever stronger. It looked as if we were desperately cling-ing on to office for as long as possible. Although it is impossible to be sure, we probably ended up losing thirty or forty seats more than might have been the case if Major had gone to the country six months earlier. For this reason, my sympathies lay with Rishi Sunak when, in mid-2024, he surprised virtually everyone by going to the country six months sooner than was strictly necessary. Per-haps he recognised that the calamitous succession of by-election losses during his brief tenure were the clearest possible intimation of his government's mortality, whenever he might choose to call the election.

In the absence of other political commitments, I had remained involved in Enfield after the 1997 election, albeit at nothing like the pace or intensity of the previous year. That summer we won a council seat back from Labour at a local by-election, and over the next couple of years I would turn up assiduously to the infrequent local Tory fundraisers and attend any community events to which I was invited. The assumption began to grow that I would fight the seat again. But that had never been my game plan. In all honesty, from the moment of my defeat I had taken a hard-nosed look at the electoral numbers and concluded that winning Enfield North back was going to take a minimum of two bites of the cherry. In the event, victory only came after three more elections. But for the same reason, I did not feel it was right to leave the local Conservatives without a parliamentary spokesman, so I had remained involved. Matters became slightly awkward when, without my knowledge, the local party petitioned Conservative Central Office to be allowed to readopt me formally in early summer 1999.

Then, once again, luck intervened. A by-election was called in mid-Cheshire when the sitting Tory MP for Eddisbury was appointed as our High Commissioner to Canberra. Though our majority two years earlier had been a wafer thin 1,185, the firm (and as it turned out, erroneous) expectation after the Conservatives' strong performance in that June's European Parliament elections was that we would win this time at a canter. Central Office decided to select a candidate in double-quick time and then get the by-election out of the way before the summer recess. I was one of around twenty aspiring candidates called for interview.

Rural Cheshire was not exactly a match made in heaven for me, though under its then boundaries the seat included the Liverpool overspill town Winsford and some suburbs on the edge of Crewe. But I was not going to turn down the offer to throw my hat into the ring when it came. Then, very rapidly, it all got rather serious. The three-stage interview process took place inside four frantic days. With a succession of strong performances, I made it through to the final three. In the end, my Achilles heel was less to do with my near total lack of agricultural knowledge and experience (the former had been well disguised at the interviews; the latter was blindingly obvious) and more to do with the perception that I was Central Office's preferred candidate.

The by-election turned out to be a high-profile and close-run contest. It also became a proxy referendum on the Blair government's proposals to ban hunting. I suspect that my taking the lead playing the rural field sports card would have made for a very uncomfortable campaign, so my near miss was probably the ideal outcome. I was now established on the national party's radar and ready and willing to fight another day. I travelled up the M6 one last time to help out on the final weekend of the campaign. Bumping into our slightly frazzled candidate, Stephen O'Brien, who was days away from becoming an MP, we chatted for a while as he waited for the imminent arrival of a leading party figure from London to join him in a walkabout in Tarporley town centre. Suddenly, the visiting dignitary arrived and I heard a familiar voice ring out behind me: 'Mark, how lovely to see you here!' I spun round and caught sight of Michael Portillo. It would not be the last time our paths would cross during the next few months.

My escapade in Cheshire confirmed categorically that I was not going to fight Enfield North again. I have remained in touch with old political friends there and have always tried to spend a day there campaigning at every election since. Politically, it turned out to be exactly the right decision – for me, at least. Only at the high water mark of 2010 – and, even then, helped enormously by a boundary change that removed Labour's strongest ward from the seat – has Enfield North returned to the Conservative fold. My successor, Nick de Bois, spent a total of eighteen years as the party's standard bearer, winning only once in five elections. We became good friends over the years, especially in his five-year stint as a fellow MP, but I am sure there were times when he must have cursed Lady Luck, rapid demographic change and me in equal measure.

Not for a moment did I feel uneasy at giving up the bird in my hand. Nor did I have to wait long for events to move at some pace. It was my fellow ward councillor, Dr Jonathan Munday, who called me at the office one afternoon in early September 1999 to tell me it was about to be formally announced that our local MP in Kensington & Chelsea had died. Alan Clark had only been MP here for the past two years but was best known for his acclaimed diaries, laced with vicious gossip and caustic insights on political ambition and motivation. I am sure he would have understood and secretly relished the fact that my first reaction on hearing of his demise was not to mourn his life but rather to calculate how this unexpected development might affect my own political prospects. How indeed? By the time the brief telephone call ended, I had worked out in my own mind what I was going to do next and how I hoped events would play out. For once in a lifetime, all those best laid plans came beautifully to fruition.

Only ten weeks had passed since my Eddisbury near-miss, but I knew full well that I had no chance of securing this latest by-election nomination. Even though it was my home seat, there were dozens of other Kensington & Chelsea activists on the list of parliamentary candidates. One of the less attractive aspects of human nature meant there was no way the locals would allow one of their own to take what they all secretly coveted. Such a plum seat was going to be snapped up by an outsider and probably someone with a national profile to boot. That clearly pointed to Michael Portillo. But, wait – wasn't everyone talking about him taking over from Peter Brooke, who had recently announced his intention to stand down from the neighbouring seat of the Cities of London & Westminster?

If you cannot be king, what better role than kingmaker? By the time that evening was out, Michael and I had spoken. My advice was straightforward – he should put his name forward and, in my judgement, he would win the nomination. In truth, whilst it was useful for him to have some inside assistance at the outset, he didn't need much help from me – or anyone else for that matter. Michael is simply a class act. He quickly won round the small number of early detractors and even in a strong field for the nomination, he was head and shoulders above the competition. By late November, he was back in the House of Commons.

All of which meant that there was now no obvious frontrunner for the Cities of London & Westminster constituency. Politics being politics, many of its younger activists had already begun to organise for Portillo. Naturally my efforts next door meant this team were well disposed to me, but they also had other favoured candidates.

I always used to think it was misleading to suggest that parliamentary selections can be 'fixed' for particular individuals, although I guess this little theory of mine was tested to destruction on the day before nominations closed for the 2024 election, when Conservative Campaign Headquarters presented the membership in the Basildon & Billericay constituency with a shortlist of one, namely the then party chairman, Richard Holden. Now that really is a fixed selection process! In the normal course of events, however, if as a potential candidate you do not shine at interview or answer questions with a reasonable level of knowledge and competence, others will clearly outperform you. Then, with the best will in the world, even your staunchest supporters on the selection committee will find it hard to hold the line.

Inevitably, the goings-on in such a high-profile central London constituency, the first in the current parliament to select a new Tory candidate, aroused the interest of the national press. Especially when political journalists were aided and abetted by disappointed former MPs expressing their dismay at being excluded or rapidly eliminated from the running. What they failed to appreciate was that many party activists across the country now craved a fresh start. It was nothing personal, but former MPs were a reminder of past divisions and a crushing national defeat. The party chairman was called upon to investigate accusations of vote rigging but gave the process a clean bill of health.

The selection dragged on for almost a month; on top of the usual interviews, it included a sweaty drinks reception for members to meet the candidates and attendance at the association's annual black-tie ball, where the entertainment was provided by comedian Jim Davidson. Sadly, none of his raucously well-received repertoire was even remotely recyclable by anyone aspiring to a political career.

Finally, it came down to a general meeting of the entire local party membership on the early evening of that first Sunday in December. The 197 applicants had been whittled down to three. Both of my opponents were old friends – my other former Enfield neighbour, Dr Ian Twinn, who would later become an MEP, and a fellow Kensington & Chelsea councillor, Warwick Lightfoot. Each of us performed and then we all returned to a designated room to await the verdict. We waited and waited and waited. By now, all efforts at polite small talk and almost an hour had passed. Ian was desperate for the loo and popped out of the room to find the nearest facilities. He had been gone seconds when, almost comically, an entourage made up of the association chairman, constituency agent and central office agent appeared before us ready to announce the result. Realising Ian had slipped away, they awaited his return. It probably was no more than three minutes, but amidst the acute tension and manic expectation, it seemed much, much longer. Desperately, I tried to catch their eyes but to no avail. I mentally made a note that any of these three gentlemen would make formidable poker partners.

Eventually – and by which time I could have gladly throttled him – Ian arrived back at the room. With the next words I heard, I realised my life would be changed for ever: 'Congratulations, Mark…'

Over the years, when explaining that moment to constituency school children, I likened it to winning the *X Factor* or some other reality TV show. Little did I realise that before long, many MPs, political journalists and the general public would also regard politics and celebrity culture as two sides of the same coin. At the risk of sounding sanctimonious, to this day, even in an era of social media overload, I have never seen politics in this light. Yet by the time I left the House of Commons, even to talk of political activity in terms of public service, a vocational commitment or the exercise of sound administration was to lay oneself open to ridicule.

• • •

On the first working day of the new millennium, I met up for lunch with my soon-to-be predecessor, Peter Brooke, at his club – appropriately enough, Brooks's in St James's Street. It was a convivial occasion, full of cricketing anecdotes and useful tips about how to handle what Peter diplomatically referred to as 'awkward characters in the Conservative Association and local community and amenity groups'. Even a quarter of a century on, I am too embarrassed and discreet to elaborate further here except to say that Peter was, as always, highly perceptive.

In essence, his more general advice boiled down to three main propositions, which that lunchtime I noted down assiduously and followed to the letter throughout my time in Parliament. First, never play partisan politics locally; putting out masses of attacking press releases (and, more recently, tweeting incontinently) never goes down well other than with the Tory Ultras who will vote for you anyway. Second, be a calm and unifying local presence such that voting against you would be like voting against the Queen. Finally, turn up to as many constituency events as you possibly can but only briefly; the constituents will be honoured by the fact you evidently have other important matters to attend to and still came, but if you hang around for the whole event, they will probably conclude that you haven't got anything better to do.

Peter never presumed to advise me again, still less to interfere, and the moment the 2001 election was called he disappeared from local Conservative Association affairs entirely. I could not have asked for a more perfect start. Keen to get some feedback, I asked Donald Stewart, the local Conservative agent, how Peter thought our lunch had gone.

'Ah, yes – all went very well. But Peter suddenly realised that the generational baton had been passed on when you mentioned that you had been at Oxford with his son. He also remarked that he had slightly got the rough end of the stick – he had taken his predecessor out to lunch when he had been selected and now he was doing the same.'

I never quite worked out whether this was a roundabout way of his expressing curiosity that I was not a member of a gentleman's club.

Although the margin of my selection victory had been eye-wateringly close, I always enjoyed a strong relationship with my local Conservative Association and its activists and councillors. In large part, this was down to a mutual understanding that there should be, and were, natural dividing lines in our responsibilities and activities. Having been a central London councillor, I knew all too well never to interfere, intervene or even to be seen as taking sides on matters like contentious planning applications, however tempting and expedient it may seem. Local councillors guard their independence jealously. And as an MP you need to hold the line that this is a local government matter – if you intervene once then it is very difficult not to get drawn in on other disputes. It also provided me with an alibi against lobbyists claiming my support for their clients' position on local issues. On these matters my lips were always sealed and very soon everyone knew it – and this made life a lot less contentious for me. It was also made much easier by the fact that for two thirds of my time as the MP, I had a full slate of Conservative councillors in my constituency.

The affluence of my constituency party meant I was able to resist succumbing to the temptation of many colleagues with less well-off local parties, who sublet office space or shared staff salaries. Some of these arrangements would unravel awkwardly during and after the expenses scandal. They also risked leaving MPs vulnerable to pressure or accusations of a conflict of interest when controversial national, and particularly local, policy issues arose.

As well as taking Peter Brooke's timeless template to heart, I was lucky. Every politician, however hard-working, is vulnerable to a clique of only three or four motivated local activists who take it upon themselves to make life hell for their MP. Their gripes might be policy or personality led, but over the years I heard some grim tales in the tea room about the antics of some local party members causing relentless misery, often over a prolonged period, for colleagues and their families.

Keeping tabs on local concerns, I was in the fortunate position of being readopted unanimously in secret ballots in advance of all six general election campaigns (including for 2019, when I only formally stepped down after my executive had approved me) barring one solitary vote against in 2010. Although the ballot was secret, I had my suspicion as to who the dissenter might be – probably confirmed when she defected to UKIP the following year.

Quickly, I got back into the swing of intense campaigning. This time round, however, there was less emphasis on my leading political action from the front. The local Tories had an office staffed by three full-time employees. During most of my time as the MP, we had over 2,000 paid up members and were reputed to be one of the wealthiest local parties in the country as well as being an acclaimed breeding ground for parliamentary candidates and MPs. There were young and middle-aged activists galore and the expectation upon me as the new candidate was to attend social events and get to know the party members and community leaders. A little light canvassing and door-knocking was only a small part of the mix. The firm assumption was that I was the MP in waiting. Having been in that position only three or so years before, I did not take things entirely for granted, but more than once I reflected on the irony that I felt infinitely more secure now defending a majority of under 5,000 than I had done in protecting twice as large a lead in 1997.

The next election could not come too soon. Although not someone naturally given to catastrophising, I began to be beset by irrational fears that I would not live long enough to see out my ambition to become an MP. I had got this far and suddenly my heart's desire was going to be snatched away. As it happens, it turned out to be a close-run thing.

The pursuit of danger for its own sake or perilous activity has never held the remotest attraction to me. Why risk breaking an ankle or worse by snowboarding or ice skating? Only under sufferance and with the children do I even contemplate the more moderately challenging fairground rides, and even then I close my eyes for the entire journey, grip the safety bar with all my might and pray the whole thing will be over as quickly as possible. Any infinitesimally small desire to take up mountain climbing came to an abrupt end on the day I spent time with the distraught mother of a fellow St Edmund Hall undergraduate, whose funeral I attended when JCR president. He had drowned in a vain attempt to save another student climber who had got herself into difficulties whilst out on an Oxford University mountaineering expedition in Wales.

Nor was I ever overly keen on taking up skiing. However, in my early thirties I was part of a group of couples who would habitually hire a chalet every year in the Swiss resort of Zermatt. More often than not, at least one of the other seven in our party would be pregnant or nursing an anterior cruciate ligament injury from a previous ski trip, so I would not always be the only non-skier. Zermatt is a wonderful year-round walking resort with picturesque villages such as Zum See and Findeln, where we would all meet up for lunch. In the meantime, I would have a leisurely breakfast, read for a while and then walk up to the pre-arranged rendezvous.

It was on one such day that my solo alpine stroll turned into a terrifying ordeal. Inexplicably, I followed a summer path sign and quickly encountered treacherous conditions. The logical thing at this point would have been to retrace my steps and find my way back on to a safer route. When walking in normal circumstances, I have always been averse to the unadventurousness of simply going back to a place in the same way I had come. So rather than doing the obvious thing, I kept on moving onwards into ever more unpredictable and dangerous terrain. Before long, I was crawling on my hands and knees across a thin ledge of sheet ice, hovering above a sheer thirty or so metre drop into a ravine.

Eventually, after a couple of hours of perilous progress in freezing conditions, I realised I was beginning to hyperventilate and shiver uncontrollably – classic signs of hypothermia. What now lay ahead of me was thick snow, but in the distance below I could see an earthy path covered in pine needles. Somehow, gathering all my strength and heading in that direction, I pushed through the snow, which first came up to my waist, then chest and finally just beneath my neck. Shuffling my way forwards, step by step, eventually I made my way down to safety. The pressure of all this unorthodox clambering had ripped to shreds the mountain jacket and corduroy trousers I had been wearing, so by the time I reached the restaurant, to the shock of my waiting friends, I resembled a vagrant. For the first time I now understood all too well those newspaper reports about intrepid British walkers getting hopelessly lost whilst hiking in foreign mountains and forests and their bodies often not being recovered for weeks or months despite the best efforts of rescue parties.

• • •

After dicing with alpine death, it was back to central London and the more mundane matter of getting myself over the line electorally. General election campaigning in Westminster and the City took on a fairly familiar pattern over the course of each of the five contests where I was the candidate. The constituency was never really regarded as anything other than safely Conservative, with the Labour Party always being seen as the main challengers.

My first opponent was an energetic Labour candidate even more youthful than me, Mike Katz. For him this was the beginning of a quarter-century-long fruitless journey to make it into Parliament, culminating in the triumph, if you can call it that, of appointment to the House of Lords in Keir Starmer's first list of nominees as Prime

Minister. Back in 2001, the local Labour Party entertained some hope that the loss of Peter Brooke's personal vote might provide an outside chance to overturn the 4,881 majority I had inherited. 'All this stuff about personal votes is nonsense,' Peter had reassured me at that first lunch. 'At most there are around 200 people I may have helped over the years whose vote won't transfer over to you automatically.' As ever, Peter's instincts proved to be on the money.

Saving a local bus service turned out to be an ideal cause on which to fight an energetic insurgent campaign. Rain or shine, over several weeks a small group of Labour activists led by their intrepid candidate stood outside the local Tube station getting concerned residents to sign a petition. To be honest, we Tories were a little slow off the mark and I was only alerted to this activity by a couple of puzzled Pimlico councillors who watched as for once our political opponents seemed to be taking the initiative. However, we had a trump card to play. Ultimately, the decision about axing or saving the bus route was in the hands of Westminster City Council, then Tory-run.

I was able to hot foot it to City Hall, meet the key decision-makers, make our case and then get plenty of photographs taken. On the day the public consultation ended, we got a glossy leaflet printed. Then, courtesy of our efficient and superior delivery network, we had it delivered overnight through the doors of thousands of Pimlico residents. I did not need to be as blatant – or, frankly, dishonest – as to claim, 'The Tories saved your bus service.' In fact, I stole my opponent's thunder far more effectively by claiming, 'This just shows what happens when our community comes together, and I want to thank the local Labour Party for their help...' When the local Labour activists peevishly criticised our leaflet, their irritation ended up backfiring. After all, failing to support that consensual and community-minded new Tory candidate would be a little like voting to abolish the monarchy, wouldn't it?

In a not uncompetitive field, the 2001 general election was truly the direst national campaign with which I was ever involved as a candidate (mercifully I was spared the 2024 calamity). Back in 1997, the Tories had been lulled into a false sense of hope by the electorate's rather cold-blooded rejection. Campaigning then was tremendously civilised – voters admitted they were very happy with the improved state of the economy, but that made it so much easier to take a chance with Labour after eighteen years. Many electors I spoke to then told me, 'I haven't quite made up my mind.' When you hear that line as a candidate, you need to understand the brutal truth – they are either too polite or embarrassed to tell you that they will categorically not be voting for you.

By 2001, many of those who had remained loyal to the Conservatives had become angry. Very angry. The two central planks of our national campaign were an increasingly excitable pitch on the issue of asylum seekers and a risible, hysterical daily countdown towards the purported abolition of the pound. Out canvassing, I came across many young professionals who would have been slam-dunk Tory voters in the 1980s but were now incredulous at the prospect of supporting the party. Broadly our vote was holding up, but it was clear to me weeks before the election that the outcome was essentially going to be a rerun of the contest four years earlier. Only on the final Friday night of campaigning did I entertain the possibility of an even more desperate situation. A group of half-a-dozen activists, plus my brother who worked nearby, met up in Marylebone. Normally we would have stuck together and canvassed as a team, but the mansion blocks and flat conversions in the area were so disparate that we decided to split up, knock on doors individually and then meet afterwards in a local pub.

Mine was an evening of unabated canvassing misery. Two affable professional couples, lifelong Tory voters, informed me reluctantly that they would be supporting Labour as a consequence of the harsh national campaign message. Several others simply refused to open the door when I rang the intercom and let them know it was the local Tory candidate calling round. Not a single person I met that evening was intending to vote for me. Feeling like a condemned man, I trudged in wretched unhappiness to the agreed meeting place to be greeted by a cheerful group of fellow Tories. They had apparently had a superbly successful trawl of the local area and proudly showed me canvass cards full to brimming with Conservative pledges. Small wonder my enthusiasm for meeting potential voters continued on its ever-downward trajectory as the years went by.

Finally, 7 June 2001 arrived – election day. My constituency count, and that for the neighbouring north Westminster seat, took place at the Queen Mother Sports Centre on Vauxhall Bridge Road, close to Victoria Station. The all-pervading smell of chlorine from its swimming baths only added to the sterility of proceedings.

My oldest friend Matthew Davidge, visiting from the US, had volunteered to be one of the scrutineers, so was there throughout the count from the moment the ballot boxes arrived. Unfortunately, he was less versed in the intricacies of the constituency, and it so happened that the first opened ballot box he caught sight of was in one of the least favourable Conservative wards in the seat. The City of London contains a polling district with a large housing association block that had been inherited from neighbouring Tower Hamlets when the borough boundaries had been regularised in the mid-1990s. Its residents were largely British-Bengali and their voting preferences retained their East End flavour.

With some alarm, Matthew concluded that I might be in for a long and difficult night. He felt obliged to call me at about midnight with this unwelcome news. For the next hour or so I half-feared the worst as I attentively followed the BBC's election night coverage on the TV at home. Then Donald, who had been the local agent since 1981, rang. 'All is well,' he pronounced and then correctly predicted our vote share margin of victory to two decimal points. My initial reaction was less joy, more an overwhelming sense of relief. After all, no part of this constituency had returned anything other than a Conservative MP since 1880. I was home and dry with a majority of 4,499 on 46.3 per cent of the vote, a level I would never in future dip below.

• • •

The new intake were summoned to attend Parliament the following Tuesday, but in the meantime, we were given a long weekend to re-cuperate. For my part, there was more pressing business to address on the City side of my new constituency. In the months leading up to the election, Hugh Kelly and I had given some thought to how my role at Kellyfield Consulting might evolve once I became an MP. The archaic sitting hours of Parliament, with their presumption that most mornings would be spent on other activity, still held sway. Family friendly hours only finally came into fashion during my first term. In 2001, Parliament sat between 2.30 p.m. and 10 p.m. Monday to Wednesday and between 10.30 a.m. and 7 p.m. on Thursday, with most Fridays set aside for consideration of private members' bills. So, Hugh and I had begun to sketch out an arrangement, with my continuing to work part-time and gradually reducing my profit and equity share in the business. To be frank, with hindsight I was utterly unrealistic about the difficulties that I would have faced trying to maintain any sort of executive role, especially as I had consistently been the company's single largest fee-earner.

No sooner had Hugh and I met up in our offices first thing on that Monday morning after the election than this problem was taken out of my hands. I had noticed with passing curiosity that in the months before my heading off on the campaign trail, Hugh would occasionally disappear unannounced during the day for several hours at a time. I was about to find out why. 'Rather than you staying involved in the business, I have been working on a Plan B. I have put together a consortium to buy you out of your share of Kellyfield.' In the circumstances, my bargaining position was not strong. But realising this, we quickly came to a perfectly amicable accommodation. A cash deal. In our initial valuations, we were only a few hundred thousand pounds apart and agreed to split the difference. Finalising the practicalities and getting the paperwork done took a couple of months. We signed off our deal on the morning of Friday 17 August before heading off for a final long leisurely lunch together.

I am afraid this is where my heartfelt views about luck and timing being central to commercial success came into play. Barely three weeks later, the 9/11 terrorist attacks triggered a sharp economic slowdown; meanwhile, the new investors in the business were determined to exploit Kellyfield's strong market reputation by rapid expansion, which involved taking on expensive new staff. A little over two years later, with turnover down by over a fifth and overheads rising by a quarter, our once highly profitable and successful SME was forced into liquidation. It may no longer have been my responsibility or problem, but it was still a desperately sad post-script to an important chapter of my life.

• • •

My first task on turning up to the Houses of Parliament was to set foot in the Commons Chamber. Although I had visited the parliamentary estate a fair few times over the years, one small superstition I retained was never to enter the Chamber until I was entitled to do so as an MP. It was a personal but moving moment, made all the more poignant when amidst a few tourists ambling around, the attendant on duty recognised me by name. Apparently, it is the fear of imposters making their way into the Chamber that is one of the things that spurs the doorkeepers to learn so quickly the names and faces of all the new intake of MPs after each election. Even this level of diligence did not prevent them suffering the mortifying experience, which I saw in my final year in Parliament, of watching helplessly as a gaggle of visitors got caught up in one of the voting lobbies during a division when an unexpected snap vote was called.

The working practices at the Palace of Westminster were so steeped in tradition as to be beyond parody. For anyone who had run a business beyond its hallowed buildings, Parliament's shambling inefficiency and outdated approach to technology (amongst many other things) must have come as a shock. This was compounded by the desperate attempts by long-serving MPs to cling to the 'way things have always been done'. I have never been averse to the formality that comes with traditional architectural surroundings, but my frustration quickly rose with those veteran politicians who seemed to worship every last vestige of Westminster life. With a mix of paternalism and resigned acceptance for institutionalised incompetence, the new intake of MPs were persuaded by the Whips' Offices that we should willingly and happily submit ourselves to the mercies of the assistant serjeant-at-arms. This pleasant and cheerful official was arguably two decades beyond her ideal retirement date and despite being an apparent stranger to the modern demands of constituency representation, she was venerated by senior MPs. She would not have lasted five minutes in any commercial organisation that I had ever been a part of.

Worse still was the absurd charade of the State Opening of Parliament. The cause of a half-day-long blanket disruption to traffic and pedestrian access in an ever-larger area at the heart of my constituency, I have long believed that this traditional spectacle should be pared back. The needs of international tourists and constitutional experts can surely be satisfied by the ceremony of the golden coach transporting the monarch from Buckingham Palace down the Mall and Whitehall once every four or five years, perhaps in the immediate aftermath of a general election. As an elected member of the House of Commons, I was always well aware of my lowly place in the pecking order within a constitutional monarchy, but it rankled that we were summoned to the House of Lords to listen to the monarch. Standing on tiptoe at the back of the chamber and looking down at the seated wives of peers dressed to the nines in ermine and diamond-encrusted tiaras, it always struck me as a bizarre way to run a legislature in the twenty-first century. When, after one such state opening, I quietly admitted to what the more religious-minded might call 'doubts', a misty-eyed colleague and keen promoter of pomp and ceremony in all its forms looked at me somewhat aghast. 'Good God old chap, are you absolutely sure that you are a Tory?'

The Conservatives had been plunged into a leadership election by William Hague's resignation on the morning after our crushing defeat. Leadership contests would become the excitable norm for my party, except during the eleven-year tranquillity of the Cameron reign. In my time in Parliament, there were four contested leadership elections (necessitating no fewer than eighteen separate ballots) and two no-confidence challenges to sitting leaders; as we know, this only became more febrile after I left the House.

I backed Michael Portillo. This came as no surprise to anyone, as I was widely regarded as one of his acolytes. We had fought neighbouring seats in 1997 and now represented adjacent constituencies. I had played a well-publicised supporting role in his selection in Kensington & Chelsea, where I had seen his undoubted abilities at close quarters in my week as his local candidate minder and driver with that most vital of assets, a Kensington & Chelsea parking permit.

But this was not quite the whole story. By summer 2001, I fear Michael's appetite to become party leader was no longer there. He realised the mountain for the Tories to climb was huge; he also knew in his heart that if his modernising plans were to be realised then he would have to betray most of the people who thought themselves to be his patrons and many of the things that people had long assumed he stood for.

To be honest, I also began to entertain some doubts. In company, Michael is charming and charismatic, and I had hoped that once the 'revelations' about his past private life had become public, he might open up a little more. If anything, it had made him even more defensive and protective of his privacy. I absolutely respect this, but sadly the celebrity-obsessed world of 2001 – and certainly ever since – does not allow aspiring top-flight politicians this luxury. In the meantime, his frenzied supporters were always demanding ever more outspoken contributions at party conference and beyond.

We now reached the all-important final parliamentary ballot to whittle down from three to two the final contenders, whose names would then be put to the party membership. I was on College Green, at the invitation of BBC Radio 4, to await the outcome. The result came through – Portillo had come third, behind the eventual winner, Iain Duncan Smith, by a solitary vote. My abiding memory of that afternoon is watching one of the other invited MP guests, Ann Widdecombe, yelping with delight, arms raised to the heavens as if overcome by some biblical revelation. But it wasn't joy that her candidate (Ken Clarke) had won through but undisguised pleasure that Portillo had lost. I suspect Michael knew only too well how deeply divisive a reputation he had; it is one thing to take on the mantle of party leadership when you are in office or tantalisingly close to it, but quite another to lead a ragtag battalion of 165 MPs (for that is what we were then) traumatised by a second massive defeat. Small wonder his heart was not in it.

Leadership dramas aside, the first few days in Parliament had passed in a blur of excitement. We started with a full day's induction organised by the Whips' Office. I suspect that these days everything is organised on a far more systematic basis over the best part of a week; equally, what we received was probably eight hours longer tuition than anything that would have been offered only ten years earlier.

The representative duties seemed overwhelming at first. The constituency mailbag was full to overflowing, as the impact of an intervening general election meant there was a pent-up supply of correspondence landing on the desk of all newly elected MPs. Needless to say, the daily three bulging bags, each holding about 100 items of correspondence, that faced me as a parliamentary newbie has now been replaced by several hundred emails, all demanding an even more immediate response. But back then, the impact was the same – without an office or staff, any new MP is simply drowning in constituency casework. You quickly work out that some of this short-lived upsurge in paperwork is as a result of the 'usual suspects', who are writing in promptly after an election on realising there is now a brand-new person to harangue. One such nightmare constituent quickly took to ringing my office umpteen times a day complaining about her council housing – I am almost ashamed to say it was a matter of much rejoicing in my office a few months later when she was rehoused to a property that fell a few hundred yards over the constituency boundary. She would now doubtless become a persistent thorn in the side for another MP's private office.

Then there are the many well-meaning non-governmental organisations (NGOs) and interest groups that send on their standard fare; the diary also rapidly fills up with commitments. You then begin to realise why the chamber of the House of Commons often appears so empty. How on earth will you have the time to attend debates? Eventually, things do settle down, but the assigning of offices and the engaging of staff all seems to take an interminably long time.

I remember, in the tea room in my first few weeks, the veteran politician John Horam telling me that when first elected in 1970 for Gateshead West, admittedly a small urban seat with only 35,000 electors, he reckoned on needing to devote only a couple of hours a week to constituency correspondence. Typically, he would do this by hand after lunch on a Sunday. A fabled MP of a similar vintage went one step further. Apparently, it was only on clearing his attic after his death that his relatives discovered several thousands of unopened letters from constituents. In a similarly cavalier vein, a Tory MP with whom I overlapped employed his wife as his constituency secretary. They would return from three months abroad each summer to adjoining desks covered in overflowing piles of letters, all of which they promptly threw away unopened on the basis that 'if it is that important, they will write again'.

I cannot think of any current parliamentarians who would be as offhand in dealing with constituents. Nowadays, it has become fashionable instead to deplore MPs for turning into super-councillors. But the dirty little secret of modern politics is that so many national and international issues have become so utterly intractable that 'holding the executive to account' (the primary constitutional purpose of those we elect to Parliament) has become the equivalent of banging your head against a brick wall.

In constituency work, however, there are admittedly more modest gains, but tangible progress can always be made with reasonable speed on pressing casework. Even in this more egalitarian era, a letter or email on parliamentary notepaper rapidly finds its way to the top of the correspondence pile at the local council, government department or public utility. Remedial action is quick. Your intervention may only be enabling a constituent to jump the queue, but activity invariably leads to a resolution of a contentious problem. Effort and reward are more clearly aligned than in much else that makes up the political process. It should come as no surprise as to why so many MPs relish constituency work and take so much more pride and satisfaction from it than most other aspects of the political process. Many MPs, especially those on the back benches, feel increasingly alienated from Westminster life, especially as it seems so detached from their existence back in the constituency where they and their activity receive genuine respect.

An early initiative in my own office was to open a box file for letters, emails and thank-you cards sent by grateful constituents. Although the obvious control experiment was never tested, I am confident that an 'ungrateful letters' file would have had far fewer takers. Naturally, come election-time, it was useful to have anonymised quotes from satisfied constituents to adorn our leaflets, but it also provided a chance for me and my private office to be cheered up by messages of gratitude from vulnerable residents. Especially after difficult days in the office, it was handy to be reminded of the many pluses that came with gruelling constituency casework. One other lesson I quickly learned was to remember that most normal people do not write to their MP other than at times of extreme stress. More often than not, correspondence with your elected representative comes as a last resort, with little hope or expectation of resolution to the problem at hand. Most people just want to be taken seriously and to have their voice heard. A rapid response and empathy often count for as much as, if not more than, getting an issue sorted.

I should like to think that I never got jaded by constituency duties, but it was always relentless. I was also wary of taking on the sort of casework in areas such as housing that was properly handled by councillors – or, in the London-wide context, the local assembly member. Inevitably, by the time I was appointed to international roles with the need to travel extensively, it was my parliamentary office that became the initial point of contact for much of the constituency work. In my first year, I held formal constituency surgeries but always felt a little uneasy at expecting constituents to attend the offices of the local Conservative Association, where they took place. These surgeries were always very sparsely attended, so before long and in the unique circumstances of Parliament being located in my seat, I used to invite constituents whose cases could not be sorted out by correspondence to come and meet me for coffee at Portcullis House. This had the dual benefit of being ideally located for public transport and in a high-security environment. Even then, in any one month I probably saw around three or four constituents with intractable issues that genuinely required a personal input.

In time, the one thing that did tire was the overwhelming sense of entitlement of some of the people I represented at either end of the social scale. Some of the wealthiest residents, often non-UK nationals, who had moved into super-prime districts like Knights-bridge and Mayfair were startlingly rude and had unreasonable ex-pectations about visa arrangements for staff and being able to have bespoke security, parking permits rights and the like. They assumed their money would talk and often demanded to deal with me and my office through lawyers or PR consultants, which I always did my best to resist.

In stark contrast, some of those living in social housing seemed to have no concept of how massively subsidised their central London housing costs were. A few would make absurdly unreasonable de-mands to be upgraded into much larger accommodation, as they had ever more children or had chosen to allow relatives to move in with them. Others requested the right to pass on their housing tenure through the generations. For every representation I received that railed at the imposition of the two-child benefit cap, I reckoned on also hearing from middle-class professionals lamenting that they could neither afford to start nor expand their families beyond a single child. Given the cost of living in central London, many of these constituents did not understand why they should be expected to subsidise others to have as many children as they wished.

In the back of my mind, I always recalled one of the pledges I had made at my selection meeting. This was to assist those middle earners in key public and private sector jobs locally, whose antiso-cial hours would be alleviated by being able to qualify for scarce housing resources. With some remorse, I must confess that which-ever way I look at it, those good intentions came to absolutely noth-ing. My efforts to rectify this pressing issue, such as they were, have been a total failure. Inner London's population is polarised as never before between the global super-wealthy and those able to quali-fy for social housing. Many of those in between, who are earning multiples of the average UK salary, are simply unable to afford to live in the heart of our capital city. This cannot be sustainable and is certainly not equitable.

• • •

I had arrived in Parliament at the high point of New Labour's for-tunes. Tony Blair and Gordon Brown were in their pomp, albeit fated to have their reputations yoked together in a comparison that in time did Brown few favours. By contrast, the Conservative Party remained subdued, realising that the long and winding road back to office would take time and probably require economic turmoil, of which there was precious little sign on the horizon.

I remember needing to bite my tongue in some early visits to the legendary tea room when listening to the woeful level of igno-rance being spouted by several long-serving Tory MPs, especially on the way the real world of business operated. Then there were those loudmouthed parliamentarians across the party divide whose pitch is that their background makes them uniquely qualified to understand the concerns of ordinary voters, when the truth is that all 650 MPs have a story to tell. One kindly senior-ish MP detected my frustration and gave me priceless advice about dealing with col-leagues, troublesome or otherwise: 'Always accentuate the positive.' I tried my level best. But there was one rural Tory who persisted in treating us to his bombastic views and homespun wisdom about the world at large. Although he fancied himself as an intriguer and intellectual of sorts, I was staggered to discover he had actually attended university, having assumed that he must be a non-graduate. Evidently his shtick went down well in his super-safe constituency, but it was no surprise to learn it had some of the lowest educational attainment in the country. I guess he was living proof that in the land of the blind, the one-eyed man is king.

Strategically, I realised it would be advisable to join a faction. I had not been averse to this as a Kensington & Chelsea councillor when I aligned immediately with the anti-establishment grouping under Daniel (now Lord) Moylan, who came tantalisingly close to securing leadership of the council in 2000. But somehow, I held back. As a result, in Parliament I became if not exactly a loner, then certainly someone who was a little more semi-detached than was advisable.

In part this came about as a result of my constituency duties as a central London MP, which meant most midweek evenings were – and would be for the next eighteen years – spent attending local events. The very nature of being the City of London's MP, of which more in a moment, also brought with it a certain need for independent mindedness, which sat uneasily with becoming overly partisan. Then I looked around at the factions that held sway in the parliamentary party and to be honest, none appealed unduly.

The strongly Eurosceptic party groups initially sought me out as a known Portillo supporter, but I rapidly realised they were not for me ideologically. I rather railed against the self-regard of the left-leaning Conservative Mainstream and nor did I really agree with most of their economic prescriptions. I guess the so-called Notting Hill Set of more metropolitan modernisers was where my views were best suited. Efforts were made half-heartedly to engage with me, but I found myself rather repelled by their near worship of Tony Blair and all his works. In my heart, I also felt strongly that for us as Conservatives, in contrast to New Labour, our gods had not failed, so why modernise wholesale for its own sake? Trying to force the pace rather than accepting that our opportunity would arise when Gordon Brown's high-spending economic model fell apart, as it surely would, struck me as essentially inauthentic.

This conclusion about the Cameron project was about a decade ahead of its time. But in politics there are few rewards or plaudits that attach to being pioneering or innovative in suggesting new ideas. It is often better to be second in promoting a fresh strand of thought in politics; innate conservatism (and not only in my party) will dampen down enthusiasm for the novel in public life, but if an idea has legs, its time will assuredly come.

One of the eccentricities of my constituency was representing the City of London. The historic commercial capital of the nation, its population has only in recent decades stabilised and risen a little. This followed more than a century of consistent decline since the arrival of the railways in the 1840s, which made commuting both possible and widespread. The Square Mile is run by the City of London Corporation, second only to the monarchy as the great surviving institution of British public life – and equally protective of its privileges and wealth. The City is the only part of the UK that retains a business vote for its local elections. It has its own police force, which predates the Metropolitan Police, and takes on several specialist national law enforcement duties. It has responsibility for the maintenance of vast swathes of public land (including Hampstead Heath and Epping Forest) and social housing estates located beyond its boundaries, and it uses its massive endowments to promote financial and professional services globally. The City's influence, financial clout and survival instinct has always ensured that, even if belatedly, it has always backed the winning side in crucial moments of English history, from the Peasants' Revolt to the War of the Roses and the Civil War.

Although my standard constituency responsibilities extended only to its 7,000 residents, representing the City in Parliament meant so much more. It involved regularly promoting private bills on the floor of the House, as well as being a leading voice in Parliament in support of the financial sector, insurance and professional services. This certainly ensured I kept abreast of economic policy and theory. There was also a massive ceremonial element, including attendance at state dinners and promoting the livery companies. I reckoned on going to a white- or black-tie dinner at least once a month. Reform of this last anachronistic corner of UK local government is probably at best (or worst, depending on your outlook) a second-term priority for the new Labour government. The senior official with responsibility for City–Parliament relations, the Remembrancer, used to remind me that unravelling and repealing the legislative labyrinth involving the City would take many years. Having had a ring-side seat in the quick-fire creation of the Supreme Court, it is clear to me that political expediency can drive rapid change, however botched the outcome. I fear it may be complacent to assume a similar fate will not one day befall the City of London Corporation.

Until the wild volatility of recent general elections, a sitting MP was almost as likely to lose their seat as a consequence of boundary changes than as a result of the fickleness or disgruntlement of the voters. The Parliamentary Boundary Commission and its work always loomed large during my time in the Commons. Indeed, one of my earliest commitments as a newly minted MP was to traipse up to Wembley to address the local public inquiry in the inauspicious surroundings of Brent Town Hall. It was agreed that the area around Bayswater and Lancaster Gate would be carved out of my constituency, although it took a further nine years for these changes to be enacted.

After 2010, the incoming coalition government arbitrarily pledged to reduce the size of the Commons from 650 to 600 MPs. Perhaps unsurprisingly, this form of parliamentary musical chairs had limited appeal and was shelved in a spat between the two party leaders. Next up came two further aborted attempts to alter constituency boundaries, which by then came at a time when the Conservatives lacked a working majority. I undertook huge amounts of preparatory work and endured a fair bit of anxiety at the prospect first of losing the City of London jewel in my crown and then later at potentially being forced into a head-to-head challenge with Sir Malcolm Rifkind for a super-safe seat (we convinced the Boundary Commissioners of a separate scheme that we devised between us, which at the time would have saved both our skins). But by the time, in 2024, that updated boundaries were eventually contested, Malcolm and I had long since retired from the House. Meanwhile, the relatively modest and favourable changes that were finally proposed and agreed for my erstwhile seat, adding 12,000 or so electors from St John's Wood, were not enough to save the constituency from Labour's landslide.

The real meat and drink of political life, of course, is advocacy in all its forms. My public speaking, like that of most MPs, improved immensely over time. I would never turn up to a constituency event without having sketched out either in my mind or on a scrap of paper a quick two- or three-minute address. As an attending MP, even if you had not been billed as the guest speaker, you were always regarded as fair game in the eyes of the event organiser to 'say a few words'. Keeping it brief was invariably the order of the day – as I used to say more often than I can remember, I have never been criticised for making a speech that is too short.

Waiting to be called to speak in debate or committee, however, was one of the great frustrations of parliamentary life. In the same way that war films misrepresent the fact that action is the exception rather than the norm, huge amounts of time in political life are spent hanging around and waiting for things to happen. Mind-sapping boredom, waiting around for others to speak before your turn finally arrives, is the fate of backbenchers keen to or press-ganged into making a contribution to parliamentary debates.

It is said that the trouble with all your dreams coming true is that you quickly discover this is not altogether a good thing. Never-theless, I spent most of that first summer as an MP on cloud nine, thrilled at having achieved my ambition, enjoying my fascinating new life and delighted to have capitalised my share of the business venture I had set up. All eyes firmly on the future. Then came 9/11 and everything changed.

Everyone remembers what they were doing on 11 September 2001 when the New York and Washington DC terrorist attacks unfolded. I was away on vacation. A few weeks earlier, we made the decision to spend that second week of September in a luxury Marrakesh hotel. It had been a close-run thing. The other option we had in mind was to head off on a rather less relaxed holiday visiting Matthew, who by then was living in Manhattan. But Morocco it was. Switching on Sky TV that day in my room to catch up on world news just before the 'top of the hour' (as their newsreaders so irritatingly describe it), I watched transfixed as confusion briefly reigned about a plane that had hit the World Trade Center before cold clarity was restored as the ghostly silhouette of a second plane swung round and crashed into its other tower.

Five months earlier I had spent an evening sitting next to Barbara Olson, one of that dreadful day's most high-profile victims. A leading US conservative TV commentator, she had been in London with her husband, the US Solicitor General and former partner with Gibson Dunn & Crutcher. That international law firm had become a client of mine and was hosting a dinner for about fifty guests in the private room of a Belgravia restaurant. Ted Olson, Barbara's husband, spoke without notes for almost an hour at the event, describing the fascinating part-political, part-legal process by which he led the Republicans in Florida after the previous November's disputed presidential election. Aware of my political activity and allegiance, Barbara was tremendous, ebullient company as we chatted away late into the evening about politics and right-wing strategy on either side of the Atlantic. On 11 September, she was a passenger on American Airlines Flight 77, which was crashed into the Pentagon. Whenever I visit the achingly affecting national memorial at the site of the Twin Towers in Lower Manhattan, I always search out for Barbara's name. So many people lost and so many others whose lives they touched, if only very fleetingly.

For a short while after these fateful events, many of those working in financial districts across the world wondered if the appetite for high-rise office buildings would be permanently impacted. The mood was sombre but determined only a few weeks later in early October, when, as the local MP, I accompanied the acclaimed architect Norman Foster at the formal start of steel ceremony for the construction of what would briefly be the City of London's tallest building, the distinctive 30 St Mary Axe, better known as The Gherkin. Everyone associated with it was keen to promote this 41-floor skyscraper as a clear vote of confidence in the future of urban sky-lines, but some genuine doubts remained. We need not have worried. Barely two decades on from its opening, The Gherkin is now dwarfed on several sides by an array of more recently completed tall towers and the City of London's skyline has been transformed.

A Conservative Party in thrall to the military and instinctively supportive of a Republican President at the White House felt at home with the outpouring of support for America in the immediate aftermath of 9/11. However, we did nothing to tap into the unease of a nation that quickly became riven with disagreements about foreign military skirmishes, which were soon becoming ominously protracted. I was as guilty as most of my party colleagues of failing to ask the searching questions about the drift to military action throughout the Middle East, beyond the initial attempt to smoke out Osama bin Laden and his followers from their Afghan hideout.

I am sure the apparent certainty of our security services and military about the threat posed by the Iraqi dictator, Saddam Hussein, played its part, but the terrible death toll, human misery and £10 billion cost to the UK taxpayer still cast a long shadow over the UK's decision to go to war on the back of intelligence that was 'presented with a certainty that was not justified', according to the Chilcot Report. We ended up destabilising the delicate balance of power in the region, to Iran's strategic advantage, and compounded the problem with a similarly naive approach to the so-called Arab Spring in 2011–12.

At the heart of military intervention lay the doctrine of liberal interventionism. At successive Lord Mayor's Banquets and in the House of Commons, I watched Tony Blair, as Prime Minister, make the case for universal values of democracy, equality and freedom like some possessed evangelical preacher. I am convinced that he genuinely believes this from the bottom of his heart, but my scepticism about this way of seeing the world has only grown over time. As the years went by, the UK made a terrible mess of military involvement in Libya and then failed to act after the use of chemical weapons in Syria.

Nonetheless, even as a backbencher I had grave doubts about the wisdom of putting these matters to a parliamentary vote. Equally, I recognised that the misapplied intelligence that had led us to signing up for war in Iraq has destroyed political trust in the executive on matters of military engagement. However, the precedent now seems to have been set to hold a parliamentary vote before UK troops are ever sent into a theatre of war. Essentially, this amounts to a virtual veto against going to war, since those constituents opposed to military action are almost inevitably more motivated in their opposition than supporters and they will bring huge vocal pressure to bear on their elected representatives.

We impose our values on others at our peril. The assumption that everyone around the world supports democracy and shares – or at least should share – our political and cultural values is not simply mistaken but deeply patronising. Ironically, it is arguably much the same mentality that lay behind the headlong rush by Christian missionaries to colonise so much of Asia and Africa in the eighteenth and nineteenth centuries.

By the time I was a Foreign Office Minister with responsibility for Afghanistan, I used to quietly despair when being briefed about the UN's nation-building efforts. It seemed to me that there was a failure to appreciate that the loyalty of most Afghan citizens, excepting perhaps those from Kabul who had been educated abroad, was primarily to their family, their tribe and their village. Structures of federal and municipal government recognisable to western aid workers lacked any credibility in the eyes of many Afghan citizens. I was once briefed by a well-meaning and highly committed NGO director talking enthusiastically about plans to roll out women's and LGBT rights on the ground in rural Afghanistan. When I suggested to her that this might easily be regarded as neo-colonialism – and presumably she had little truck with the original version – she seemed unable to understand the need for the west to make a far more convincing case for our humanitarian interventions.

• • •

The political map of London throughout my time in Parliament contained a small oasis of Conservative blue at the centre, largely surrounded on all sides by a sea of red, Labour inner-city strongholds. This made it essential to work across party lines, and what never ceased to surprise constituents was how effective working relationships can be struck up between neighbouring MPs of different parties. Frank Dobson sought me out straight away to assure me that he had no intention of 'playing silly buggers in the local press' and was duly comforted that I was similarly minded. I took this to be a slightly more earthy interpretation of Peter Brooke's earliest words of wisdom and we always got on well.

The toxic racial politics within Tower Hamlets meant that neither Jim Fitzpatrick nor Rushanara Ali ever had any cause to see me – or any local Tories for that matter – as a troublesome opponent. But the local Labour MP with whom I had most contact was Karen Buck in neighbouring Westminster North. We never personalised any dispute and always had a highly productive working relationship on a full range of local matters. The hospital used by most of her constituents, St Mary's in Paddington, was located just inside my patch. There were some serious issues around its perennial funding shortfall and increasingly dilapidated estate. It would have been easy when in opposition for either of us to play the partisan political card on this, but we both concluded that our constituents stood to benefit more by our putting on a united front with the Department for Health and the hospital's senior executives.

The South East Bayswater Residents' Association also straddled our two constituencies, and at its annual summer garden party, Karen and I invariably spoke as something of a double act. This always went down extremely well with local residents. I guess most had come to see politics within the prism of the Prime Minister's Questions pantomime and the frequent remark was how much more refreshing it was to see politics being conducted by grown-ups.

One aspect of my life that sadly was not operating so harmoniously was my marriage. Michele and I had met through mutual university friends and were wed just before Christmas 1994. She worked punishing hours in corporate finance and subsequently as a director with two stockbroking firms at the same time I was building up Kellyfield Consulting. One memory that will linger for as long as I live was my being at home alone one weekend when we had been married for about four years. She was away in South Africa with clients, finalising a major transaction. I sat quietly in our living room and was enveloped by a warm sense of sheer happiness and contentment about our life together that all but brought me to tears. My political and business successes during this period would not have happened without her unstinting support.

But the years continued to pass and slowly but imperceptibly, the two of us began to drift apart. Children never seemed to be on the agenda. We hardly ever exchanged a cross word – I probably regarded this as a reassuring sign when perhaps alarm bells ought to have been ringing. For us both, I fear an increasing amount of dissatisfaction became bottled up. She has made her reputation since our marriage came to an end as the CEO of a succession of medical charities. I have always appreciated how fortunate I was to have spent over a decade together with her.

· · ·

The first serious signs of cracks in my marriage began just as Elizabeth Truss entered my life. Liz later insisted that we had first briefly met whilst out campaigning at the Uxbridge by-election in summer 1997. Neither of us could have possibly suspected then that the circumstances that would trigger a subsequent by-election in that far-flung outpost of north-west London suburbia would also propel her to the shortest premiership in the history of the office. But that all lay almost exactly a quarter of a century ahead.

Meanwhile, by the time I had become an MP her name was already familiar to me as a fellow party activist in London. Liz then set up C4C in the aftermath of another dismal Tory performance in the capital at the 2001 election – although two of our eight national gains were in seats on the Essex borders, our vote share in London as a whole was lower than it had been even four years earlier.

Conservatives For Cities, to give it its full name, was a fairly transparent vehicle for self-promotion by a clearly ambitious young politico. In fairness, over the next few years, with characteristic energy, Liz organised plenty of speaker meetings, drinks parties and policy papers on urban issues. At the time, she identified the urgent priority for fast-track planning reform, increased housing density and affordable childcare. This perky, positive and conventional socially liberal agenda was all a far cry from her later descent into the world of faintly paranoid conspiracy theories and accusations of being thwarted by the 'deep state'. Sadly, the prescription for that ever-elusive Tory urban recovery has changed not one iota, but the opportunity to transform lives has been wasted by the Conservatives since 2010, all too often opting for government by announcement or gimmick rather than implementation and action.

So, to the romantic, dimmed lights of early autumn on England's self-styled Riviera. It is October 2002 at the Highcliff Hotel in Bournemouth, with Conservative Party Conference in full swing. I am chatting away at a packed late-night bar with an Oxford contemporary, Philip Hollobone, who will finally make it to Parliament at the third time of asking at the following election. We have always been on diametrically opposite wings of the Conservative Party over Europe, immigration, gay rights and much else besides, but despite it all we have remained firm friends for the past forty years. I fear that the mutual distrust and antagonism in the party nowadays means few such relationships persist, which does not augur well for the future.

But I digress. Unobtrusively, Liz sidles over to join us and for the next half an hour, the three of us gossip away about current affairs, the future direction of the party and, something close to the heart of both of my companions, candidate selection. As we part, I wish her all the best in her search for a parliamentary seat and as a throwaway line say, 'Please get in touch if I can be of any help.'

By the time I next made it into my parliamentary office the following Monday morning, a friendly email awaited, taking me up on my offer and seeking advice about selection interview techniques. Within the week we met and then began to stay in touch over the next year, getting together for coffee or lunch on an increasingly regular basis. Even then, Liz came across as an impulsive bundle of energy, totally obsessed by the workings and machinations of politics. During this time, we worked together as she approached with laser-like precision the nerve-racking process of getting select-ed – the parroting of slogans, blind partisanship and presenting it all with a veneer of absolute confidence. She was in her element. Despite still only being in her late twenties, Liz got mighty close to selection in several Conservative-held seats and never seemed more than momentarily disheartened by the succession of near misses. With such toughness in the face of adversity, it hardly needed saying that it was simply a matter of when rather than if she would find herself a constituency.

Resourcing for opposition parties is best described as being on a shoestring. Many of the shadow Cabinet had served in govern-ment, so the sparse level of help came as something of a culture shock after so many years of relying on the assistance of the civil service. Having joined the front bench, it was all hands to the pump amongst the depleted contingent of 165 Conservative MPs as future manifesto writing and an election beckoned. I was asked to prepare the first draft of the party's international trade policy, and Liz was in her element as we worked enthusiastically together on this over several weeks. To my surprise, our work was incorporated virtually word for word into the party platform, and to my amusement, as International Trade Secretary she was still using the phrase 'free and fair trade' that we had coined all those years ago.

This is where I had my first exposure to her quirky approach to problem solving and policymaking. Liz has always prided herself in being dismissive of the conventional, almost to the point of parody. By contrast, she is genuinely excited by the new, the untried and the untested. She steadfastly refuses to be told what to do but is always open to maverick ideas and proposals. It is no surprise that in her earliest political activity at school she would not have seen the Conservative Party as an obvious fit, but her libertarianism, orthodox economic views and social liberalism have become more mainstream over the years.

Part of this process of broadening minds involved lending each other books, which unfathomably the other had not already got on their shelves or read. For her part, she passed on a well-thumbed copy of Ayn Rand's *Atlas Shrugged*, the almost unreadable bible of libertarian philosophy. Having ground my way through its 1,000 plus pages of dense print, I resolved for each of my (now) three published books to employ an editor and steer well clear of wildly impractical political theory.

In return, I lent her *Liar's Poker* by Michael Lewis, the story of reckless greed, excessive ambition and impetuous risk-taking on the Wall Street trading floor. I assume this must also have been an inspiration of sorts to Liz, though we all had to wait almost two decades to understand precisely what that inspiration was.

Gradually we came to see more of each other, so that before long barely a day would go by without our at least speaking over the phone. Some years later, a mutual friend who knew us well at this time remarked on the evident chemistry between us and how we both became so much more animated when talking of each other. But it was only at the end of 2003 that the intensity of our friendship turned into the relationship that later became so well documented.

Liz was always exhilarating to be around. She could turn on a sixpence from being a wide-eyed wannabe hanging on my every word to instead becoming an opinionated, stubborn and somewhat belligerent know-it-all. In equal measure, her manic energy was intoxicating, disconcerting and exhausting. Not to mention at times utterly infuriating.

Inevitably, there is something very unreal in any affair, especially when both parties are married and living with their spouses as we then were. The mundanities of clearing the dinner table, putting out the rubbish or even settling down together to watch television play no part in your shared existence; instead, there is the anticipation and elation of a few precious hours spent in each other's exclusive company and the thrill that comes with never quite being sure whether this is the last time.

Nevertheless, in my heart I was painfully aware that our marriages were in very different places. Every three or four months, beset by what I took to be a mixture of guilt and indecision, Liz would seek to cool things down. I quickly worked out that the best response to this was to step back and make no attempt to contact her. Within a week or so, she would be apologetically back in touch and we would quickly carry on as before.

In early 2005, she was finally selected in the marginal Yorkshire constituency of Calder Valley and threw herself into an intense three-month general election campaign, giving up her public affairs job at Cable & Wireless. I travelled up a couple of times and watched her in action, leading from the front with an utterly obsessive approach to politics that I already knew I did not have in me. She motivated her activist base with total self-belief, living, eating and breathing canvassing schedules, delivery networks and press relations. It was awesome to watch, albeit an electoral battle fought in vain as she missed out by under 1,400 votes.

Back in London, Liz and I now continued life where we had left off; she was job hunting and I was part of George Osborne's opposition Treasury team. A very intense couple of months followed as we saw a lot of each other. Then Parliament went into recess and we both headed away on non-overlapping family holidays and in my case, on two overseas delegations. This meant we would not see each other for almost two months.

I am not sure I have ever really subscribed to the theory that absence makes the heart grow fonder, but I remember feeling very unsettled that summer as I tried to work out how to resolve the uncertainties of my personal situation. Clarity came in September when Liz told me that she was staying with her husband. I knew in an instant that my own marriage was over.

Westminster is a cauldron of gossip at the best of times and as my marriage fell apart, there was naturally speculation as to its causes. Liz also had her detractors, and it was her decision to put herself forward as a potential candidate for the Bromley & Chislehurst by-election after Eric Forth died in mid-2006 (a much-missed character, he was the only serving Conservative MP to die during my entire time in Parliament) that led to someone tipping off the *Daily Mail*. Our past relationship now became public knowledge.

The story was something of a one-day wonder, not least because neither of us went on the record, despite journalistic persistence. Whatever the temptation 'to tell your side of the story', giving an interview in this sort of situation only serves to give further oxygen to a story by providing journalists with a fresh angle to take. The likelihood then is that the story, such as it is, will run out of control.

If I had thought this was the last the world would hear of this private grief, I had reckoned without the Turnip Taliban. That phrase was invented by my old friend, Richard Spring, who represented one of the neighbouring East Anglian constituencies to Liz's eventual seat. He was outraged when, over three years after the *Daily Mail* article had been published, some leading figures in the South West Norfolk Conservatives sought to overturn Liz's selection on the basis of the story. In reality, this was never going to happen

– the party leadership had invested too much in the promotion of an A-List of more diverse and female candidates, in tune with the values of modern Britain. Nevertheless, it was a deeply unpleasant baptism of fire for Liz and her family but once again reinforced the powers of self-belief and resilience that were central to her political progress.

When eventually we became parliamentary colleagues, our relationship was always cordial and matter of fact. Neither of us would exactly go out of our way to make conversation, but nor did I ever feel any sense of awkwardness when we walked past each other on the parliamentary estate or exchanged a few words together in the division lobbies.

The sole exception that comes to mind was at the parliamentary party getaway at an Oxfordshire hotel just before the EU referendum. People were milling around near the bar before dinner and Liz and I got into conversation. I teased her about her forthright public support for Remain and suggested this might owe more to her personal loyalty to Cameron and Osborne and the confident expectation that she was backing the winning side rather than her real convictions on the issue. A snort of mock indignation greeted my insinuation that she was no more than an opportunistic careerist and we laughed away together, almost like old times, then asked each other about family and friends. This exchange must have gone on for about five minutes when she suddenly stopped short. We both looked around and realised that quite an audience of fellow Tory MPs were watching our animated conversation with a slightly quizzical look.

So, to one of the political questions I have been most frequently asked in recent times. Did you ever see Liz Truss as being a potential Prime Minister?

Well, yes and no. In her defence, she has many of the qualities that are essential to reaching the highest rank in politics – limitless ambition and self-belief, raw intelligence, resilience and an overwhelming sense of personal destiny. But the only questions that ever really need to be asked about anyone's Prime Ministerial prospects are when and in what circumstances will the vacancy arise? In summer 2022, both these factors worked perfectly to Truss's advantage. After a succession of Cabinet roles in which she had been subjected to relentless criticism and ridicule, being tipped for the sack at virtually every reshuffle, she came to the fore under Boris Johnson in the International Trade and Foreign Office briefs. She was then the beneficiary of the 'anyone but Sunak' movement when a deeply divided party, unreconciled to Boris's defenestration, voted for his replacement. All those years of hard graft as a party activist, association chairman, three-time council and parliamentary candidate now stood her in the best possible stead. She alone understood what made the ageing party membership tick, so it came as no surprise to me when she wiped the floor with Rishi Sunak. He, by contrast, had spent his twenties behind a desk at Goldman Sachs or studying for an MBA in California before being parachuted in to a super-safe seat without ever having previously stood for public office.

On the other hand, there was startlingly little to suggest that she had either the powers of inspirational leadership or the administrative capacity to focus on delivery and implementation. No one doubted her genuine passion for theoretical policy ideas. But any grand plan to cut taxes and slash public expenditure flies in the face of demographic reality. The UK's population is fast getting older and more dependent on the state. Meanwhile, her mantra of 'growth, growth, growth' was never backed up by the remotest evidence of how she would implement the practical supply-side measures that someone with hands-on business experience would have instinctively understood as being essential. Nor was there any recognition that the two most obvious things needed to implement these supply-side measures, namely the liberalisation of planning and immigration, would be most bitterly opposed by the party grassroots who had just elevated her to the premiership.

She had entered government as a junior Education Minister, intending to transform childcare provision. Acting like a bull in a china shop with her officials, she found herself totally outmanoeuvred by her Liberal Democrat coalition partners and we ended up with the worst of all worlds – a more expensive, unresponsive and bureaucratic system. Next up, at the Department for Environment, Food and Rural Affairs (DEFRA) she implemented worthy but marginal innovations in the export of agricultural produce (notoriously pork and cheese), but a host of unsolved problems were left to her successors. These included indiscriminate reductions in the budget of the Environment Agency that compounded flooding and sewage discharge issues, failings in the regulation of privatised entities under DEFRA's watch and a failure to prepare farmers for the consequences of the Brexit that so many of them supported, assuming that their Common Agricultural Policy cheques would continue to roll in.

As Justice Secretary, she had the misfortune to inherit an expensive prison reform programme promised and announced by her predecessor, Michael Gove, but not cleared with the Treasury. She then put her career before her duty to defend the independence of the judiciary by failing to criticise the *Daily Mail*'s attack on judges (the controversial 'Enemies of the People' headline) after Brexit-related court proceedings. This destroyed any remaining credibility she had with the judges, although from my regular lunches as a constituency guest at the Central Criminal Court at the Old Bailey, it was also clear to me that some of this was motivated by misogyny and the patronising attitude that is always directed towards non-lawyers in senior government legal positions.

By the time she had been demoted to Chief Secretary to the Treasury, I was also a Minister of State and we had several productive meetings over the workings of the Prosperity Fund and Official Development Assistance. It was one of those rare situations in dealing with the Treasury where there was a clear 'win-win', and Liz was as motivated as me to ensure that some of the then gargantuan aid budget could be legitimately siphoned off for economic collaboration projects under the Foreign Office's watch. But her brusque and impatient manner with civil servants – both hers and mine – regardless of their expertise or seniority struck me as an unusual strategy for getting the best out of those entrusted to execute the radical changes she has always clamoured to achieve.

At the Department for International Trade and the Foreign Office, she exploited to the full the opportunities for self-promotion in the aftermath of Brexit. Truth be told, almost all the trade deals that she signed with great fanfare were a mere matter of cutting and pasting arrangements that had already been agreed whilst we were members of the EU. Even the much-heralded deal with Australia soon appeared less desirable than it had seemed at first when UK farmers examined the small print after it had been signed. Not that this was any barrier to Liz placing herself at the forefront of a series of profligate communications campaigns, whose extravagant cost alone seemed to run counter to the low-spending, free-market principles apparently so dear to her heart.

In reality, her entire decade-long ministerial career had been an object lesson in relentlessly talking a good game about individual freedom, smaller government, tax cutting, economic growth and promoting market solutions but actually delivering next to nothing.

None of this would of itself have necessarily been fatal to her prospects of making more of her time as Prime Minister. But she lacked the self-awareness to realise the need for trusted advisers in her close team, whose outlook would help temper her over-confident personality excesses. Having made it to 10 Downing Street against the odds and in the face of doubters and critics, she was determined to do it her way. In her mind she had been pragmatic for long enough – and now no one was going to stop her.

Late in August 2022, my old friend Matthew Davidge and I exchanged emails between London and New York. He had first met Liz almost twenty years earlier as our friendship was in its very early stages and was incredulous that she was now only a matter of days away from becoming Prime Minister: 'God save the UK. Liz is actually going to make it!'

In the weeks that followed, he frequently reminded me of my reply: 'Strewth, I guess I now know how the first line of my obituary will read, but the likeliest scenario is that Liz's tenure will be calamitous. I reckon it is by no means impossible that we shall have to go through the whole process of choosing a new leader again within six months.' As ever, my innate optimism shone through.

•   •   •

I have always contended the one thing that virtually all national politicians have in common is an element of single-minded determination. At the very least, this is an essential ingredient in the process of getting into Parliament, which, as we have seen, is not really a process for the faint-hearted or risk averse. No one becomes an MP without a degree of planning and, more often than not, some malice aforethought. It is certainly true that many a ruthless operator has not caught the break needed either to get selected in a safe constituency or been able to win a marginal seat in a good year for their party. By the same token, the accidental MP, inspired by idealism alone and entirely absent of opportunism, is a purely fictional construct – although if Hollywood is to be believed, they always seem to be left-leaning erstwhile investigative journalists.

Politics also attracts a disproportionate number of people who find the work all-consuming, the lifestyle glamorous (for a time, at least) and are possessed by a burning ambition that sacrifices conventional domesticity. Worse still, any semblance of a distinction between work and leisure has been made virtually impossible by the relentless demands of 24/7 media, not to mention its social offshoot, plus demanding constituency duties. There are a multitude of motivations for those entering Parliament and despite rumours to the contrary, the great majority, in my experience at least, are motivated by a sense of duty, public service or a burning desire to change the world. However, as the reality TV virus has mutated, even I have begun to worry that too many people in politics are chasing fame, glory and money and regard the entire political process as the middle-class educated equivalent of being a celebrity.

On the other hand, until recently, many MPs sought to remain in politics often well past their sell-by date because they grew overly accustomed to a way of life unlike anything else. I realise the political class does not elicit much sympathy, but do not underestimate the number of MPs who hang on in Parliament simply because they have no clue what to do next and fear leaving the warm embrace of political status. Even now, it is instructive to see just how many of those who lose their seats are desperate to return. Essentially a unique form of self-employment, parliamentary life is not work as most of our constituents would recognise the concept.

My progress through the ranks in opposition was fairly conventional. Within two years I had joined the front bench. To my consternation, I was asked to join the Whips' Office. I had a near-sleepless night contemplating turning down the role; then I proceeded to love my time there to the extent that I was deeply disappointed when nine months later I moved on to become shadow London Minister. There is an old parliamentary saying that once a whip, you are always a whip. I am not sure this really applies any more. The Whips' Office is no longer the alternative career track it once was. The turnover of MPs serving briefly as whips means the office is no longer a law unto itself.

But it is interesting to note that in spite of this fluidity, none of the last nine Conservative leaders has ever served as a whip; given recent tumultuous times, I suspect that represents an important gap in each of their political education. In my time there, I understood all I ever needed to know about parliamentary process and procedure, a fair bit about human nature and motivation, and learned about the balance between individualism and teamwork in Parliament. Maybe I was too junior to be brought into the inner sanctum when it came to the fabled dark arts of the Whips' Office… or perhaps they only really exist in more lurid imaginations. There was plenty of gossip, of course, but relatively little that came as a massive surprise.

To my regret, the Tory opposition of the time fervently opposed changes to working practices in the Commons. Needless to say, we were outvoted, so all-night and even most late-night sessions virtually became a thing of the past. The truth is that law-making is an activity that expands to fill the time available for it; the advent of the guillotine has not, with very few exceptions, notably impaired the quality of legislation. Curtailing the absurdity of all-night sittings and filibustering for the sake of it has had more impact on the takings at parliamentary bars than on appropriate scrutiny. Despite all our huffing and puffing when the changes were made, after we returned to office in 2010, the clock was not turned back. A good thing too.

The perceived power of the Whips' Office to make or break careers is also a little exaggerated. Parliament remains a place where the burnishing of a prior national reputation or the specialist subject knowledge of an expert attracts a mix of awe, envy and suspicion. In a very British way, it isn't done to seem to be too clever, but it is noticeable that many of those complaining most loudly about this very real tendency to dismiss those who seem too clever have usually done themselves few favours by arriving in Parliament and being publicly dismissive of opinions other than their own. But the institutional memory of the Whips' Office is not what it was. Many of the most ambitious MPs have an understandable tendency to fixate on the smallest setbacks and assume their political career is finished or at least badly impaired. The incident will haunt you for so long as you remain an MP. The Whips will always treat you as suspect. The dizzyingly quick ministerial merry-go-round of recent years has surely put paid to this theory. Probably the most serious damage to the reputation of the Whips' Office as a centre of power and influence, however, has been done by the straightforward loss of patronage. The membership of select committees, for example, is no longer in the gift of the whips but subject to a secret ballot of MPs.

In more recent times, the Whips' Offices have come in for intense scrutiny and scathing criticism at their collective failure to provide better pastoral care to MPs. In fairness, they were never really set up as human resources departments and issues around mental health, for example, have represented a new challenge to personnel professionals the world over. The trouble is that the primary purpose of any government whips' office is to 'keep the show on the road' and this applies even in opposition to a large extent. All too often, the imperative becomes to minimise bad publicity, cover up misbehaviour and protect the public reputation of the party rather than properly assist, discipline or deal with troubled MPs. Perhaps it is inevitable that this catalogue of failings has led to an ever-louder clamour that these responsibilities within the parliamentary estate are passed over to external agencies.

I reckon I learned a lot even in my brief stint as a junior whip. How much I put this newfound knowledge into practice for my own benefit was another matter. If anything, my time in the office played up to that existing character-flaw-cum-tendency to look at life from the viewpoint of a semi-detached observer. It certainly heightened my sense of the absurd and I struggled to take even some of my most senior colleagues all that seriously when I became aware up close of some of their flaws and foibles. Come on, Field – accentuate the positive, accentuate the positive.

Next up was my time as shadow London Minister. As far as I recall, over the eighteen months or so in this role I spent the vast majority of Friday and Saturday nights turning up dutifully to drafty halls or tastefully decorated living rooms (well, one or two were a little on the chintzy side, but let's not dwell on that) in far-flung suburban London venues, drinking red wine of variable quality, chatting away with well-meaning local Tories invariably old enough to be my parents and then making a speech, taking questions and talking up the electoral prospects – or at least the future potential – of the Conservative candidate they had so sensibly selected. It was all good for the soul, but glamorous it was not.

In my first departmental role, I was fortunate to work under Caroline Spelman, who was always collegial and supportive. She twice let me attend shadow Cabinet in her stead when it was clear that all she would be asked about was the state of the London campaign and she allowed me to lead from the front bench on London-flavoured opposition day debates. Then, as the 2005 election approached and it became clear that the party was likely to make some significant headway in the capital, she helped get my bid with the leader's office over the line for some additional resource to publish a London manifesto. The brilliantly efficient special adviser for all seasons Sheridan Westlake turned this round inside forty-eight hours, and we received an endorsement from the *Evening Standard*, which had backed Labour at the two previous elections.

Much as I should like to take personal credit for the fact that at the 2005 election the Conservatives made eight of our thirty-two gains nationally in London, our success was really down to a plunge in the Labour vote share as a result of the Iraq War. The Liberal Democrats were the main beneficiaries of these defectors, but we also managed to surpass our dismal showing in the previous two elections and came through the middle to win back an array of constituencies that had been regarded as safely Tory before 1997. I spent eight days of a notably showery April campaigning in our target seats and our new faces in London included a cluster of future ministers: Justine Greening, James Brokenshire, Stephen Hammond and Greg Hands. It had been an exhausting campaign, with my own election night ending with the graveyard slot on a BBC Radio 4 election night special panel between 4 and 6 a.m. and followed by an appearance on breakfast TV, broadcast rather incongruously from a pub on the south bank of the Thames.

By the time I had woken from my slumber early the next afternoon, the party was facing up to a third leadership resignation since I had become an MP less than four years previously. Michael Howard announced his intention to step down but wanted a prolonged contest to allow a rule change that would return the right to vote for party leader to MPs alone. This caused an almighty row, and he was eventually forced to back down. Naturally, he had a point and recent history in both main parties suggests that leaving this decision to a membership whose judgement is at odds with MPs is a potential recipe for disaster. But by the same token, once that cornerstone of democracy 'one member, one vote' has been established, it becomes fiendishly difficult to make the case for restricting the franchise.

My work in an essentially campaigning role meant that over the previous year, I had only half an eye on what was happening within the parliamentary party. Somewhat under the radar, David Cameron had rapidly amassed the patrons, media advocates and true believers that every top-flight politician needs if they are to bamboozle their way to prominence and power.

After a third successive defeat, and with a parliamentary complement still under 200 MPs (Labour managed to surpass this benchmark even under Michael Foot in 1983 and Jeremy Corbyn in 2019), Cameron offered the beleaguered Conservative Party hope. He also had two key qualities that had been in short supply over the previous decade and a half. First was a youthful energy and good looks that had never been an obvious first priority for our leaders. Second, he was the self-styled 'Heir to Blair' – if we couldn't beat them, we had better join them. Ironically, at the very moment the British public were falling out of love with Blair and his New Labour project, the Conservatives, in some desperation after that third crushing electoral defeat, signed up for this tribute act.

Ideologically, I should have been more on board with this project than anything else on offer. But personally, the two of us did not get on. Cameron always gave me the impression that he had been untouched by modesty or doubt from a very early age. He reputedly divided colleagues into two classes, team players and wankers; I was never under any illusions as to which of these categories he had me down for. Whilst I was essentially a moderniser and recognised that his programme would be popular with the many metropolitan professionals living in my seat, it always struck me at its heart as insincere. But in the fullness of time, I contemplated that the disagreeable experience of being sidelined by the emergence of your own generation taking charge was perhaps the rather less palatable reason why I couldn't bring myself to admit much sympathy for what he and his followers stood for.

Cameron was capable of being charm personified, especially during the course of his rapid ascent to the summit of UK politics, as he sought to impress senior party figures. But as time wore on, anyone outside his inner circle who had the temerity to disagree with him could expect a response of dismissive petulance.

More recently he has attempted to rehabilitate himself and his reputation, which had taken a battering over Brexit and the unravelling of his post-premiership commercial interests, by returning to the fray during the last months of the Sunak government as Foreign Secretary. It remains to be seen what international liquidators and criminal investigators will reveal when the full story of Greensill Capital's demise comes to light, but it is difficult to disagree with the

House of Commons Treasury Committee, which found that Cameron had displayed 'a significant lack of judgement' in his dealings with the disgraced Lex Greensill.

• • •

Parliamentary trips overseas have always attracted a certain amount of criticism. Political journalists, all manifestly innocent in the matter of all-expenses paid travel, would fall over themselves gleefully to write up lurid tales about MPs' boondoggles whenever the latest register of interests was published. Hand on heart, I cannot say that each and every one of the delegations I joined were strictly necessary. Sometimes you might get a call late in the day from a chum asking you to make up the numbers on a trip and with nothing much else in the diary, you would take up the offer. Once you acquired a reputation as a good travelling companion and easy-going company, the offers would keep on coming. Most trips involved a substantial number of meetings, which were always tricky to endure if conducted through interpreters. But the host countries would want to go out of their way to ensure that there was plenty of time in the schedule for guest parliamentarians to be whisked through the main tourist attractions.

In my second summer recess, I visited Washington DC for the first time in the course of a fascinating two-week-long British-American Parliamentary Group programme that took in a state capital (in my case, Denver in Colorado) and a long weekend in a congressional district. I was keen to spend time with a Republican representing an equivalent inner-city district to my own constituency. This request turned out to be something of a problem. Even then, there were no Republican congressmen to be found in the heart of New York City,

Los Angeles, Philadelphia or San Francisco. We eventually settled on Mark Kirk, a first-term representative whose district included some of Chicago's northern suburbs. He provided lavish hospitality and in later years we met up in London and Washington, where he subsequently served a term in the Senate. Other trips included my first visits to India and China – two countries I would become much more familiar with in the years to come. The omnipresent Conservative Friends of Israel hosted a delegation of new MPs to the historic quarter of Jerusalem, Tel Aviv and the West Bank. Also in the Middle East, I joined teams visiting Jordan and Qatar, then very much up and coming, with its peninsula of liquified national gas storage facilities as far as the eye could see.

Those pesky political journalists would be amused to learn that one of the most troublesome aspects of overseas visits arose over airline upgrades. Often the whole delegation would be upgraded as a matter of course, but nothing caused more playful provocation or anxiety than some of us getting the nod and others ending up stuck in economy class. As David Ruffley used to put it emphatically, 'I didn't become an MP to turn right when getting on a plane.' I always seemed to get the lucky break, but it may have been something to do with normally turning up in a smart blazer at the check-in desk. It was on the way back from that fact-finding mission to Doha that the most acutely embarrassing episode arose – for me, at least. Alone of the delegation, I had been upgraded to first class on the Qatari Airways flight; I tried to avoid letting the others know, but then it came to boarding the plane. At this point, I was escorted by two beautiful air hostesses as if I were some billionaire plutocrat and ushered into a smart black limousine, which whisked me across the tarmac from the departure gate on a journey of little more than 100 yards to the front of the plane. Predictably, this sequence of events as it unfolded was met with utter derision on the part of my fellow parliamentary passengers.

But the most memorable of all the visits I made during my early years in Parliament was a six-day trip in 2003 to Syria. We met Bashar al-Assad, then less than three years in office but full of talk of reform and developing his country as a regional hub for technology, tourism and much more. He was softly spoken but clearly much influenced by his late father's military and secret-service entourage. It came as no surprise to learn that his was something of an unexpected presidency after the death of his older brother in the mid-1990s in a high-performance car crash. The young al-Assad looked every bit the studious eye surgeon he was training to become before fate intervened, and it has always been difficult for me entirely to equate this image with that of the ruthless and murderous dictator he became when Syria was plunged into civil war less than a decade later.

Beyond Damascus, we visited Aleppo and the breathtaking archaeological sites at Palmyra, now almost utterly destroyed. On the Lebanese border we walked around the beautiful and almost intact medieval crusader fort of Krak des Chevaliers. But the two episodes that struck me most deeply were our visit to a small village an hour's drive from Damascus, which had been a Christian stronghold since the time of St Paul. Its people, like many minorities, believed their interests were best protected by the rule of dynastic dictatorship; the community leaders there had no truck with the notion of democracy, which to them represented only the prospect of their rights being trampled over by the tyranny of the majority. This struck me as an important insight that the west has tended to ignore in many of its recent overseas military adventures.

The other memorable event on that tour was the drinks party

attended by many of the Damascus great and good and hosted in our honour by the British Embassy. It was impossible not to be impressed by the sophisticated and urbane Syrian attendees. However, on closer questioning, it was clear that all these successful business-folk, whilst extolling the virtues of economic reform and international trade, were beneficiaries of exclusivity deals, quotas and state controls that keep at bay any overseas and domestic competition. They all seemed to own apartments in Paris, London or New York – so where would they make their lives if the al-Assad regime were to come under threat? Naturally, the regional upheaval of the past decade has weighed heavily on my mind whenever I think of that visit. Some of those we met must have struggled grievously – or worse. But I suspect many others have bailed out and in leaving Syria have deprived the nation of a viable ruling class that might help rebuild that tragic land from the rubble.

• • •

I happen to believe that there are still some MPs who regard it as a cardinal sin to speak to the press. Some, but not many. Even whips, who used to be told under pain of death to steer clear of journalists, can often be seen in Portcullis House having a coffee with political correspondents. It stretches the imagination that all they are talking about is the weather or their next overseas travel plans. What hasn't changed is the woeful lack of media guidance received by all bar the most senior politicians. I reckon this has helped make for a general imbalance in the relationship that is not to the credit of the political trade. It was the early twentieth-century US journalist and satirist H. L. Mencken who patronisingly proclaimed, 'The relationship of a journalist to a politician should be that of a dog to a lamppost.' I always felt that in an ideal world, the political class should seek to impose the exact inversion of this in their dealings with the fourth estate. Unfortunately, witnessing the fawning of all too many senior politicians in the presence of journalists and particularly newspaper proprietors has been one of the most depressing, and at times contemptible, aspects of political life over recent years. Apart from anything else, in a world of increasingly atomised media the (overstated) influence of old school newspaper owners and columnists has been massively in decline.

I used to enjoy the company of most political journalists and some with whom I still stay in touch I guess should now count as friends, but I was never under any illusion, even amongst that select band, that whenever I was in political difficulties, they would probably run a story without fear or favour. Rightly so. I make no complaints on this score.

Now I appreciate that politicians complaining about the media is a little like farmers moaning about the weather. However, the cavalier approach to fact-checking and detail of much of the UK media makes it an international outlier. No European country has a tabloid press to match the tawdry content of our UK equivalents, and only a little over a decade ago the best-selling *News of the World* was forced to close down amidst the phone-hacking scandal, which resonates in the law courts to this day. It is fashionable to deride the dullness of style and content in the leading US newspapers, but their strict rules about multiple sourcing every detail and rigorous fact-checking, as well as allowing a right of reply, compares favourably with our own press.

Over the years, I have read the reportage of many stories where I have either been involved or know many of, if not all, the story's intricacies. It is rare for there not to be a slant in the reporting (and my complaint here is seldom a matter of out-and-out partisan bias), which then makes me inherently suspicious of the accuracy of every other story published in which I have had no prior knowledge. Whenever any proposal is made to find a mechanism to arbitrate against these failures in ethical standards, the tabloid press scream blue murder and accuse government of seeking to undermine press freedom. Yet with breathtaking hypocrisy, the UK's beleaguered print media is always the first to demand stricter regulation and control against the social media outlets that are undermining their business models.

My complaint about much that passes for day-to-day political journalism in the UK is its overriding obsession with triviality. In contrast to some highly perceptive political commentary, newspaper and website readers are fed a diet of politics reported through the lens of theatre or, worse still, as a game. Our media still focuses on the day-to-day breathless coverage of politics as soap opera and thereby fails to hold neglect in government properly to account. The absurd charade of Prime Minister's Questions (PMQs) dominates TV coverage on a Wednesday. I was so appalled, and frankly bored, by this dreadful spectacle that in my final decade in Parliament, I was only present for PMQs on the two occasions when immediately after the pantomime was over I had been summoned to respond as a Foreign Office Minister to an urgent question.

I suspect that a whole host of departmental failure is never properly reported on because that would take too much effort – why bother when domestic drama can fill the programme or pages? Offhand, I can think of three episodes in my time as a minister where a suitably diligent level of investigation by journalists would have uncovered a glaring government error. Although we all spent an anxious few days, there was never any need on the part of ministers or civil servants to cover up the mistakes that had been made. Instead, we watched as the political press circus moved on relentlessly to its next nonsense destination. We all give lip service to the ideal that politics is a serious business that needs to be conducted by worthy people, but then the microphone gets passed on to charlatans and narcissists who make for apparently better copy.

CHAPTER 5

A DIFFERENT PATH

7 NOVEMBER 2006

Even by the usual standards of parliamentary life, the morning of Tuesday 7 November 2006 was a hectic and varied one for me. By the time it came to an end, my steady and predictable upward political advance had come to a juddering halt. Unexpected and a little unpleasant this may have been at the time, I was quickly left in no doubt that this turn of events was for the best. Where uncertainty began to creep in was working out how I should best plan for the future.

I have never really been much of a breakfast person. To my mind, the first meal of the day is normally devoured snappily on the way out of the door. Only where time permits, which essentially means in the vacation setting of a hotel, do I ever allow myself the luxury of breakfasting in a leisurely fashion. Business breakfasts satisfy neither of these conditions. But they are increasingly part of modern-day commercial life. It is all too often the fate of politicians to find themselves on the menu, singing for your strawberry smoothie and chocolate croissant. That's how it was for me on that chilly autumn Tuesday morning, with my first port of call the modern serviced offices occupied by the London Chamber of Commerce and Industry in the heart of the City of London.

By then I was the Conservative Party's culture spokesman, but despite the frontbench convention that you do not veer into subject matter beyond your brief, my breakfast time address inevitably touched on more general economic themes. I then fielded, with moderately unguarded responses, a range of penetrating questions from a knowledgeable City and lobbying audience about financial services, tax policy and infrastructure projects.

There were several familiar faces in the audience that morning, and one who has remained a friend and wise counsel ever since, Laura Montgomery, reassured me: 'That was great, but the party really should be using more of your business background and economic knowledge.' I was aware of her close links to the party leadership, and a decade later, under her married name, she would become a life peer as Baroness Wyld in David Cameron's resignation honours list. Given what happened later in the day, the next few times we met she was always endearingly anxious to reassure me that she had not reported back my breach of etiquette. It had genuinely never occurred to me that she had.

By mid-morning, I was in the midst of back-to-back meetings over coffee in Portcullis House with representatives from the worlds of museums, publishing rights and libraries when my pager vibrated with a message to head over to the Leader of the Opposition's office. Winding up my final meeting a little more briskly than usual, I made my excuses and then set out on the three-minute walk and busied myself straightening my tie in an attempt to calm my rising nerves. It wasn't long before I got an inkling of what was in store.

Immediately ushered in by one of the entourage working in the leader's team, I was momentarily amused to have been placed in the exact seat at the boardroom table I had occupied a little over two years before, on the last occasion I had attended the shadow Cabinet by invitation. But that was then and this was now. David Cameron sat opposite me and to his left was his chief of staff, another former Oxford contemporary, Ed Llewellyn. In the years ahead, Ed would stay intermittently in touch with me, usually using me as a sounding board for the party's mood on Europe. Perhaps I am reading a little too much into it, but I also reckoned that he wanted me to know that in his eyes at least, I was not entirely beyond the pale. Most recently, we have spent time together in a rather more enjoyable setting, over a glass or two of claret, sitting out in his Paris embassy garden when Ed was our ambassador to France. I used to stay overnight at the residence in Paris following meetings at the OECD when I was its UK ministerial lead.

Cameron seemed almost reluctant to get to the point, talking in a circuitous way about the need for positivity from his frontbench team but also recognising the contribution I had made in my various frontbench roles. I sensed at once where this was leading, and I would like to claim that my unnerving him by my silence was all part of some deep psychological ploy. My negotiating experience in the world of business had taught me that a strategy of saying nothing is often a highly effective weapon in tense meetings. The truth on this morning was that my mind was firmly on my next engagement, for which I was now running late. I had been invited as a special guest of honour at a lunchtime party for an elderly constituent celebrating her 100th birthday that very day.

Duly relieved of my frontbench duties, I arrived only fashionably behind schedule at the nursing home just as the candles were being lit on a huge celebratory cake. It was a pleasure finally to deliver a short speech with absolutely no one caring whether or not I was sticking to the party line or expressing sufficiently loyal partisanship.

There was even a rather curious postscript to this story. Shortly after the 2010 election, the great niece of my centennial constituent wrote a sweet letter informing me that her elderly relative had died. However, she had lived long enough to use her postal vote for me at the general election but had then passed away before polling day. This is the sole legitimate way in which a vote by someone deceased can be cast and counted. My immediate and strangely comforting thought was that it also meant that she was not around to see that day's nemesis, Mr Cameron, make it to Downing Street.

• • •

The seventeen months between the 2005 election and my departure from the front bench had been eventful on many fronts. I have already touched on the changes that were afoot in my personal life. In the immediate aftermath of the election, I had been promoted to shadow Financial Secretary to the Treasury under the new shadow Chancellor, George Osborne. We had already worked together during the second half of 2003 as the two most junior whips, but now for the first time I saw at close quarters how he operated.

For George Osborne, politics was only ever about power: where to find it and how to exercise it. Not really about ideology, nor even any burning sense of public service, although perhaps I am being a little unfair on that point. I came to respect his professionalism and work rate. However, from the very first time we met, I never quite got over the feeling when thinking about Osborne that had he been only two or three years younger, he might easily have arrived

ABOVE My parents enjoying an evening out with army friends in Singapore shortly after their wedding in the then British colony in November 1962. My father never really came to terms with life outside the military but adored my mother, who, after becoming a refugee from eastern Germany twice by the age of fifteen, provided stability to the family as I grew up.

LEFT My first day at school in Aldershot, a few weeks before my fifth birthday in 1969. Despite the disruption that came with frequent changes in schooling as my family moved around the south-east, I had a very happy childhood. My own political awakening can be traced back to the threat posed to my education as I was about to begin secondary school.

ABOVE There were rather too many carefree days for my tutors' liking during my time at Oxford. When I wasn't engaged in student politics and journalism, there was always an active social life to pursue. Here I am with my closest friend Matthew Davidge and his then girlfriend in 1986. Matthew and I have lived on different continents for the past three decades, but if anything it has tied us closer together.

LEFT All good things have to come to an end. Graduation day, 1987, in the exquisitely atmospheric front quad at St Edmund Hall in the company of my sister Antonia and my brother Dominic. One of the joys of middle age has been growing closer to my siblings.

As a newly elected MP in 2001, standing proudly within the precincts of the Houses of Parliament and surveying my famous constituency. Little did I realise then the turbulence that was to lie ahead during my time in Parliament as a consequence of, to name a few, terrorist attacks, the global financial crisis and Brexit.

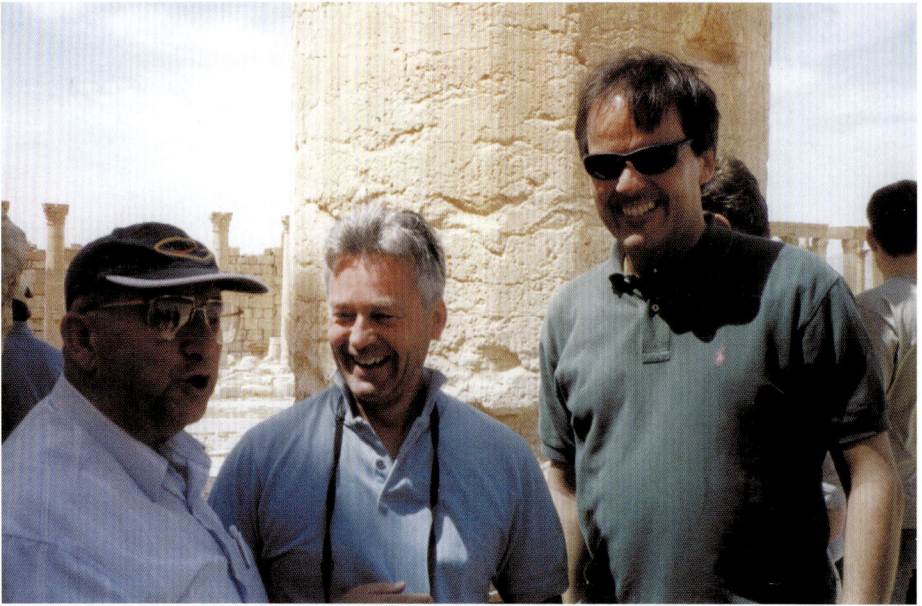

On a parliamentary delegation to Palmyra, Syria, in 2003, surveying the breathtaking archaeological ruins, many of which have since been destroyed during the country's tragic civil war. Here I am with future Foreign Office ministerial colleague Alan Duncan, who was always an easy-going and amusing travelling companion.

The Conservative Party's efforts to diversify its candidate base predated David Cameron's controversial A-List imposition. I was the shadow London Minister in the run-up to the 2005 election, and one of our stars in the making was local nurse Evett McAnuff, who stood for the Conservatives in her home seat of Lewisham West. Here we are standing together on the terrace of the House of Commons.

For all its bustle and noise, central London remains a patchwork of ancient villages. As the local MP, I would be invited to attend and speak at countless residents' associations and amenity societies, which many in the community would faithfully support. Here I am addressing the Pimlico-based Westminster Bangladeshi Association in 2006.

Perfect April sunshine greeted mine and Vicki's wedding day at St Margaret's, the parish church adjacent to Westminster Abbey, in 2007. We are accompanied by our team of ushers, dear friends from every part of my life. (*Back row, left to right*) John Cullen, Peter Wilson, William Wellesley, Dominic Field, Jeremy Hunt. (*Front row, left to right*) Graham Davies, Matthew Davidge, groom and bride, Stephen Hammond.

Catching them young! Usually we were expected to campaign in more marginal constituencies in London, but uniquely the May 2010 general election coincided with local elections in the capital. My then two-year-old son Frederick was already a dab hand on the streets of inner-city Belgravia with a blue balloon!

I was blessed with a highly supportive local Conservative Association throughout my time in Parliament and can honestly say that cross words were never exchanged. The team pictured here in Tachbrook Market, Pimlico, in 2011 includes husband and wife councillors David and Angela Harvey, the fabulous campaign organisers Kate and Andrew McCarthy and my eventual successor, councillor Nickie Aiken.

My Foreign Office responsibilities were for the entire Asia and Pacific region, which included relevant United Nations Security Council meetings in New York. Here I am attending and speaking at an urgent debate on Afghanistan in 2017 sitting alongside Rex Tillerson, who was US President Donald Trump's first Secretary of State.

Where do the years go? Our two children have grown up so fast and we have watched with wonder as they form their own independent views on the world around them. They are already seasoned travellers – here Frederick and Arabella are standing alongside Vicki in the country lane leading to our finca in rural Mallorca in 2021.

in Westminster and come under the spell of Tony Blair and Peter Mandelson, with whom he had so much in common. I suspect that in this parallel version of reality, our George might well have become a leading figure in New Labour's younger generation.

But back on planet Earth in mid-2005, Osborne set to work building a loyal team of acolytes who would serve him so well over the next decade. Into our support team came an irrepressibly enthusiastic junior executive from the Bank of England called Matt Hancock, of whom much more would be seen and heard in the years ahead. Matt had been a notably energetic and effective minister – pre-Covid, at least – and at one time a credible contender for the party leadership. His fall from grace amply underlined the risks that come with mixing politics and celebrity, not to mention having an unshakeable belief in one's own publicity.

Osborne's other big find at this time was Rupert Harrison, who had seemed set to enter the Commons with high hopes and expectations at the very moment Hancock's time in politics was coming to an inglorious close. It wasn't the first time I had met Rupert – that had come on the campaign trail in 2001. He and his girlfriend Joanna Orpin (now Mrs Harrison) were then Bayswater constituents and, unusually for such young metropolitan graduates at that election, they were strongly Conservative. Or at least Jo was. As I canvassed their basement flat one Saturday morning, she answered the door and warned me that her fiancé was wavering a little. Dragged out of the shower and wrapped in a towel, Rupert was urbane and charming, and for the first and I fear only time in my life, I was able to persuade him of my suitability. Unfortunately for Rupert, the election of 2024 was the first time in over two centuries that the good burghers of Bicester & Woodstock, where he was our candidate, decided against electing a Conservative representative to Parliament.

I guess my mistake during this period was working on the presumption that the shadow Treasury roles were likely to be only a temporary billet for us all. It was widely assumed another reshuffle would shake everything up yet again when a new leader was finally in place at the end of the year, so I spent more time learning about economics and finance whilst I had the chance. Life was a whirlwind of briefings about all aspects of that year's Finance Bill, as well as getting to understand Islamic financing and various esoteric fiscal instruments. With hindsight, I might have been better advised ingratiating myself with George and his soon-to-be influential team.

At the height of his power and reputation, immediately after the 2015 election triumph, there was an imperiousness about George Osborne as he surveyed the political landscape. I remember at this time his hosting a packed Treasury support group meeting for the new Tory intake. In the manner of a mafia boss, he proceeded to introduce by name each and every one of his previous parliamentary private secretaries and aides who, by implication, had risen to the ministerial rank they now held on his coat tails.

For someone so skilled at playing the game three or four moves ahead, Osborne can be forgiven for not recognising the emergence of Jeremy Corbyn as Labour leader as the poison pill to his prospects it turned out to be. Corbyn's leadership may have made Labour unelectable, but his half-hearted embrace of the Remain cause at the EU referendum meant the opposition were severely underpowered in their support for Remain. With such a close referendum result, this was a critical factor in condemning the nation to Brexit.

• • •

Given I represented the heart of the capital, the prospect and threat of a terrorist attack was never far from my mind. The police and security services had briefed me privately after the horrors of 9/11 and then again early in 2004, when Madrid's main railway stations were bombed in a co-ordinated series of attacks with fearful loss of life.

London's turn came on 7 July 2005. That morning dawned with the capital enveloped in a blanket of excitement. My alarm went off early and mercifully, I was able to do BBC radio interviews in my dressing gown from the comfort of my study. Against the odds, the day before London had been awarded the 2012 Olympics; in my previous role as shadow London Minister, I had spent a quiet Friday in March walking around the east London canals, disused railway lines, abandoned factory sites and overgrown open space that had been earmarked for development, so I was able to talk with passion and insight about what lay in store for a small but largely forgotten quarter of the city.

By the time I made it into the office, that sense of euphoria had been replaced by confused news reports about power outages paralysing the Tube network. Very briefly the media narrative changed to that hardy staple, old-fashioned British cynicism – if we cannot run an underground railway, what hope of London hosting the Olympics? Then came a phone call from the office of a senior Metropolitan Police counter terrorism officer. Confusion turned to certainty. Catastrophic loss of civilian life in four locations – two in my constituency at Aldgate and Edgware Road stations. The reports remained muddled and wisely I decided to take with a pinch of salt an excitable message from Conservative Central Office, as I was about to do the rounds of TV studios, that suggested the death toll might run into the hundreds.

This was also the day of my local Conservative Association's major fundraising lunch at the Savoy Hotel. I turned up there at the appointed hour, half expecting no one else to show. In the event 250 or so of the 400 guests were there and the overwhelming feeling was one of defiance and a sense that 'the show must go on'. To do anything else would be to play into the hands of the terrorists. Understandably, our usual guest speaker at this annual occasion, the party leader, was stuck in Parliament, and so with five minutes warning and without a script or even notes, I spoke from the heart about what the day's tragic events must mean for those of us who value living in a free and open society. I still reckon it was the best speech I have ever made.

More media followed in the afternoon and well into the evening. By the time I was interviewed on the same BBC radio station on which I had spoken first thing that morning, the death toll had become clearer – thirteen of the fifty-two innocent lives lost had been taken in my constituency. It had been a traumatic day and for the relatives of those killed and the many with terrible injuries, the pain, suffering and life-changing anguish was only beginning. Trivial things stick in the mind. For me it was the noise of slamming car doors and loud chatter outside the restaurant over the road from the house where I then lived. Late at night this would normally be the cause of irritation; on this terrible evening, the sounds of people just getting on with their everyday lives was strangely reassuring.

• • •

Andy McSmith has a lot to answer for. Then the political editor of *The Independent*, he had written up a lead political story as 2004 was coming to a close. He suggested that I might be a dark-horse contender to become party leader, in the event that the Conservatives decided to skip a generation after Michael Howard. Whilst

David Cameron and George Osborne were also mentioned as leading rivals, I suspect this story and the follow-up elsewhere in later
weeks saw my card being marked in the eyes of some. Most people
would be mildly flattered by such attention. In all honesty, I wasn't
– not even for a moment.

Over the years, I suspect all MPs are asked by constituents, who
assume that everyone entering the House of Commons has at the
very least a secret ambition to be Prime Minister, whether they are
angling for the top job. I never, ever wanted it – or thought it remotely possible. I knew instinctively that high office was not for me.
Perhaps I was never someone overly burdened by glorious purpose,
a misplaced confidence in my abilities or the level of obsessive drive
that marks out party leaders from the rest of us. By normal political
standards, I recognise that I lack either an overwhelming ego or
a burning desire to drive forward specific reform in some aspect
of public policy that will bring with it immortality. The nature of
my local constituency party, with its vast number of parliamentary
aspirants, meant I could see all too well that political ambition has
few boundaries, and two of the 2024 leadership contenders were
former ward chairmen of mine. But as I was wont to say of the many
pushy Young Turks habitually involved in the Cities of London &
Westminster Conservative Association, at any one time two thirds
reckoned they could do a better job than me and by definition, the
other third probably could.

As you may already have gathered, one of my other faults – if you
can call it that – was that I could never take the internal workings
of politics entirely seriously or at least not half as seriously as many
other MPs. I fear it was never easy fully to conceal this from some
of my more bumptious, sectarian-minded or committed colleagues.
I soon concluded that there are an astonishing number of elected

politicians who probably have no place in a run-of-the-mill office environment – not that this has ever been an impediment to their being promoted to ministerial office.

I could see all too well which way politics was going, but blind loyalty for its own sake and being wheeled out for media interventions that focused only on infantile partisanship and repetitive sloganising was never going to be my bag. In a world where 'attack dogs' were feted, I settled for being a placid pooch. On the other hand, it was depressing to see the waste of potential talent this almost anti-meritocratic approach threw up. There were many MPs who refused to 'play the game' despite being precisely the sort of people who would probably have been well adjusted to, and make a success of, the rigours of political administration.

Ambition is a strange bedfellow. As a teenager, I had it in spades. But at that time of life its focus is strictly limited within the prism of conventional academic or specific extra-curricular success. The complications all come later, when an overriding sense of ambition for the sake of achieving glittering prizes threatens to distort all of life's other priorities.

As a prospective politician, my single-minded pursuit of a parliamentary seat was all-consuming. But even this apparently limitless personal ambition began to ebb away fast once that goal had been achieved. It was as if making it into the House of Commons had finally sated something that had been burning inside for as long as I could remember. I suspect the nature of my constituency, with its exceptional attributes, only redoubled this sense. Meanwhile, I recognised that entering Parliament meant many of my political contemporaries were ramping up their drive and ambition; for me, it was a time for putting a foot on the brake. I realised in my own mind even at the time that my approach to politics made a mockery of any media suggestion that I might be heading for the top job.

Perhaps politics had simply been the vehicle for fulfilling the instinctive sense of purpose I had in my early adult life. I was good at politics; I was naturally ambitious, so the pursuit of political office became the obvious mechanism for my aspirations. What I only began to appreciate later was that I lacked the all-consuming hunger and self-belief that is so integral to sustained progress in the pursuit of political success. Politics provided me with status and autonomy, but something was definitely lost from the very moment all my dreams had apparently come true.

In the fullness of time, I look back and wonder whether I was ever really temperamentally cut out for the rough and tumble of modern-day frontline politics. Hand on heart, despite allowing it to dominate my twenty-something hopes and dreams, I am not so sure now that politics was ever the right fit for me.

I also recognised the longer I remained in Parliament that my own priorities were evolving. The overwhelming sense of privilege and opportunity in having a public platform meant that in my earliest days as an MP, there were very few media opportunities I would turn down. But television is an essentially artificial medium. Its main frustration for politicians is that the ever-shorter attention span of viewers means live TV often gives you painfully little chance to develop a theme before the presenter is interrupting your flow or bringing in other panellists. Once filming in the studio has commenced, you are also acutely aware of your every facial expression and the need to concentrate at all times whether or not you are on camera. None of this makes for enhanced verbal fluency, so the tendency is to speak in pre-prepared soundbites. The inherent danger with agreeing to pre-recorded TV is that the editing process will leave only newsworthy or incriminating clips.

Despite this aversion to the medium, as a central London MP there was many a time on a Friday or at weekends that I would get a desperate call from Central Office or the broadcaster direct at very short notice, asking me to appear on TV when a major news story had broken or to deputise for a colleague who had pulled out of a show. Over several years, I was a regular on the Saturday morning newspaper reviews for Sky News, which was a little more enjoyable and expansive, not least because it was rare to appear alongside other politicians and the subject matter was more varied.

I much preferred doing radio. The highly experienced Carolyn Quinn was professionalism personified on BBC Radio 4's *Westminster Hour* before she retired, and over the years I appeared on the MPs' panel over sixty times on that flagship live Sunday evening programme. There is always more time on radio to develop your answers. Being able to refer to notes that I had sketched in advance, following discussions with the production team, eliminated the nerve-racking high wire act of reciting prepared lines that is part and parcel of appearing on TV. Paradoxically perhaps, I think it also added to the spontaneity of proceedings.

Truly ambitious politicians have a near-obsessive desire to drop everything to get on TV and radio or feature in the newspapers morning, noon and night. For them 'all publicity is good publicity'. The rise of a vast array of social media outlets such as Facebook, Instagram and TikTok has only added to this frenzy of activity. Predictably, the MPs most engaged in feeding the sewer that is social media also shout loudest when their posts provoke anonymous threats of violence.

I realised I was losing my sense of drive and ambition when fairly soon after becoming an MP, I began to pass on media opportunities. The early thrill of seeing my name in print had soon turned to nervousness and a familiar sinking feeling as I worried that the published quote in my name would lead to trouble – a stern call from a colleague or my whip or follow-up stories in the other parts of the media. Quickly, I came to the conclusion that it was far easier to avoid the risk of an anxiety-filled evening or weekend by saying nothing at all to enquiring journalists rather than feeding the media beast. This was definitely not the reaction of an ambitious politician on the rise.

• • •

In the eyes of party colleagues, every MP is at least partly defined by the intake with which they entered Parliament. Superficially, the thirty or so new Tory arrivals of 2001 must be regarded as an especially high-quality vintage. Despite being a small intake, it contained two Prime Ministers and the third-longest-serving post-war Chancellor. Around half of us ended up as ministers, but in my view some of the most thoughtful and interesting characters have remained resolutely on the back benches. It is often remarked upon with some disbelief that the great anti-slavery campaigner William Wilberforce spent his entire thirty-two years in Parliament as a backbencher. The presumption is that in the modern age, this far-sighted hero of one of the greatest humanitarian causes would be a senior minister. I have serious doubts that this would be so. It is far more likely, I fear, that if Wilberforce were a politician in the current era, he would be dismissed as something of an obsessive crank and certainly insufficiently conformist or 'on message'.

John Baron was the first in the class of 2001 to take on an opposition

departmental frontbench role. A former army officer, he promptly resigned over his refusal to support the Iraq War. Restored for
a while to the front bench, as a former Fusilier John consistently
made the case in opposition and government for greater military
spending, although never seemed willing to support actually putting our troops in the line of fire and voted against action in Libya
and Syria. Mild-mannered, polite to a fault and always convincing
on the media, the fact that much more was not made of his clear
talents – for many years he authored an asset management column
in the *Investors' Chronicle* – speaks volumes for the imperfections of
the system. I can imagine he has long been dismissed as 'unsound'
by the leadership, despite the manifest meretriciousness of many
holding ministerial office in recent years.

I first met Richard Bacon, another of the 2001 intake, when we
were both recently out of university. Soon we were co-editing the
Bow Group's magazine and I recall a memorable morning in late
August 1990 walking across Hampstead Heath together to interview
the then political editor of *The Guardian*, Hugo Young, at his stylish
home on Christchurch Hill. The first Gulf War had just begun, and
our interviewee magisterially pronounced that as a consequence,
'Margaret Thatcher is now safe from challenge.' Yet within three
months she had been ousted. Ah, the stark fallibility of the punditry
is one of the few things that has remained reassuringly consistent
throughout my time in politics.

Back to Richard – he has always had an endearing Tigger-like
intensity and energy about him. For much of his time in politics,
this has attached to a passion for innovation to help boost house
building by promoting prefabricated construction at scale. It was
typical of him that when I made contact in 2023 after he had failed
to be readopted as a candidate in his South Norfolk constituency, he

brushed off any disappointment and reassured me that he still had so much more to do in shaping the intricacies of housing strategy before leaving Parliament. Given that we burned our way through sixteen Housing Ministers in our fourteen years in office, it seems rather sad, if not surprising, that space could not be found for someone with Richard's evident knowledge and enthusiasm at some point along this hapless procession of stop-start policymaking.

A couple of days after leaving my frontbench role in autumn 2006, I was called in to chat at length with the Deputy Chief Whip, Andrew Robathan. I had got to know and rather like him when we had both been on the deputation for the inaugural Conservative Friends of India visit to New Delhi, Mumbai and Srinagar three years earlier. His own elevation to his then role owed much to time and chance, so he was keen to impress upon me that 'nothing is for ever in politics'. Having entered Parliament in 1992, he was almost the last of his intake to make it to a frontbench position in 2001.

Later, Andrew became one of the core team organising David Cameron's leadership campaign. The appeal of that operation was not immediately obvious to everyone, but Andrew was a true and early believer. Cameron had been widely assumed to be laying down a marker for a future leadership contest by running, whilst simultaneously re-affirming his place in the shadow Cabinet pecking order. Evidently, even from the outset, that is not how his acolytes saw things. When Cameron won against the odds, Andrew found himself very much on the inside track and eventually became a Defence Minister and later still went to the House of Lords.

Andrew made frequent entreaties to me, but he was not going to get me to waste my time, as I saw it, sitting on a select committee. I was determined to enjoy my newfound freedoms away from the front bench to speak and write openly about economic and financial affairs, especially as it was now clear to many in the City of London that it was only a matter of time before the economy, which had been in an almost unprecedented fourteen years of continuous growth, was heading for a slowdown. Few predicted the severity of financial crisis that engulfed the western economies in 2008, but the application of economic gravity meant it was clear the good times had to come to an end sometime soon.

Now I had left the front bench, I realised I was essentially faced with three main options. Working my passage back into favour with a sustained campaign of sycophancy was never going to work for me and even if it had appealed, I reckoned I would be trailing behind a long line of more accomplished performers of that particular art.

Option two was to wait on events and hope the pendulum would swing back. There are few certainties in political life, but I worked on the basis that Cameron was going to be around for quite some time. As all students of history know, treachery is only ever a matter of dates. So, whilst my instincts about the tenure of the Cameron regime turned out to be right, in the six years after his departure there were no fewer than four changes of leadership. This led to many spectacular and unanticipated turnarounds in individual fortunes, as MPs who seemed to have been banished to a life on the back benches were spectacularly returned to ministerial office. And vice versa, lest we forget.

But very soon, the third option opened up for me – to use the fact that I was the MP for the City of London in a time of financial upheaval and crisis to build a personal platform of sorts. This I did as a politician with 'something to say', albeit with a sensible, thoughtful perspective rather than as a talking head parroting the party line or an attention-seeking maverick. 'A cheerful rebel' was how several political journalists at the time described me; I did not see myself as especially rebellious, but the term rightly recognised that I lacked the anger and stubborn resistance that we would all see from many 'outsiders' in the years to come.

The Conservative Party's favourite political strategist, Lynton Crosby, never disguised his irritation at the media freelancing of backbench MPs. 'If you absolutely have to be on Twitter [the platform now known as X], then for Christ's sake never, ever tweet when you are either angry or drunk,' he would tell meetings of the parliamentary party. Crosby had made his name transforming the electoral fortunes of the Liberal-National coalition in his Australian homeland. Always capable of sharp and pithy asides, his other favourite piece of advice to us all was, 'You lot have got to make up your minds – are you players or commentators?' In truth, he was a more soft-spoken, thoughtful and cerebral figure than these anecdotes make him appear. I think the last time we bumped into each other was on one of my rare trips to the Royal Opera House, so there was evidently more to him than the brash populist image often portrayed in *The Guardian* and on the BBC. I suspect Lynton was happy enough to play along with all this, provided he was respected and feared in more-or-less equal measure.

• • •

However, it was now pretty clear which path I would have to take. With all the spare time I now had on my hands, and at the very moment the financial markets had become the biggest news story, I set about researching many problematic and intractable economic issues. I was fortunate enough to have connections and expertise in the City of London at my fingertips. In addition, very soon the *Daily Telegraph*, *City A.M.* and the newly established but already highly influential Conservative Home website were regularly running the fruits of this research. I initiated parliamentary debates and in time published two collections of essays with the slightly provocative titles *Between the Crashes* (2013) and *The Best of Times* (2016). For the best part of the next decade, I was indisputably much more commentator than player.

The passage of time all too often treats opinion pieces written in the heat of battle harshly. At the risk of sounding rather immodest, I don't think that applies to my books. Rereading many of the essays I wrote in the first half of the 2010s reinforces the foreboding I felt even then that economic policymaking was dangerously awry. I was certainly assisted by my City contacts and network, but looking back, I reckon my own judgement as to the likely outcome of events has proved prescient.

As far back as 2013, I was lamenting that the Office for Budget Responsibility 'has served to entrench rather than challenge conventional wisdom'. Two years on, I was an early outlier in expressing alarm as to the wisdom of relying upon foreign investment to sustain our ever-larger deficit. A recurring theme in my essays even then was the anaemic level of economic growth and the failure to devise any sustainable strategy to counter it. So too the distorting orthodoxy of the Treasury and the Bank of England well before it became fashionable, in certain quarters at least, to do so. Then there was the urgent – and still unresolved – need to turn our finest economic minds to a lasting reform of the public and private pensions system and developing a more effective regulatory and compliance structure to protect the City of London from money laundering and financial engineering. But above all was my repeated warning that the UK was living way beyond its means despite all the talk of austerity, a problem made ever more serious by the reluctance to expand the tax base rather than constantly looking to take more people out of income tax entirely.

One of the first themes in my sights when Labour was still in government was its vastly expanded use of the Private Finance Initiative (PFI). Most of its much-vaunted 'investment' in public services since 1997 had been deliberately placed off the public balance sheet, which in essence disguised borrowing to fund current consumption by gradually repaying capital and service costs for the new hospital wing or upgraded school building over periods as long as twenty or thirty years.

The main reason criticism of PFI was so muted at the time was that private sector operators were all able to make hay as professional advisers in the process. Every PFI – and its rebranded twin, Public Private Partnerships (PPP) – contract turned into a lucrative payday for consultants, lawyers, architects and accountants. For facilities management contractors and operators, the plan was that the money would keep flowing in for every last designated replacement or upgrade for the length of the contract. Until, as we saw most spectacularly with the recent collapse of Carillion plc, the gravy train came to a juddering halt.

Two conversations with senior business figures linger in my mind from this time. I was endeavouring to understand exactly what was going on – all in, there would in time be about 700 projects under PFI/PPP with a capital value of £56 billion. What I wanted to discover was their true impact on the state of the public finances. My first conversation was with the CEO of a leading conglomerate that had reinvented itself; expanding rapidly, his company was now up to its neck in public sector contract work. Almost messianic in his advocacy of public-private collaboration, he brushed away any suggestion that PFI might turn out to be poor value to future generations of taxpayers. Amidst his pyramid sales scam patter, it was simply impossible for me to pin him down on precisely how the risk of project or service delivery was being transferred to the private sector. I came to the conclusion that he simply did not understand the mechanism – this from the CEO of a company annually entrusted with schools, prisons, roads and hospital building programmes in all corners of the UK, not to mention billions of pounds of public money.

My worst fears were confirmed within weeks when I invited myself for coffee at the modern City offices of a Magic Circle law firm. The partner, whom I had known for some years, quietly closed the door to his office as my questioning became more intense. 'My biggest worry, Mark, is that many of these off-balance sheet financings have been so poorly negotiated by the government that we are avoiding some very tough decisions that will need to be made about future public spending. But when the balloon goes up, we shall all suffer.'

The trouble was, we were all in on it. Not just well-paid professionals but MPs too. The last £1 billion plus hospital PFI scheme to make it in under the wire in 2005 was for Barts Healthcare, whose flagship hospital was in the City of London, so even I have to plead guilty. PFI was the only funding game in town, so whilst in a Commons debate both Diane Abbott and I expressed our doubts about the means of financing (she wanted it paid for directly out of taxes), we both implored the Health Minister to give the proposal the go-ahead post haste on behalf of our constituents. The annual servicing costs for this PFI contract have risen sharply with the return of inflation and in 2023 stood at a little over £150 million. This already cash-strapped NHS trust, which is crying out for more medically qualified staff and whose waiting lists continue to rise, has to pay back the historical fixed costs associated with this contract before it can even take its day-to-day running costs into account in its annual budgets.

As if the economic illiteracy were not enough, my political concern was that off-balance sheet financing of this sort would also severely limit the room for manoeuvre of a future centre-right government. The consistent repayment costs would be making sustained reductions in public expenditure all the more difficult to implement. This is precisely how things have played out, but I believe it is important to remember that the coalition government's austerity squeeze has only compounded a problem that was already in train once PFI had become so widespread. We see this in the deep reductions in discretionary expenditure by the Health and Education departments over the past decade. So too in local government, where the budgetary constraints imposed by PFI repayments and then austerity have resulted in many now financially troubled local councils signing up for ever-riskier borrowing on property investments, which are fast unravelling as interest rates return to historic norms.

There were some half-hearted efforts in the early days of the coalition to try to claw back from contractors the sometimes-egregious returns they stood to make from long-term PFI/PPP contracts. But many of these contracts had already been repackaged and sold on for vast profit, so predictably the excessive costs tied up in these deals will be left to government – or perhaps more accurately, to future generations of taxpayers. And it gets worse – some of the infrastructure built in the earliest PFI schemes is fast reaching the end of its natural life. Yet at the same time as we need to find the money for its urgent replacement, the taxpayer may still be paying the bill for the last years of the original contracts.

My background in business made me an obvious candidate to

take on the chairmanship of the All-Party Parliamentary Group on Private Equity. I knew the senior figures at the British Venture Capital Association well and had always stood up against the simplistic criticism that private equity was an industry made up of asset-strippers. It also struck me that innovation and rigorous management were often enhanced by private-equity-led ownership. However, in time I also came to see that the generous tax treatment of private equity holdings left the door open to financial engineering for its own sake and that some elements of that advantageous tax regime are still overdue for reform.

In a parliamentary debate, I drew a distinction between genuine risk-taking entrepreneurs and private equity investors, both of whom qualified for entrepreneurs' taper relief on the sales of their holdings. In good times, the role of private equity is more that of a financier rather than risk-taker, which makes the treatment of 'carried interest' in private equity funds all the more difficult to justify. This has become part of a perennial debate about the widening gap between rates of income and capital gains taxes. For a short time towards the end of the Thatcher era, it looked possible that the two might be equalised. We may yet return to this – although it is likely to be a rallying call from the centre-left that there should no longer be any distinction between the rewards to labour and capital. This would, in my view, be a sensible and overdue simplification of our tax system. The UK tax code, packed with exemptions and complication galore, is now the world's longest at over 10 million words, having in recent years surpassed the oft-criticised Indian version.

The other concern, tax treatment aside, which I expressed back in 2008 and has only worsened over time, is the cost and regulation facing public companies. This has only helped make the private markets yet more attractive. If the government and the City of

London are serious about enhancing the international reach of our London Stock Exchange, we need to address this challenge. Like it or not, every time a UK company seeks a primary listing in New York it is regarded as a grievous blow to our prestige and, especially post-Brexit, raises concerns about the UK's international clout. Slowly but surely, these decisions also diminish the available pool of stocks for institutions and individuals wishing to invest here.

But in time, it was the potential for financial engineering that concerned me most. Private equity investment became seen as a means of loading up previously healthy balance sheets with debt in order to pay out hefty dividends on an attractively tax-efficient basis to the new ownership team. A number of high-profile retailers found themselves seduced into private equity ownership before quickly becoming overwhelmed by unsustainable debt. Closer to home, it was in 2011 that I first became aware of the ownership issues at Thames Water that would blow up so spectacularly over a decade later.

Anyone who has walked on the central London shore of the River Thames during the past decade will have seen the colossal Thames Tideway tunnelling that is being built to renew the early-Victorian sewer system. London may no longer be home to as much extractive industry as it was in the 1850s, but its population has risen three-fold. An upgrade was long overdue, particularly in view of the ever-more-frequent instances of drainage overflows resulting in raw sewage being discharged. Thames Water made a persuasive case to do this properly – let's install a made-to-last fifteen-mile super sewer at a cost of £4 billion rather than a £1.5 billion patch-up version.

Then came the discussion about paying for all this. Until only a few years before, Thames Water had around £1 billion of reserves on its balance sheet, but it had then been bought out by the asset management wing of an Australian bank, Macquarie Group. Substantial dividend payments and the loading up of debt became the name of the game – all apparently sustainable given the ultra-low interest rates that then applied. Wave goodbye to those prudently accumulated reserves! And under the terms of Ofwat's environmental guidelines, the entire cost for the blue riband upgrade could be charged to the householders and businesses in the Thames Water region.

When I spoke about this on the floor of the House, I recognised that making the case for my constituents to pay an additional £70 per year over the next fifty years (naturally, it has turned out to be a lot more than that) would be less difficult than the task facing well over a hundred other MPs in the more distant parts of the Thames Water empire – in rural Gloucestershire, for example. At least my constituents could see the vast work being carried out in their name and would tangibly benefit from the tunnelling work.

The UK's privatised water industry became a favourite destination for financial engineering of this sort. Below the radar, apparently rather dull and invested in by pension funds who saw water as a safe and reliable asset, by the late 2000s its dividend policy had been upended. Its hapless regulator seemed to have taken its eye off the ball. Senior water company executives were absurdly overpaid, in the manner of captains of industry rather than custodians of a regulated monopoly. In London, along with the sewage discharge issues that have made headline news, we will soon be faced by a serious shortage of drinking water. This will be extremely costly to fix. Taking water back into public ownership may be popular but would be vastly expensive given that – as with PFI – the companies who benefited from leveraging the balance sheet have long since departed the scene.

Even before the financial crisis engulfed the City of London, it was a matter of increasing anxiety to me as the local MP that too much that happened in the world of financial services gave succour to the critique that people working in banking put their own interests before clients, let alone the wider public. Financial engineering of the sort that was soon to beset Thames Water was, as we were soon to discover, only the tip of the iceberg.

No one disputed that there wasn't an urgent need to get more stuff built – infrastructure accounted for 12 per cent of public spending in 1970 but barely a quarter of that at the turn of the century. But what, where and how? As a constituency MP, I recognised there were seldom many votes, let alone a great outpouring of public support, for large projects causing great disruption in the locality. Endless traffic disruption, demolition of homes and wrangling over compulsory purchase terms became a running sore in my patch over the Crossrail development.

My unequivocal support from the outset for the new cross-London train link won the approval of non-voting businesses but implacable opposition from those Soho and Barbican residents most inconvenienced by the works. Essentially, an MP needs to weigh up the national interest with genuine constituency concerns. I could see the wider benefits of Crossrail – or the Elizabeth Line, as it was later called. The same applied to Heathrow Airport expansion. I consistently voted for the third runway (which I still suspect will never be built), although I recognised that until technology caught up it was likely to result in a diminution in the quality of life of many central London constituents, my family included, living below the flight paths.

I am sorry to say that, in stark contrast, I believed the case for HS2 was a calamity from the very outset. The Conservatives when still in opposition latched onto the proposal for a north-south high-speed rail link in order to cloak ourselves in a visionary, environmentally friendly, long-term transport policy. It also provided us with a useful political alibi for opposing Heathrow expansion at the time, a policy designed to make us electorally competitive in a handful of west London marginal seats. The commitment to level up after the Red Wall seats had been won in 2019 meant that we still felt unable to put this woefully defective project out of its misery, until Rishi Sunak finally lost patience with the ludicrous overrunning cost.

At the outset, the full HS2 had been expected to cost £32.7 billion. The truncated version on offer – now with no Birmingham to Manchester or Leeds branches – is still expected to come in at around three times that cost. The underlying logic was originally a reduction in travel times, an argument which always struck me as odd. No disrespect to our Mancunian friends, but reducing the journey time from the north-west to London by forty-five minutes surely makes the capital an even more attractive commuting option, rather than an inspiration to head north? Then the goalposts were changed – it was all about additional capacity, apparently. This in the rail industry which has been the recipient of huge levels of public subsidy for over a century and whose users are predominantly relatively well-off Britons.

My implacable opposition to HS2 has been long-standing, but even I could not have imagined the catalogue of incompetence and wastefulness that has followed. The feeding frenzy for those environmental consultancies, urban architects, surveyors and assorted professional advisers who have feasted on HS2 whilst departmental ineptitude has held sway has been nothing short of scandalous. Constant Treasury questioning of the next chapter of cost overruns had until very recently been superseded by political indecision and a moral cowardice to make definitive decisions as the public justifications for this notorious white elephant have changed over time. In the meantime, the really pressing transport need in the Red Wall continues to be for an overhaul and upgrade of the lines that link Liverpool, Manchester, Sheffield, Leeds and Newcastle.

Vying with HS2 as one of the biggest fiascos in this space, albeit mercifully not at such cost, is an infrastructure project closer to home for the political class: the seemingly endless saga over repairs to the Houses of Parliament, a UNESCO World Heritage Site no less. As a matter of courtesy to me as the local MP, I was brought into the loop as early as 2016 by those senior parliamentary officials overseeing the renewal and restoration. 'I suspect that I shall be long gone by the time the work is underway,' I chuckled more in jest than any expectation of foresight. Two years later, almost half a ton of masonry crashed down one morning from the ceiling of my lower-ground-floor ministerial cubbyhole of an office. Had I been there at the time, my earlier prediction might well have been instantly realised. Incidents like this across the oldest parts of the parliamentary estate, dating from the mid-nineteenth century, were becoming ever more common.

Nevertheless, acutely worried about adverse press reaction as the projected costs have predictably escalated, MPs have found themselves paralysed by indecision. Initially, we voted to decant at enormous cost to allow for many years of uninterrupted work to fix our beloved asbestos-ridden, rodent-friendly Victorian fire hazard. This plan incorporated the building of a temporary and identical debating chamber at an office block somewhere nearby in Westminster.

Winston Churchill insisted, without consultation, on rebuilding an exact replica after the total destruction of the Commons chamber by enemy action in 1941. Apparently, today's MPs are still in thrall to Churchill's whim. Surely a sensible course would at the very least have been to rebuild a chamber that comfortably houses all 650 MPs and ideally in a semi-circular format that reflects the international norm? This plan was later shelved and replaced by an even larger budget allowing MPs to stay on site whilst works would take place piecemeal around them over several decades.

Later still even this decision was countermanded, so that a final, final decision is still pending. Small wonder no sensible company seems willing nowadays to sign up for any major or high-profile infrastructure project in the UK. To be fair, we are not alone. Witness the farcical delays and mammoth cost overruns with the building of a modern Berlin airport fit for purpose, which has been a national embarrassment to many Germans. Nevertheless, our recent infrastructure travails are fast turning the UK into something of a laughing stock.

● ● ●

All such a far cry from Margaret Thatcher in her pomp. An appraisal of her time at the helm still divides British opinion. I suspect it always will. But one thing is for sure – in the 1980s no one accused Britain of being an international laughing stock.

The longest time by far I spent in the former Prime Minister's presence came early in 2007, at the very time when those PFI, private equity and infrastructures issues were in the forefront of my mind. The outgoing dean of St Paul's, The Very Revd Dr John Moses, had always been very kind and thoughtful to me in my early years as the local MP. It was an unexpected pleasure to have been invited to a final intimate lunch at his Amen Corner home, a stone's throw from the cathedral. Even more so when I discovered that I was one of only ten guests and at the narrow rectangular oak table I would be sitting opposite the guest of honour, Baroness Thatcher. I had been warned that at this stage of her life, relatively recently widowed, she had 'good days and bad days'. Two things were unwavering, however. Her immaculate dress sense and her acute sense of punctuality. Not a hair out of place nor a moment delayed.

As the meal began, conversation was at best rather faltering. Amidst the chatter, the acoustics were a little difficult. I worried that the baroness was having one of her bad days and I racked my brain for a theme, any theme, that might open up conversation. Sitting to my left at the end of the table was Dr Claire Gilbert, the renowned ethicist, who at the time was a lay canon and would later migrate to Westminster Abbey. She remembered me from university. At the mention of the word 'Oxford', Baroness Thatcher's face lit up as if someone had flicked a switch. For the next hour it was as if we had all been transported back six decades as she spoke with passion and excitement about her undergraduate days. Involvement in the Conservative Association, men coming back from the war, May balls attended, walks across Port Meadow and in the parks. It was remarkable and unforgettable. It is often said of elderly folk who are facing up to dementia that they cannot recall recent events but sometimes have a pitch-perfect memory of the distant past. So it was on that lunchtime, and it was an astonishing treat to watch and listen to Margaret Thatcher on top of her game.

Before that year was out, there was another Prime Minister entering Downing Street: Gordon Brown. He had been an all-powerful figure at the Treasury. Deeply partisan, he epitomises the traditional tribal party loyalty to Labour that we Conservatives are simply unable to match. It was noticeable that during the Jeremy Corbyn era he simply went to ground – it would not have occurred to Brown to publicly criticise a Labour Party leader. These days, by contrast, it seems nearly miraculous when a former Conservative premier has a good word to say for his or her Tory successor – or vice versa.

Brown's partisanship meant he was congenitally incapable of giving any credit to his political opponents. When coming into office, he never acknowledged the fact that he had inherited a strong economy, nor when bragging of the number of quarters of continuous economic growth would he ever recognise that the first twenty-two had not come on his watch. At each Budget, as he rattled off future revenue projections, I noted with amusement that the UK economy always seemed to be a tantalising three years away from balancing the books (although in fairness, much the same happened under Chancellor George Osborne).

Public spending was redefined as 'investment' by Brown; this didn't change the fact that we overspent, pumping ever more money into unreformed public services as he took for granted that the sustained upsurge in tax receipts from financial services would continue forever. Time and again at Budgets and autumn statements, with a hubris that verged on the foolhardy, Brown boasted that he had 'ended the cycle of boom and bust'. This, of course, was why the Conservative line held sway for many years ahead that Labour's profligacy, rather than the recklessness of lightly regulated bankers in the US property and derivatives markets, had brought the global economy to its knees. To my disbelief and despair, George Osborne had pledged to stick to Labour's spending plans on the very eve of the financial crisis. But Gordon Brown's determination to lap up all the credit for economic success in the good times made him vulnerable when everything turned to dust.

Shortly after he left the Treasury, the financial crisis hit and it all came crashing down. Brown's reputation may have lay in ruins, but the G20 summit that he convened in London in early 2009 was his finest hour. He, and his unflappable successor as Chancellor, Alistair Darling, led the global political and economic community with a rescue plan that saved the western economy from a potentially catastrophic depression. In response to a slip of the tongue at Prime Minister's Questions, he was ridiculed by Cameron, Osborne and Oliver Letwin, who rolled around on the front bench screaming, pointing and giggling like overgrown schoolboys. Whenever I look at that photograph it still makes me cringe with embarrassment.

So, I take a contrarian view of Gordon Brown. I do not highly rate his record as Chancellor, but in the circumstances, which were in part self-inflicted, his performance as Prime Minister is better than most political historians will give him credit for. I suspect the British people shared this grudging respect for Brown as PM, which is why Labour's defeat in 2010 was only a conventional reverse rather than the rout that so many of its MPs told me they were anticipating in the early months of that year.

• • •

On the domestic front, little went right for Gordon Brown. A serious missed opportunity was over the parliamentary expenses issue, where visionary political leadership had long been lacking. The expenses scandal had been a slow-burning issue during much of my time as an MP, but it blew up spectacularly in May 2009. The nub of the problem was that over many years, MPs had habitually voted down salary rises proposed by the senior salaries review board. Instead of transparent increases in remuneration and the resulting one-day wonder of confected press outrage, they/we voted instead to take the pay rise under the counter in the form of a vastly inflated second home expenses entitlement. A freedom of information (FOI) request to reveal the full details of thirteen MPs' expenses claims had been challenged by the parliamentary authorities and a rearguard action in the courts took place over several years to prevent disclosure.

Now I need to confess at the outset that I was scarcely a dispassionate observer on this issue. As an MP with a central London constituency, I was one of the small number who was ineligible to claim for a second home. This was a source of more than passing irritation, since unlike virtually every other colleague, I was unable to make up in expenses what I was 'losing' in repeatedly foregone salary rises. On the plus side, when the balloon went up, central London MPs were not directly impacted by the controversy. My constituency neighbour, Frank Dobson, caught up with me in the lobby at the height of the scandal and in his inimitable style reflected, 'Fuck me, Mark, what a mess! But at least me and you can sleep easily at night!'

Evidently, second home expenses had become a de facto salary supplement in the eyes of virtually every MP who claimed them, which is why the details when revealed were so damaging. And why until that point party managers were so determined to prevent full disclosure. For several years I had been confronted by dumb insolence from the Whips' Office as I complained about some of the scams in the system and warned repeatedly that this would not survive contact with public discovery. Looking back, I suspect that compared to the senior whips, I knew barely the half of it. In fact, barely the half of the half of the half of it. But what I did know was that we were collectively sleepwalking into disaster.

Then in January 2009, tucked away at the bottom of the Order Paper, which details daily business in the House of Commons, was a bland motion in the name of the apparently unimpeachable duo of Harriet Harman and Sir George Young, which would have sneakily exempted parliamentary expenses from FOI requests. This motion had been cooked up and tabled just days after the courts had finally declared that the full FOI disclosure should apply not only to the thirteen named MPs but to all parliamentarians past and present. Somehow an eagle-eyed journalist or two got wind of this and predictably a huge storm broke. Next up there was a rearguard action to redact or edit out huge quantities of detail of expense claims going back many years (notionally on privacy or security grounds), without which the real story would never have emerged.

Within weeks, the *Daily Telegraph* had purchased a stolen disc containing the full, unredacted details. A massive research project at the newspaper involving dozens of staff being assigned to the story followed, and during May and June a vast swathe of expense claim documentation was published. Predictably, the *Daily Telegraph* came under fire from politicians across party lines for compromising their security and handling stolen goods. In truth this was public interest investigative journalism at its finest, but it would not have happened if senior figures from all political parties had not fought this out so tenaciously over the years in the courts. But there was rough justice too. Some of the most high-profile casualties committed minor, but eye-catching infringements (Peter Viggers never actually claimed let alone received money for his notorious duck house) whilst I am well aware of several individuals whose serious transgressions over second home designation slipped under the *Telegraph*'s radar.

Gordon Brown flunked his brief opportunity to show leadership on the expenses issue. Governments inevitably suffer more when these meteors hit, but he could have made a heartfelt apology to the public and then sought to draw a line under the past with promises of strict punishments for future offenders. Instead, he characteristically tried to make partisan political capital by conflating expenses (where Labour were the worst offenders – all six members of the Commons who went to prison for false accounting were on their benches) with second jobs (where Conservatives have been, and continue to be, the main beneficiaries) in proposing onerous new rules on outside earnings.

David Cameron had a 'good war' on expenses but at a price. Those closest to him were protected as the earliest revelations about the shadow Cabinet were met with his instant insistence, at the pain of demotion, that controversial claims be repaid in full. He was no less decisive in dealing with backbenchers, but older, more independently minded MPs felt less well looked after as the revelations went on and on. This resulted in a long shadow of distrust with some in the parliamentary party, which arguably contributed to more than a few of his party management problems over the European Union in the years ahead.

· · ·

The backdrop to the 2010 election could scarcely have been more challenging for the Labour government. The financial crisis had necessitated huge bailouts of the banking sector, with two of the UK's Big Four, RBS/Nat West and Lloyds, the recipients of an eye-watering amount of government support running into tens of billions of pounds. Western economies had been plunged into a deep but short-lived recession, but no one thought we were strong enough yet to raise interest rates above the emergency levels that had been set in March 2009 at below 1 per cent. Equally, no commentator or mainstream economist could possibly have imagined that thirteen years would pass before they would be raised above this level. UK soldiers were dying in Afghanistan, although in comparison with the conflict in Iraq, now subject to an uneasy ceasefire, much of the British public regarded this conflict as a just war. The expenses scandal had claimed the careers of scores of MPs who were standing down.

With a certain amount of exhaustion, Gordon Brown finally went to the country on almost the last possible day, to coincide with local elections in May. In London, a general election took place on the same day as all-out council contests for the first time ever. Benefiting from being on the coat tails of the thirty Tory local government candidates in one of the Conservatives' then flagship councils, I enjoyed spending all my time in the constituency working alongside them. The weather was warm and dry for the most part, and in the event my majority rose into five figures for the first and only time during my tenure. But from the outset I had my doubts about the overall outcome and won the office sweepstake along our part-corridor of Portcullis House by predicting almost exactly the national result. Sadly, these powers diminished with age and experience and in the two subsequent elections I fought, my predictions were well off beam.

So, a hung Parliament beckoned. The Conservative leadership must have known they faced the unpalatable prospect of a no-holds-barred internal analysis of our faltering election campaign. For all its professed love of modernisation, the leadership had complacently gone into the election believing that an old-fashioned appeal based on spouting a few simplistic slogans about change and repeatedly rubbishing Gordon Brown would see us swept to victory.

It had been taken for granted by those advising David Cameron that their man needed only to turn up at the TV debates to win them. Yet suddenly and unexpectedly, Cleggmania exploded on the scene. From the time of the first TV debate, just three short weeks before polling day, it became horribly clear that we had not sealed the deal. Whilst many of our local Westminster canvassers had been faithfully reporting unease from party supporters about Cameron's resolve and likeability for months, it had been widely assumed by central office that he was universally popular with those key 'floating voters'. Nick Clegg's emergence on the national stage changed all that.

The Conservative campaign lacked a strategic bite, with even our one great revolutionary message, the Big Society, failing to ignite much enthusiasm. To many purists, the case for Conservatism was never really put. The leadership had taken fright when the first instalment of deficit reduction plans announced at the previous October's party conference had been poorly received at the polls. Our double-digit lead halved overnight and never again was an explicit mandate for tough economic measures either sought or received. By the early hours of the morning after the election, as the outcome became apparent, an audacious leadership fightback swept into action.

If the Conservatives were disappointed at the outcome, the Liberal Democrats must have been shell-shocked. Election day had dawned with universal expectations of significant gains – some commentators were predicting a 100-seat haul and all reckoned on a substantial uplift from the 22 per cent vote share five years earlier. As it became apparent that the breakthrough had not taken place and that the party's seat tally had in fact fallen back to fifty-seven (nine net losses to the Tories being partly rebalanced by four gains from Labour), Nick Clegg must have appreciated the necessity of shoring up his own position. This was as good as it was likely to get. A rapid second election would almost certainly see the cash-strapped third party being badly squeezed. Clegg needed to seize the initiative from this unexpected position of weakness.

For our part, the Conservatives had secured almost fifty more seats than Labour. But we were still twenty seats short of a majority and the leadership must have taken fright at the prospect of going it alone. Necessary and urgent action was required to deal with the domestic deficit, and many feared the worsening economic situation in Greece was likely to lead to eurozone contagion. Immediate action to deal with these twin issues risked any new administration becoming unpopular very quickly. The assumption that a quick second election in October would see the Conservatives swept to an overall majority may have turned out to be wildly optimistic. In short, the window of opportunity to reinforce this near win might be impossibly narrow. The fear must have been that a minority administration 'doing the right thing' ran the real risk of being ousted in a confidence motion if the economy continued to deteriorate. I reckon it was from such a bleak analysis of the economic and electoral runes that the enthusiasm grew from both Cameron and Clegg for a fully-fledged coalition.

Part of the difficulty lay in the fact the electorate had seemed unwilling to grasp the seriousness of the national economic situation. The imposition of ultra-low interest rates and pumping money into the economy through quantitative easing seemed at odds with the backdrop of grave financial crisis. Complacency began to creep in, and during the run-up to the general election there seemed little public appreciation that an era of financial reckoning now lay ahead. The case for empowering people, a smaller state and responsibility was never made – and arguably this was to continue throughout the Conservatives' time in office.

Over the weekend, coalition talks gathered momentum. All the while the Tory parliamentary party was kept in the dark as negotiations continued apace. My whip called me, but, evidently speaking from a script, it was to ask me in very general terms about concessions around proportional representation. At no point did he address the issue of my potential support for the concept let alone specific terms for coalition, which was now being discussed openly and excitedly in the press.

Then as the new working week began, events moved swiftly with a keen momentum of their own. On the Monday evening, once the Liberal Democrat negotiators had apparently opened up a line of communication with the Labour Party, an emergency meeting of Tory MPs was convened. Whilst I have never been one for conspiracy theories (there is more than enough incompetence in the world of politics – or business for that matter – to explain most missteps), I quickly came to the conclusion that this was probably choreographed by our leadership. A feverish atmosphere was being whipped up that the Liberal Democrats were about to steal a march on our rightful advance to Downing Street. Few suspected that this gambit may have owed more to Clegg needing to keep his own left-wing supporters happy by being seen to offer the Labour government terms. But it softened us up to make concessions.

Four days on from the election and David Cameron had still not made it through the door of No. 10. Those Labour MPs I knew and spoke to seemed relatively relaxed. After all, they had not been humiliated at the election and with 258 seats, sixty more than we had secured in 2005, many must have calculated on their reasonable prospects of bouncing back at the next election. Above all, there was the electoral arithmetic. The harsh truth was that even adding together all the Labour and Liberal Democrat MPs still left the putative partners a full eleven seats off an overall majority. In reality, a deal between the 'progressives' was never on the cards.

Not that any such cold-blooded perspective or analysis was put to Monday's crucial Conservative parliamentary party meeting. On the contrary, the swollen ranks of Conservative MPs, who packed out one of the largest committee rooms, were treated to an impassioned plea from Cameron that failure to seal the deal now risked our being left at the altar as the forces of anti-Conservatism united. Uncertainty leading to the prospect of a second election within weeks or months must also have sounded especially unpromising to the 140 or so Tory MPs who had been elected for the first time just four days earlier. These were the circumstances in which the Conservative Party was bounced into coalition and making an offer of a referendum on whether to adopt alternative vote instead of first past the post. Persuasively, Cameron explained that it had been the Liberal Democrats who had dismissed out of hand the prospect of a 'supply and confidence' deal to allow a minority administration. The alleged third 'option' of coalition and accepting proportional representation without a referendum had almost certainly never been canvassed and I guess it was only floated theoretically to suggest that our negotiating team had won some concessions. So, the leadership got its way. A salutary lesson in the ways of democracy. Not a single elector voted for coalition, though in fairness they never had the option put to them. But lest it be forgotten each of the parties had entered the election campaign expressly stating that a clear outcome to the election was essential for the nation's future well-being.

There was a final chapter to this story. A visibly relieved David Cameron displayed a small sign of humility after the party had voted for his coalition proposal, as he faithfully promised to pay more attention in future to party management. Within three weeks, and by now safely in Downing Street, he unilaterally announced his intention to change the constitution and membership of the Conservative Party's independent backbench committee. The activities of the 1922 Committee have come to the fore in recent years with the never-ending succession of leadership elections and challenges. David Cameron was neither the first nor last party leader to tire of the machinations of the 22, even though it plays an important role as a safety valve for internal unease and dissent. But from the word go, he gave the appearance to many of his backbenchers of being far too busy running the country to bother with party management. He and his team carried on as if they had secured a majority of eighty in their own right, when in order to shore up their position it was the Liberal Democrats who had been showered with ministerial office and influence.

Despite frequent speculation to the contrary, I never doubted for one second that the coalition would last the course for the full five-year parliament. After all, the two leaders' personal political survival depended on it holding together. Plenty has been written about the coalition government by those who were members and supporters of it. My observations are those only of an outsider. However, given what has followed, there is in my view an understandable but mistaken tendency to lionise the coalition years.

The impression of a steady hand on the tiller during that period masks the fact that too many tough decisions were flunked. Look around today at some of the most pressing domestic problems we face. We were well aware of many of these from the earliest days of the coalition, but the political establishment of the day chose to commission further independent reviews or postpone painful decisions rather than commit to action. The arguments over energy capacity, social care, the viability of state pensions, the state of the criminal justice system, house building and planning reform have barely changed since 2010, but a lack of political resolve has turned challenges into crises. The coalition's easy economic consensus and illusion of political stability also enabled the can to be continually kicked down the road over public spending.

To coin a phrase, the coalition government failed to fix the roof when the sun was shining – in relative terms, at least. Ultra-low interest rates gave the appearance of economic stability and certainty, but too much risk was mispriced and its torrid impact is only now coming to the fore. Above all, I would contend that the fast track to Brexit began the moment the coalition was formed. The distrust between the Conservative Party leader and all too many of his parliamentary troops meant that a certain steel entered the soul of the latter. They were going to get their referendum and it was going to be very difficult to persuade many that any reform deal in his name was worth the paper it was written on.

· · ·

Amidst all this political drama and tumult, there was an oasis of calm. Well, perhaps not calm, but once again my private life had become a source of stability and pleasure. Vicki and I met when I was shadow Minister for Culture. Her career was in media and hanging out with her clients and friendship group represented an exciting departure for me. She had grown up in and around Conservative politics – her mother and stepfather had served as local councillors – without being either taken or repulsed by the political bug. In a bid to escape from the intensity of Westminster life, one of our very best early decisions was to buy a plot of land in the rural central plain of Mallorca. The little finca we built there was an ideal getaway over the years.

We were married at St Margaret's, the parish church between Westminster Abbey and the Houses of Parliament, on the final Saturday of April 2007. It had been the most fabulously sunny month, as English Aprils sometimes are. But as our big day approached, I became convinced that month's more conventional showers would finally rear their head. They did but only on the morning after our wedding, by which time we were en route to our honeymoon in the Caribbean. So, the everlasting memory of our wedding day was of warm weather, spring blossom and a massive crowd of tourists taking photographs at what they assumed was a central London celebrity wedding in their midst.

Frederick arrived on 19 December, on the twenty-fourth anniversary of my receipt of that acceptance letter from St Edmund Hall. All my friends remarked how fatherhood was the making of me. Before you have children, particularly if you have left this momentous rite of passage until your early forties, you cannot imagine what life will be like as a parent. The moment you cross that threshold it is as if it has always been so. The most natural state in the world.

Arabella made her first appearance three-and-a-half years (less one day) later – she had to make do in the anniversary stakes with sharing a birthday with Paul McCartney. Well, it's a long and winding road. My nagging worry in the months before she was born was how could I ever love someone as much as I adored my firstborn? This was a genuine concern, which naturally was dispelled from the very first moment I held her close after her birth.

Vicki has always been the lynchpin of our family life. Until I left Parliament, she took on the overwhelming share of childcare and running the home. Working from home during the pandemic and beyond has been a timely wake-up call as to what this has entailed. But we have watched with wonder and pride as our beloved children have developed into independent and strong-minded young personalities.

Time for a small confession. My unwitting but crucial role in the celebrity careers of Sally Bercow and Nadine Dorries is about to be revealed. Entrepreneurial to her fingertips, Vicki had run her own business since her early thirties. On graduation from Oxford University (she matriculated in the year I left), where she had been as active in the drama scene as I had been in politics, Vicki began work as a theatrical agent. She specialised in placing talent – some household names – into media deals. A very different world from politics… or so I thought.

A matter of months before the formation of the coalition government, I attended a black-tie dinner at one of the plush Park Lane hotels. Our host was *The Spectator* magazine, and the guest list included a smattering of politicians, businessfolk and other 'friends of' the UK's leading centre-right political weekly.

On arrival, I glanced at the seating plan. My luck was in – either side of me were Anya Hindmarch, the luxury handbag designer, and Nancy Dell'Olio, the Italian lawyer and media personality at that time best known for having been the girlfriend of the former England football manager, Sven-Göran Eriksson.

I had a wonderful evening. Needless to say, my two neighbours probably went home cursing the fact that they had drawn the short straw being stuck next to some dull politician, but for my part, as well as being struck by their insightful analysis of contemporary politics, I learned more than I might have imagined about the Italian legal system and the precarious economics of the luxury accessories market.

Fellow guest George Osborne sauntered over mid-meal looking somewhat bemused. 'Who have you bribed to get yourself on this table?' he asked. I reckon it was the one and only time he has ever shown the slightest hint of envy towards me and my lot in life.

Coincidentally, only a week later Vicki and I were both guests of my constituent and old friend David Buchler at the English National Opera (ENO). As well as being internationally renowned in the field of corporate turnaround and restructuring, David is the ultimate opera buff. He is a walking encyclopaedia of venues and performers and in view of the ENO's perennial financial precariousness, his involvement there as deputy chairman brought together two of his many expert interests.

Who else should be there in our small party that evening but Nancy Dell'Olio? One thing naturally led to another and having introduced the two of them, Nancy and Vicki not only got on like the proverbial house on fire but quickly struck up a fruitful commercial relationship. TV bookings on *Have I Got News for You* and *Strictly Come Dancing* followed, as did a column in the newly launched *Sun on Sunday*. Which got my wife thinking – who else amongst my contacts in and around the political world might be similarly equipped to develop a media or celebrity profile?

Whisper it softly, but Sally Bercow was a Tory in her student days. In fact, we first met in the early 1990s in Blackpool at a party conference when, as Sally Illman, she was already coming under the spell of her future husband, John (or perhaps it was the other way round). Her politics moved sharply leftwards from then on and in due course the future Speaker of the House of Commons would follow suit. Nevertheless, it should not be forgotten that as an aspiring candidate in the early and mid-1990s, John Bercow was universally regarded as a big star in the making within Tory Party ranks. He had already made his name helping Conservative Central Office clean up the image of the party's student wing following the disbandment of the Federation of Conservative Students. His tub-thumping, unapologetically Thatcherite speeches, full of robust economic and social policy prescriptions, were always a huge draw at party conference.

It was no surprise when Bercow was rapidly snapped up as the candidate for one of the party's safest seats for the 1997 election, and even the Blair landslide at that contest did not deprive him of a five-figure majority in Buckingham. Newly elected, he was for a short time even talked of as a modern-day Disraeli, a break from Conservative tradition whose unique style would help bring the party back from the wilderness and into office once again. Recollections may vary on this, but I never thought that the Jewish connection between the two was ever made in an overtly antisemitic way. The comparison to Disraeli owed more to the fact that Bercow did come across as something of an outsider, rather odd looking with his strange articulation and florid but essentially Victorian-era speaking style. Unlike Disraeli, however, he lacked the patience and tactical nous to carve out his own path in Conservative Party politics.

His time as Speaker ended in bitter acrimony, but I always respected the fact that he took seriously his overriding duty to act as the champion of backbenchers rather than as a government mouthpiece. Urgent questions became the norm as opposed to an infrequent occurrence – and rightly so. Whilst it meant plenty of my ministerial mornings being disrupted as I prepared frantically for an ordeal in the chamber, I have always believed that government has far too much control of the parliamentary agenda. Enabling MPs to contribute to far more spontaneous debates and statements on issues of the day is a worthy legacy to John Bercow's decade as Speaker.

Sally Bercow was never one to settle for standing in her husband's shadow. Not only was that something of a literal impossibility, but once I had introduced her to Vicki, she proved bright, feisty and infuriating in equal measure. The path to securing a slot on reality TV involves much cloak-and-dagger negotiation, so agents usually earn their fee and more. In 2011, Sally made her splash on *Celebrity Big Brother* and whilst she was voted off first by the public, her performance in the house opened the door to plenty of other opportunities.

Fellow housemate Paddy Doherty was a former bare-knuckle boxer from the Irish traveller community. Much to everyone's surprise, he and Sally hit it off to such an extent that with Vicki's help, Endemol commissioned a spin off reality TV show. *When Paddy Met Sally* featured the stark contrast between living in a grace-and-favour apartment in the Palace of Westminster and life in a wind-swept north Wales campsite.

Vicki then secured her a weekly *Daily Star Sunday* column. Most celebrity guest columns are to varying degrees ghostwritten, but unusually Sally penned all of this herself, with its content and style invariably being well received. Several months in, her contract came to an abrupt halt. Budget constraints at the newspaper meant that all columnists were being forced to take a significant reduction in their weekly fee. Sally's petulant reaction to this on social media was that she wouldn't even use the *Daily Star Sunday* to line her cat litter tray, which predictably brought to a grinding halt any prospect of contract renegotiation. It was also a precursor to the altogether more serious trouble she would get herself into the following year with incontinent, finger-on-the-trigger tweeting over sex abuse claims. That episode ended in the High Court, with an abject public apology and payment of substantial damages for defamation.

It was perhaps inevitable after this introduction to political celebrity that my next port of call as a talent spotter was with a near office neighbour of mine on the fourth floor of Portcullis House. Nadine Dorries was, according to taste, already regarded by her Conservative colleagues either as a breath of candid fresh air amidst a bland and fusty party or woefully ill-disciplined with erratic judgement bordering on the unhinged. I must confess, I always had something of a soft spot for Mad Nad, as she was quickly christened, although I suspect in these more politically correct days no one would get away with that nickname.

The Boris Johnson era was still many years away, so at that time Nadine was not only a bundle of free-wheeling energy but evidently unfulfilled in Parliament. She was already beginning to make something of a name for herself as a proudly forthright and outspoken Tory from working-class roots, someone willing to engage openly on touchy subjects like poverty and homelessness.

Early in 2012, I arranged for Nadine and Vicki to meet up. Before long, the prospect of a lucrative appearance on *I'm a Celebrity... Get me out of Here!* loomed. Nowadays, politicians on reality TV are ten a penny, but Nadine's jungle appearance really was a ground-breaking deal as she was the first politician to take part.

One big problem. Filming was in Australia. It was also taking place during the parliamentary term. One month's leave of absence was urgently needed. A carefully crafted email from Nadine to the then Chief Whip, Andrew Mitchell, resulted in some confusion as to whether she had been given consent to head out to the Australian jungle or not. In view of her less-than-supportive approach to the Cameron/Osborne leadership the whip was withdrawn, and it would take a tortuous six months or so after her return from filming for it to be formally restored.

In the meantime, the path towards Nadine the best-selling author had already been laid. It started with a three-book deal – the Four Streets trilogy set in the Liverpool of her childhood – and with a big PR campaign, Vicki kicked off her writing career. With over 3 million novel sales to date, it was definitely one of Vicki's better ideas, and even many of her political opponents have written admiringly of Nadine's story-telling ability.

The world of performing arts and literature is littered with cases of the talent's head being turned by the financial possibilities that their initial, unexpected success quickly brings to light. Usually the writer, singer or artist watches awkwardly as this all unfolds but does their level best to please everyone. It normally takes gentle tact to balance the interests of the home-grown associates who have worked tirelessly to bring you out of obscurity with the demands of the major-league agency now offering untold riches and exposure. This is awkward but not impossible to achieve. Unfortunately, such diplomacy was never Nadine's style.

Life is too short to hold this against her, but elements of her blatant disregard for doing the conventional thing by those who had supported her from the outset have played out for all to see in recent years. Few of her closest friends, let alone seasoned political commentators, thought she was likely ever to grace the ministerial ranks, but then all bets were off once Boris became PM. Suddenly, having a celebrity past and the ability to blurt out the first idea that comes into your head regardless of the facts came into fashion. Turning up brazenly ill-prepared to select committee hearings on key departmental priorities, such as the Channel 4 privatisation policy, was no longer regarded as behaviour beyond the ministerial pale.

And so, to the final chapter of the Dorries public playbook – the protracted War of Nadine's Resignation. The near three-month-long saga of will she, won't she stretched the meaning of the phrase 'immediate resignation' to the limits of the English language, all the while keeping Nadine at the centre of public attention. Regrettably, her erstwhile Mid Bedfordshire constituents never had much of a look-in as this all played out over the summer of 2023.

Behind this was also probably a keen realisation on Nadine's part that her media brand and status as a sitting MP were more closely intertwined than she had originally thought. She never forgot the need to retain a suitable platform to launch her final journey of literary distinction. With an unusual degree of unity, book reviewers were quick to dismiss her two hastily written post-parliamentary works of instant history, *The Plot* and *Downfall*, as the products of a feverish imagination. It was even more remarkable, given the deep and antagonistic divisions within today's Conservative Party, that every one of her anonymous briefers appeared to share her niche views on the betrayed brilliance of Boris Johnson and the backstabbing scheming of Rishi Sunak.

More worryingly to my mind is the fact that we all seem to have accepted that politics is now little more than a subset of the entertainment industry. On this basis, the electorate are no longer regarded by many politicians or political commentators as citizens to be engaged in serious debate but as an audience to be entertained. It says something about our appetite for sincere political discourse when Penny Mordaunt, a serious contender at two contests for the top job, is remembered more for her appearance on a celebrity reality TV programme and for gracefully holding a sword during the King's coronation than for any policy initiatives or lasting achievements in a ministerial career that spanned almost a decade.

Unless and until we all recognise that politics is a serious business, which needs to be conducted – at least by its ministerial participants – in a sober and serious fashion, I fear we will all suffer. The celebrity culture that plagues public life has often allowed politicians to get away without proper scrutiny because trivia and sensationalism is so much easier to report and understand in a world where the general attention span has become so limited. The golden rule in modern politics is that the more people protest that it is all about ideas and policies, the more certain it has become a matter of communication and image.

* * *

We have now reached early 2014. Some sustained economic growth has cheered politicians and voters alike. My friends and connections in the City assure me with some relief that the financial crisis is now firmly behind us. Why then are we about to celebrate, if that is the right word, five years of emergency interest rates? Is it not high time to take the UK economy off what was billed as temporary life support?

Trying to understand and explain the strange economic and political crosswinds of this time was one of my main preoccupations. It meant a series of fascinating discussions with financial academics and market insiders, whose observations and concerns helped crystallise my own thinking. In summary, my increasing concern was that the neo-liberal financial orthodoxy that had held firm since the late 1970s had been badly shaken by the events of 2008, but the reaction of policymakers worked on the assumption that despite their unprecedented market intervention, it was desirable to return to the status quo ante. Needless to say, this was not always an easy argument to make from the standpoint of the City of London.

Nevertheless, the *Daily Telegraph* published a 2,000-word opinion piece of mine in January 2014, which I believe has stood the test of time. I argued then that since the financial crisis, UK government monetary policy had been driven by an overwhelming desire to minimise the impact of the economic shock. The baby boomer generation that had enjoyed – and continued to take for granted – an expanded welfare state, cheap goods, never-ending lines of credit and the benefits of inflated house prices had been broadly protected, notably by rock-bottom interest rates. Less consideration had been afforded to those excluded from this influential and sizeable cohort – today's young people, who grapple with sky-high rents and house prices, increasing personal debt and less secure employment. Even then there were rumblings about the maintenance of the pension 'triple lock' and the raft of pensioner benefits that were likely to be protected for a further electoral cycle. So little has changed in the decade since, and the intergenerational tensions and divisions in UK society have become only more entrenched.

I further observed that history indicates that policies designed, with the best intentions, to insulate from short-term shocks often have serious long-term consequences. Back in the 1930s, the impact of the Great Depression was cushioned by restrictive practices and cartels in British industry, which had already been subject to widespread consolidation after the First World War. The National Government of the time drove through tariff reform, which was supported across the board. The 10 per cent levies on imports were designed to insulate manufacturers from international competition, which focused emphasis towards empire rather than global markets. This featherbedded UK business in those difficult times, but it did lasting damage to Britain's longer-term competitiveness, as became evident from the 1950s as the US dominated after the Second World War. This is what happens when domestic companies have little incentive to modernise and innovate.

I argued then those five years of ultra-low interest rates had similarly provided UK businesses and individuals with a welcome breathing space. But emergency monetary stimulus, including the multiple helpings of quantitative easing (QE), never comes without cost to longer-term economic interests. The so-called zombie companies that have been allowed to continue in existence, as lending banks have felt no need to pull the plug on non-performers, has tied up capital and labour in non-productive activity. Even in 2014, I was clear that this low-interest-rate strategy augured ill in the face of fierce global competition, particularly if we were serious about economic growth in the years ahead.

What only became abundantly clear much later – although some of us had already by then recognised some of its distortive impacts – was that the QE experiment would be a disaster for those of us who believe in sound money governance. Governments across the western world – except those such as Portugal and Greece, caught in the eurozone straitjacket that has turned out to be something of a blessing in disguise – were given free rein to borrow and spend well beyond their means. Asset prices were driven up, creating a toxic wealth gap that has undermined any true sense that we were all in this together. Ironically, the big fear at the time was a Japanese-style deflationary spiral and QE was regarded as the best means of avoiding this. However, controlled deflation enables a gentle fall in the cost of living and it is the best mechanism by which society naturally redistributes wealth for the benefit of all.

Regrettably, policymakers continued the policy of rock-bottom interest rate levels for almost a further decade after these words of warning. The twin economic shocks of Brexit and the pandemic were an easy alibi as central banks and governments continued to kick the can down the road. In the meantime, a whole generation reached adulthood and spent a decade of working life assuming that the near-zero cost of borrowing was the norm. They took out mortgages, student loans and other debt on that basis. Events since the end of 2021 have come as a rude awakening for many of them. But I fear the distortions deeper in the economy will take longer still to become apparent. It was no coincidence that my collection of essays covering that deceptively calm few years in the middle of the last decade was entitled *The Best of Times*.

So, how best to restore fairness within society? The divides between old and young or between rich and poor seem as intractable as ever. So too the unequal rewards between labour and capital. With the recent return to office of the Labour Party, I believe we may finally be reaching a crossroads in public policymaking here. Much of my political life was spent amidst arid debates about inheritance, mansion, and wealth taxes, with fairly clear divisions along party lines. It was no surprise that the case for annual taxes on wealth and property assets were always strongest in central London. Those who rub shoulders with the fabulously wealthy living in the City of Westminster, Camden or the Royal Borough of Kensington and Chelsea have some genuine cause to believe that tweaking the tax system to make the rich 'pay their fair share' will sort out the nation's deficit at a stroke.

The stark reality is that in the UK as a whole, there are woefully insufficient numbers of the super-rich to bring in the game-changing sums that many on the left assume will be raised by a targeted wealth tax. The most affluent and moneyed living on these shores are also the most highly mobile if taxes are set at too punitive a level. We have already seen this under a Conservative administration as the virtually immediate consequence of abolition of the non-dom status. The simple reason that the middle class always face the brunt of tax rises is that there are so many of them. For any Chancellor of the Exchequer, this will always be the most efficient and straightforward means of raising the largest sums.

Inheritance tax now raises so much money for the Treasury (up from around £2.2 billion to over £7 billion annually over the past twenty years) that its abolition is a non-starter. Nevertheless, many of the arguments against it remain sound. It is in essence a form of double taxation, levied on income that has already been taxed during the deceased's lifetime. For the very well off, it has traditionally been easy to avoid by lifetime gifts and estate planning. As we all now know, agricultural land had historically been exempt, but modestly well-off people, whose assets are essentially tied up in the family home where they live, have no means of avoiding it.

I used to speak and write about all these issues, which were understandably close to the hearts of many of my central London constituents. Shortly before I left Parliament, I wrote an article for a local glossy magazine proposing that the time was ripe for a radical overhaul of council tax bands as well as a substantial uplift in the inheritance tax threshold, to be introduced alongside a reduced rate of capital gains tax payable on the sale of a main residence. At that time, I also proposed, on grounds of equity and simplicity, to return to a theme that Nigel Lawson had touched on during his long tenure as Chancellor – namely, moving towards equalisation in the rates of income and capital gains taxes.

In the past, politicians of all parties have placed such long-overdue

reforms to taxes on property and wealth into a box marked 'too difficult to implement'. The clamour for fairness across the generations
and in our ever more polarised communities is probably now loud
enough for action; it will be interesting to see how the Starmer/
Reeves government will finally respond.

As the 2010–15 Parliament drew to a close, my strong interest in
economic affairs and the state of the financial markets remained
undimmed. Recognising that in the eyes of the British public the
rehabilitation of bankers and banking still had some way to go, I
sought to promote vigorously the City of London's fee pool – the
array of ancillary services that fed on banking transactions but had
also been able to strike out and develop strong international reputations in their own right. The law, accountancy, insurance, management consultancy and corporate communications had all thrived
and were critically important service exports.

• • •

But gradually my parliamentary interests and activities were taking
on a more international flavour. The cadre of Conservative colleagues regarding themselves as foreign affairs specialists was both
ageing and diminishing with the expectation that modern MPs
would be more constituency and domestically focused in their work
and interests. By now I had spent some years on the Intelligence and
Security Committee, so as the situation in Syria deteriorated into
civil war in mid-2013, I was asked for the first time by a national
newspaper to write an opinion piece on foreign affairs.

US President Barack Obama had failed to back up with action
his threat of 'enormous consequences' if the al-Assad regime were
to use chemical weapons. As evidence stacked up that sarin gas had

been used to murder hundreds of civilians in rebel-held territory, the clamour for western intervention grew stronger. The initial plan was to arm rebel groups, but I remained unconvinced that such a decision would not come back to haunt us. On this basis, we might be arming ISIS fighters, who if they had been living in the UK would be subject to 24-hour police surveillance. There appeared to be little consensus amongst our NATO allies about the objectives behind intervention or any medium-term humanitarian strategy. Perhaps more important still was the risk that we would be dragged into a civil war that might well escalate throughout the region on Shia-Sunni dividing lines.

Early the following year, Russia annexed the Crimean peninsula in Ukraine. This took place in the aftermath of the coup that had seen the overthrow of Ukraine's pro-Russian government. President Putin calculated from the outset that the conflict in Ukraine was one that western leaders wished would go away. He came to a similar conclusion eight years later when ordering a fully-fledged invasion, but the west reacted with more resolve this time.

I had hoped in 2014 that the west would take steps to reduce our reliance on and exposure to Russian oil and gas. Moreover, through the selective use of economic sanctions, visa cancellations and international blacklists, we had a rare chance to isolate and antagonise Putin's political and financial backers. These strategic opportunities passed us by and we, especially the people of Ukraine, would all pay a higher price when Putin came back to finish the job.

It had been a testing decade. The aftermath of the prolonged upheaval in the financial markets and the unpopular, failing military adventures in Afghanistan, Iraq and Libya had battered the confidence of the US and its western allies. Academics and forecasters were charting the apparently inexorable advance of China to the extent that many predicted the size of its economy would overtake the US in the early 2020s.

In March 2014, I travelled to Beijing, Tianjin and Shanghai on China's eastern seaboard and concluded from what I saw that it would be hasty to write America off too soon. China's opaque financial system and the imminent squeeze on the labour market as a demographic consequence of its one-child policy were portents of trouble ahead. So too was the rapid urbanisation exacerbating the inequalities between existing city dwellers and the vast numbers of migrant workers relocating from rural areas. High-profile corruption investigations of senior figures in Chinese public life may have owed more to domestic political score settling, but this was already making foreign multinationals more nervous of investing in China.

As I travelled on the impressively efficient high-speed train, I passed countless empty skyscrapers in ghost towns and cities, the clearest sign of an overheated property market. This has been a feature of Chinese economic reporting ever since. My comforting conclusion was that for the foreseeable future the US could rest easy – the challenge to its position as the pre-eminent economic superpower still lay some way off.

CHAPTER 6

AN UNEXPECTED OFFER

---

15 JULY 2015

'I've got some good news and some bad news.'

Coming from a consultant oncologist these words would be alarming enough – from the mouth of the Chief Whip on the Ides of July, only slightly less so.

The oak-panelled rooms lying at the heart of Parliament must have given the impression of unrivalled grandeur back in the 1850s when the Palace of Westminster was virtually entirely rebuilt after a catastrophic fire. But for anyone familiar with the US version of *House of Cards*, our Chief Whip's office was by comparison rather tired and dated. Mark Harper was new to the post and the bare walls betrayed that fact. His predecessor had presumably taken away whatever artwork and personal effects had previously adorned the room. For a moment, this stark environment recalled less the epicentre of the government's enforcement of discipline than the base of someone craving anonymity on a witness protection scheme.

With a wry and knowing smile, I thought it best to take the good news first. Harper came straight to the point: 'The Prime Minister and I want you back in the team. He has asked me to tell you that at the next reshuffle he will bring you into the ministerial ranks, but in the meantime, he would like you to take on the chairmanship of the party's international office.'

I had no need to ask about the bad news. I had spent five enjoyable and highly educational years on the Intelligence and Security Committee (ISC) and had been sounded out just before the election by the previous Chief Whip, Michael Gove, about staying on in the new parliament and perhaps even becoming its Chair. To be honest, it had seemed an attractive proposition. This would have allowed me to retain my independence, and as I had absolutely no expectation of being recalled to the front bench whilst Cameron was in office, it was probably as good as it was likely to get. But evidently this was no longer on offer.

My mind was racing a little. It was neither ingratitude nor irritation that made me suspect that this sudden bid for my services may have owed at least as much to the leadership's need to free up slots on the prestigious ISC for senior former Ministers than any burning desire to bring me back on board. That's how things work. On the other hand, after nine years in the wilderness, this was an olive branch and it would be foolish and churlish for me to spurn it. The Conservatives had unexpectedly won the general election in May; we were going to be in office for at least five more years – surely it was better to be inside the tent than out?

Right up until the exit poll on election night, my working assumption had been that we were likely to be back in hung Parliament territory but this time probably in opposition. After my own declaration, my parliamentary office team and a few activist friends came back to our apartment and we all watched TV in rising excitement as other results came in from around the country. I felt happy for individual colleagues who had belied the dismal opinion polls and been re-elected against the odds.

But as that night's drama unfolded, I felt strangely semi-detached, almost totally unable to share any sense of ownership or the joy that everyone else was feeling as the party's national triumph became clear. In the period after the election this had left me feeling despondent and more than a little ashamed of my reaction. Harper's unexpected offer might not have been all that I had been looking for, but to refuse it would be to double down on that mean-spiritedness.

I looked Mark Harper in the eye and took him by the arm. Fellow MPs are supposed not to shake hands as we are all 'honourable members', but this tradition, like that of not applauding speeches, is fast dying out. Neither of us were to know then that there would never be another David Cameron reshuffle. That by the time the next Prime Minister honoured the promise that had been made to me, it would be Harper who found himself banished to the back benches. That he would languish there for over six years and through three premierships, trying, as I had done, to carve out his own distinct path before finally being recalled. That is the world of politics. I would always be grateful for Mark's support and his candour, regrettably not a universal virtue amongst Chief Whips in my experience. As I left the spartan surroundings that afternoon, I reflected on the curious concurrence that my most recent visit to this office almost five years earlier had been to formalise my appointment to the ISC.

• • •

Back in 2010, I had spent almost a decade in Parliament without becoming more than vaguely aware of the existence of the ISC, which some mischievously refer to as the Spooks Committee, the oversight panel for the UK's security services. In view of the sensitivity of its work, the ISC remained, almost uniquely, a select committee appointed by the Prime Minister.

One Sunday evening shortly after the 2010 election, I had joined Michael Fallon, whose London flat is in the same street as mine, for an early evening drink. He had narrowly missed out on becoming the first elected chair of the Treasury Select Committee and was musing about what to do next. He told me that as a consolation he had been informally offered one of the prized positions on the ISC, but on reflection had decided to stay involved in the financial and economic arena. As Michael spoke about the scope of work on the ISC my interest was pricked, and he gave me his blessing to put in my own late bid for a slot on this committee. This I did the following morning. Three months had then passed without a further word. My assumption by that point was that nothing was going to come of this. What I hadn't reckoned on was that behind the scenes, some security vetting was quietly taking place.

Out of the blue, the then Chief Whip Patrick McLoughlin called me in for a meeting. Well, it was not exactly without warning. I had made it clear some weeks earlier that I was likely to vote against the government on one clause of a small piece of legislation, which adversely impacted a small cluster of central London constituencies, including mine. My small rebellion would not make any material difference – the coalition's majority meant they would get their business through, but this way I would keep some vocal constituents happy. Patrick got down to business: 'Well, Mark, I am very keen to put you on the Intelligence and Security Committee, but that is going to be difficult if you vote against the government.'

'I understand that, but given that the ISC requires independent-minded scrutiny, I am sure you wouldn't want someone who caved in at the first sign of pressure? Perhaps we can come to an accommodation, and I will support the government on the programme motion [which sets out the timetabling and procedure once a bill is agreed]?'

With that, we had a deal.

Only in the early 1990s had the UK government even publicly avowed that it had security and intelligence capabilities. Having done so, the clamour for parliamentary scrutiny became impossible to resist. Whilst security issues are still only sparingly regarded as appropriate fodder for routine debate in Parliament, the ISC provides parliamentary oversight for the three agencies – the Secret Intelligence Service (MI6), the Security Service (MI5) and Government Communications Headquarters (GCHQ).

Generally, the ISC was made up of former ministers, normally with hands-on security experience in the Foreign, Home or Northern Ireland Offices. So, my appointment was unusual – the only other members without prior ministerial experience were Menzies Campbell, who had been leader of the Liberal Democrats, and my colleague Julian Lewis, who had a long-standing interest and expertise in counter espionage. Over the next few years, there was a tremendous *esprit de corps* within the nine-member committee.

We were led by the former Foreign Secretary, Sir Malcolm Rifkind. Robin Butler, one of the two peers, had been Cabinet Secretary to three premiers. The other member of the Lords, Michael Ancram, I already knew well from his time in the Commons. On the Labour side were Hazel Blears, Paul Goggins and George Howarth, who were always insightful and a delight to work with. For me, the countless informal conversations we had on tour were the equivalent of a rolling seminar in life at the heart of government. I squirrelled away and would later make plentiful use of what I had learned.

The sensitivity of the subject matter meant that we had to attend a nondescript, secure government office building a short walk from Parliament for meetings in order to access and read the copious paperwork that became meat and drink to us all. None of this material could be sent to us via email or read either at leisure or at a time of our choosing. The committee regularly travelled to meet the heads of the agencies and see in action their new capabilities and methods of work. We routinely took evidence behind closed doors from the agencies and ministers with security responsibilities. This was the era when substantial investment in cyber capabilities brought GCHQ to the forefront and placed a little more into the shade the overseas intelligence work handled by MI6.

Nonetheless, we invested much time and energy into relationships with our counterpart committees across the Five Eyes community. This was the grouping of security services in the English-speaking world, which had been brought together after 1945 to collaborate closely and who continue to share vital intelligence in peacetime. We would meet annually on a rotational basis in the US, UK, Canada, Australia or New Zealand.

The massive expansion since 9/11 of the US security and intelligence infrastructure has not been without some domestic controversy. This vast American security complex, made up of seventeen agencies based in and around Washington DC, Maryland and Virginia, reflected changes in American foreign policy. This had all happened stealthily and with very little debate. It was widely held that too much openness only served to aid the enemy. Whereas in times of war or during the four decades of Cold War against Soviet Russia the enemy was an identifiable state, international terrorism was now normally conducted by non-state actors. Their tactics were often brutal and murderous, and the US military and security felt justified in responding in kind. The enemy had no restraints on their action, went the argument, so why should we? President Obama came to office in 2008 pledging to release all those imprisoned beyond the jurisdiction of the US courts in the Guantanamo Bay detention camp in Cuba within his first term. It remains open to this day.

The ideological underpinning to all this goes back to the late 1940s with the creation of the Central Intelligence Agency (CIA), which enjoys wider powers and less legal restraint under domestic law than equivalent overseas intelligence agencies. From its earliest days, the CIA has been engaged across the world in fomenting regime change and military coups, as well as providing ongoing financial and logistical assistance to insurgent groups whose interests the CIA believes are more closely aligned to the US than the incumbent government. The leaks of vast swathes of classified documents in the early 2010s by Chelsea Manning and Edward Snowden revealed the methods and methodology used, some of which risked opening our own security services to legal challenges if they were complicit in the secret operations being carried out.

It was during a Five-Eyes oversight conference in Ottawa that we first learned of concerns from our American and Australian counterparts about the influence of the Chinese-owned technology provider Huawei. Back in the UK, we undertook extensive research and produced a detailed report titled *Foreign Involvement in the Critical National Infrastructure*, with a range of general recommendations which for a time helped inform government policy. We published investigations of the national security implications of access to communications data and of the brutal Islamist terrorist murder of Fusilier Lee Rigby on the streets of Woolwich in south-east London.

Home Office initiatives on counterterrorism and surveillance are perhaps better known and understood than some of its work on countering ideological radicalisation and indoctrination. This we also keenly monitored. In more recent years, there has been far more research undertaken about religious fundamentalism and the scourge of non-violent radicalisation. We eagerly sought guidance from academic specialists in this controversial field of study. The ideological motivation behind theocracies has some paradoxical similarities to extremist political indoctrination, namely that the avowed priority of those holding power is on religious purity and obedience rather than the needs, desires or improved living standards of the people living under their control.

As we are witnessing in the latest and renewed surge of violence in the Middle East, the leaders of terrorist cults, such as the Iranian-sponsored Hamas and Hezbollah, are unbiddable. All too often, mainstream opinion in the west assumes that the granting of greater democratic rights, improving the living conditions of residents or drawing more equitable borderlines on maps will at a stroke solve long-standing religious and racial divisions. What we learned was that the fanaticism that lies at the heart of religious fundamentalism knows of no such compromise or doctrinal doubt. I fear that peace and harmony, even on our own streets, will remain elusive until this troublesome fundamentalism is properly understood.

Developing an expertise in highly absorbing work of this sort is something that does not really leave you. The critical faculties that I developed working alongside senior former ministers and mandarins with experience and insight in the national security field have given me a lasting interest in intelligence. I still voraciously follow newspaper reports and television documentaries on global security – and always with a sceptical eye on what we are told is the 'official line'.

To take one example, the use of unmanned aerial vehicles, or drones, was still at a very early stage of development at that time, but they have since become a devastatingly effective means for the pursuit of strategic objectives. As we have seen in the war in Ukraine, they enable decisive military action from states without the need to put boots on the ground, in an era where there is diminishing appetite from western electorates to engage in overseas military adventures.

Drones have been employed beyond traditional battlefield surveillance and are now regularly used in deadly tactical raids on military, and increasingly civilian, targets. Of more concern under international law is their increasingly widespread use in the extra-judicial elimination of enemies in a non-combatant context. Whilst technological development has continued apace and drones have become an ever more essential aspect of international warfare, this has not been matched by an overhaul in the conventions, laws and regulations governing their use.

As drones become ever cheaper to produce, their widespread use by non-military personnel and untrained operatives amounts to a kind of democratising of the field of battle. We in the west rejoice at their decisive deployment to eliminate terrorists from afar. But as always, we need to be careful what we wish for. Before long, as their cost and operational capability comes within the grasp of terrorists and criminal gangs with extortion in mind, we may come to regret their widespread availability – not to mention the impact of the full capabilities of AI coming on stream. The potential misuse of AI to infiltrate news and media organisations is already well understood, but its related pernicious abuse of cyber and other defence platforms is not far behind.

• • •

Graduating from the word of espionage oversight to a senior international role in the Conservative Party may not have seemed the most natural move, but the two roles turned out to have more in common than might immediately meet the eye. To my initial surprise, I enjoyed my new job immensely.

Reporting for duty, I found party headquarters an unexpected hive of activity. They were located on two floors of a stylish Victorian building, reassuringly only five minutes' walk from the gates of Parliament. The modern, open-plan layout resembled a City dealing floor and was a far cry from the rabbit warren of small rooms in which the fabled Conservative Central Office of the 1970s and 1980s had operated.

Staffers, mainly twenty-somethings, were bustling around and it was clear that my first – and most important – task was to commandeer a small bank of desks and computers to house my team. That done, I popped in to meet Andrew Feldman, who, as party chairman, had the only designated office in the entire building. He was now my direct reporting line – or 'boss', as we used to describe it in the last century. Feldman had been a close Oxford friend of David Cameron, who had elevated him to the House of Lords. As a consequence, he was able to straddle the political and fundraising aspects of the party chairmanship, which had often in the past – and would again in future – result in an unsatisfactory co-chairmanship arrangement.

With his trademark charm and brisk efficiency, Andrew assured me that he would support me to the hilt in making what I wanted of the role. He proved true to his word and we worked harmoniously together. Many months later, he revealed that I had been rather foisted upon him with a warning from No. 10 that I might prove difficult to manage. 'I have to say that you have been a dream to work with. A real team player, professional, hard-working and reliable. I really cannot see what all the fuss has been about you.'

The admiration was mutual and Feldman's reputation at Conservative Campaign Headquarters (CCHQ) burnishes to this day. In no small part this was down to his awesome brilliance at fundraising. Typically, national political parties ramp up campaigning activity and employee headcounts in the run-up to general elections, only to scale back drastically once the election has been won or lost. For many party staffers, one minute they are working all hours until polls close, co-ordinating campaigns in key marginal seats, uploading data, arranging online advertising and managing the national or local media. Then virtually the day after the election, they find themselves being made redundant.

By contrast, on the morning of the May 2015 election Feldman had reputedly been able to report that the party was in surplus to the tune of £7 million once all outstanding bills had been settled. This was an almost unheard of achievement, reflecting both Feldman's financial wizardry but also the expectation that we might be heading for a hung Parliament and the distinct possibility of a second election in quick succession. Liberated from the potential of that financially ruinous outcome, CCHQ was suddenly awash with cash. The decision was taken not to drastically downsize the operation but instead build up some institutional memory.

This was the upbeat environment that greeted my arrival as chairman of the international office, which works in partnership with centre-right parties across the world offering training, capacity building expertise and active support at election time. I was further bolstered by the simultaneous appointment of Colin Bloom as my director, the full-time CCHQ professional running the department. The ever-changing nature of political life means you might work closely and intensely alongside someone for a period, then have little to do with them for many years before once again your paths cross.

Although it would only be for the next two years that Colin and I were a formal team, he has remained a friend ever since, both in Parliament and beyond. He made it his business to find me some consulting work to help tide me over immediately after I left politics; meanwhile, he led and authored a well-received independent review into how government should engage with faith groups. His connections in the world of centre-right US politics are legendary, and he was already predicting the emergence and ultimate triumph of Donald Trump in early 2016, when so-called expert media opinion was dismissing the populist phenomenon as a flash in the pan.

One of our early priorities was bolstering our team. Colin and I set about recruiting two highly impressive women who have both since developed careers working in senior diplomatic relations and international justice roles. Carlotta Redi was a bubbly, diminutive legal academic who, somewhat ahead of the times, we recruited by an interview over Teams. She joined us from Edinburgh University via Italy. Our Mediterranean credentials were enhanced further with the arrival of Marta Corti, a fluent Spanish speaker whose organisational skills kept us and our international partners in order.

After the fall of communism, the Major government had set up the Westminster Foundation for Democracy and provided annual Foreign Office grant funding for initiatives between UK political parties and their ideological counterparts. An even more important element of our funding came from the Alliance of Conservatives and Reformists in Europe (ACRE), the breakaway centre-right grouping in Brussels dominated in numerical terms by MEPs from the UK and Poland.

I attended the annual conferences of our sister parties in Germany, the CDU and Bavarian CSU, where my faltering few sentences in rusty A level German were always politely received by my hosts. Needless to report, they bore little comparison to the excellent spoken English of everyone under the age of forty attending these conventions. My Swedish was non-existent and, whether in Malmö, Stockholm or Karlstad with the delightful and fun-loving Moderate Party, I was put to shame by the flawless English spoken by all the locals of whatever age.

In Africa, we worked alongside the International Republican Institute, whose charismatic and impressive European resident director was Jan Surotchak. Despite his exotic sounding name, Jan was a third-generation American who hailed from Pennsylvania. He linked us up and looked after our security needs in Kenya and Nigeria, where tight elections were likely to be disputed in the courts and on the streets. Meanwhile in Ghana, the pro-business party of President Nana had won office at the third time of asking. We attended a colourful inauguration in Accra and the following day a church celebration in his home village, an hour's drive in armoured convoy away, which had been decked in bunting as far as the eye could see.

We explored new partnerships in Israel, Iceland and Lebanon and sponsored a Caribbean conference in Jamaica with the three regional centre-right premiers then in office. Our host in Montego Bay was Andrew Holness of the Jamaica Labour Party, which confusingly is the pro-business, conservative grouping in that island's two-party system. Our sister party in St Lucia, also then in government under Allen Chastanet, went under the even more unlikely name of the United Workers Party.

One of the added advantages of my taking on the international role was that it enabled me to retain the services of my chief of staff, Julia Dockerill. Now better known as a political figure in her own right under her married name, Julia Lopez, she had joined me essentially straight out of Cambridge in early 2006 after a gap half-year travelling. She had assiduously avoided student politics but was always confident of her Conservative beliefs, and at the time she joined my office we both saw this as a starter job for perhaps two or three years.

I don't think a political career of her own featured anywhere in her thinking for some time. However, her role in my office soon evolved to managing other team members, including the excellent Joanna Thomas, who went on to become a special adviser in the Sunak government. Julia then started speech and article writing, where she quickly acquired that most valuable of attributes – to me, at least – of 'knowing my voice'. This typically meant I was able to sketch out a few ideas on paper or chat briefly with her and be confident that she would produce an opinion piece or speech that usually would require little more than the odd tweak before being fit for purpose.

Julia soon became invaluable to me, and I realised my challenge was to find ways of advancing her role sufficiently that she would develop new skills without feeling the need to move on to pastures new. Her love of travel fitted beautifully with my new responsibilities, and she joined me on many of the overseas conferences. By then she had also become a local councillor in Tower Hamlets and began for the first time to contemplate going into Parliament herself. As luck would have it, the configuration of desks at CCHQ placed the candidates' department adjacent to my international office team, so she was soon able to ease her path onto the approved list.

With breakneck speed, inside five weeks after the snap 2017 election was called, she was selected and then elected to Parliament for

Hornchurch & Upminster on the east London and Essex border. Julia's initial majority was almost twice as large as I had ever managed. In her first parliament, which turned out to be my last, we saw less of each other as I was in the Foreign Office. Less happily, our paths also diverged on Brexit when Julia decided in the end, after much soul-searching, to vote Leave. Then, as an MP in a virulently Leave-supporting seat, she ended up as one of the irreconcilable Spartans voting down three times the deal that Theresa May put to Parliament. Under Boris Johnson she became a minister and had the unusual distinction of remaining in the same role as a Minister of State in the Department for Digital, Culture, Media and Sport under all three of the 2022 Prime Ministers.

• • •

I was thoroughly enjoying my early weeks and months as chairman of the international office when, as is so often the case in politics, out of a cloudless sky came a biblical rainstorm. Unfortunately for a few days that autumn, this came pouring down on me.

One of the few journalists I would count as a personal friend is Isabel Oakeshott. We have known each other since I was the shadow London Minister, which is when she started in the lobby with the *Evening Standard*. Our children are of almost identical ages, and over the years our families have socialised together on a fairly regular basis. Isabel soon became one of the youngest political editors at the *Sunday Times*, but more recently she has found herself at the centre of several major political controversies.

One of those controversies arose on the publication of *Call Me Dave*, the unauthorised biography of David Cameron that she co-wrote with the Tory peer Michael Ashcroft. Ashcroft had been a crucial financial supporter to the Conservatives when the party's fortunes were at their lowest ebb during the early Blair years. When, in the run-up to the 2010 election, Labour sought to make political capital out of Ashcroft's complicated tax affairs, Cameron swiftly froze him out – this book was widely regarded as Ashcroft's revenge for that ruthless treatment.

Amongst several outlandish claims in the book was that whilst at Oxford, Cameron had joined a notorious all-male dining club whose initiation ceremony involved placing one's penis into a dead pig's head that had been laid out on a platter. This implausible but not entirely unbelievable story had apparently been given to Isabel by an Oxford contemporary who was now a serving Conservative MP. Predictably, this saga became known as Piggate. It even has a detailed Wikipedia entry of its own.

An enterprising young tabloid journalist on *The Sun* produced a photofit line-up of six Tory MPs who had been Cameron's university contemporaries on a whodunnit theme. Given that the other five were signed up members of the Cameron appreciation society, the finger of guilt quickly pointed to the sixth on the list. That, needless to say, was me. The gaping hole in this convenient little theory was that the half-dozen prime suspects were by no means an exhaustive list of those Tory MPs who had been at Oxford at the same time as the Prime Minister.

Suddenly, the story went viral and all hell broke loose. Unfortunately, Cameron was abroad in a Muslim-majority country in Asia at the time, so the dubious tale of a decades-old student prank involving the penetration of an unclean animal dominated his press conferences. The book extracts were regarded by a usually cynical press corps as gospel truth and for day after day made the news headlines. It was on one Saturday morning, as this compelling absurdity of a story was just beginning to make waves, that the self-assured Downing Street director of communications, Craig Oliver, made contact with me. I was ambling across Hampstead Heath with my family and vividly recall trying my best to concentrate on the fifteen-minute mobile phone conversation as my darling children were splashing in puddles and trying to push each other into the waterlogged and overflowing ponds.

Everyone knew about my friendship with Isabel. To be fair, I had never considered myself a stalwart of discretion around journalists, but I baulked slightly at the clear insinuation that I would so readily spill the beans on my party leader. However, a quarter of an hour on, I was confident that I had assured and convinced Craig of the facts of the matter. Namely, that I was not the source of the story, that I had never attended the dining-club in question and nor for that matter had I even previously been aware of these bizarre details, let alone passed on to a journalist such a juicy snippet of historical gossip.

Any wishful thinking on my part that this explanation had resolved this matter was quickly dispelled. The astute and perceptive Tim Shipman, who had moved into the political hot seat at the *Sunday Times* in Isabel's stead, subsequently told me that I was still Downing Street's prime suspect. A charitable interpretation was that the press team wanted to kill the story rather than allowing speculation about its source to continue into further news cycles. There were other ways of looking at it, of course.

Mercifully, journalists eventually found other earth-shattering events worthy of coverage. My own bit of amateur sleuthing came up with a more plausible suspect for the leaked story, which was quietly confirmed to me. I would have done nothing further with this piece of private intelligence had events not played out in an unexpected way a little over a year later, when the Tory colleague in question started making some very disobliging observations about the Conservative Party in general and the Cameron administration in particular. I felt it might be helpful for the Chief Whip to be made aware of my knowledge to assist in rebutting any further attacks. When I revealed the truth to Gavin Williamson, by then the sixth Chief Whip in as many years, he was beside himself with amusement that this little mystery had apparently been resolved. 'Is it OK if I tell David Cameron?' he asked. Although by this stage Cameron was no longer either Prime Minister or an MP, it still seemed a timely and entertaining way after all these years to finally draw a line under our differences.

● ● ●

In the immediate aftermath of my appointment to the international chairman role, the imminence of the UK's promised referendum on EU membership meant I was suddenly in great demand, with representatives of the London-based diplomatic corps keen to keep tabs on political sentiment. After the Brexit vote, these lunch invitations ramped up further as ambassadors became almost desperate to find out what was going on in Westminster and to report back with some authority about the UK government's thinking and tactics.

This may not have been exactly what I had in mind as I spent my twenties and beyond fantasising about life as an MP, but there must be worse lines of duty than sharing fine food and wine in highly agreeable diplomatic company whilst talking with as much confidence and authority as I could muster as we all tried to make sense of what was happening.

For the first time in several years, I was required to attend the party conference. My new position meant I was run off my feet with endless bilateral meetings, sometimes but not always as a diary filler for centre-right ministers from overseas governments who were in attendance. I was also responsible for writing and presenting a daily early morning political briefing. This was delivered to our largest-ever number of sister party representatives, who had flocked to Manchester for the conference now that we were back in office without the Liberal Democrat deadweight. For the first time, I even found myself on the invitation list for most of the smartest late-night parties.

There was even a sun-kissed Indian summer that October, in Manchester of all places – it was almost too good to be true. David Cameron's conference speech was full of the vision, confidence and spark you might expect from the all-conquering hero. Little did the Conservative family know, as it returned to London with a real spring in its step, that this would be his last. For him – and his brand of modernising Conservatism – it would never be 'glad confident morning' again.

We were now on the final leg of the road to the EU referendum and what became Brexit. Cameron's reputation and legacy will be forever tarnished in the eyes of many by his alleged recklessness in calling the plebiscite in the first place and his failure to deal with its aftermath by resigning the moment it was lost. On both counts, I believe this is unfair. All our main political parties had at various times in the previous decade pledged to let the people have their say over Europe, as the EU's direction of travel became more centralising. In view of the fact that Cameron had led from the front with a renegotiation package that he then put to the people, it was never plausible for him to have stayed in post once that vote had been lost. This rejection and reversal were surely more powerful even than a parliamentary vote of no confidence.

In 2011, I had been one of the eighty-one Conservative MPs who defied a three-line whip to support a referendum. The overwhelming majority of that group was strongly Eurosceptic, but I was by no means the only one of the 'rebels' in the Remain category. I felt strongly that, after the controversies over Maastricht, the repeated assurances made during the negotiations for the unratified EU Constitution and Treaty of Lisbon meant the time for the British public to have its say was long overdue. Realistically, as the decades-long unease festered about the nature of the UK's involvement in the EU, it was always a matter of when rather than if this matter would at some point be put to a vote.

What I had hoped for then was a simple and quick-fire in/out referendum rather than the protracted renegotiation that Cameron suddenly proposed in January 2013. What I totally misjudged – and in fairness, this reflected the cosmopolitan inner-London seat I represented – was the strength of national feeling on the immigration issue, one of the four baskets open for renegotiation. Certainly, the protections for nations outside the eurozone that Cameron negotiated on behalf of the City and the financial services industry represented, in my view, a notable and positive improvement.

Life was not made easier in these formal discussions by Cameron's unilateral move, before he even reached Downing Street, to remove the British Conservatives in the European Parliament from the main, centre-right grouping, the European People's Party (EPP), and set up a rival alternative. History will record that this fateful, tactical decision was taken by Cameron and his campaign manager George Osborne in the midst of the 2005 Conservative leadership election in order to curry favour with a sizeable group of right-wingers, who were unconvinced by the other candidates on offer. This gave a much-needed boost to a campaign which, for some months that summer, appeared to have run out of steam.

As a regular attender of Anglo-German conferences hosted by the centre-right Konrad Adenauer Stiftung, I spent countless hours over the years trying to explain to bewildered and incredulous German politicians and academics why we had left the EPP and why our continental centre-right friends should not take it to heart. But the more I have reflected on that tactical decision, the more damaging I believe it was. Many of our closest EU friends and allies were angered and dismayed. Perhaps more importantly, at the very moment that Cameron and his team needed to build trusted alliances with partners in Europe and ensure they fully understood the nuances of UK politics, we had deliberately placed ourselves beyond their close embrace.

But in the final analysis, for many the EU referendum was a battle between the heart and the head. It was a battle we on the Remain side were losing hands down. A week or so before the vote, I had an opinion piece published in the London financial newspaper *City A.M.* where I tried to belatedly set out what I saw as the emotional case for continued membership.

Without even mentioning the pride I felt on a personal level at the European blood that flowed through my veins, my heartfelt words poured out. Seven decades of European peace and reconciliation after centuries of warfare. Our crucial and enduring role alongside the US in the institutional, cultural, moral and physical rebuilding of the continent after the Second World War. In a dangerous and uncertain world, maintaining our values pointed to ever closer interconnectedness and interdependence. How it would be a miswriting of history to suggest that in 1940, when we stood alone, our isolation was either desired or desirable. Over four or five centuries it had never been the British way to walk away from international difficulties. Our nation's proud freedom, security and prosperity would always hinge upon displaying a proper respect for the fortunes of our neighbours and allies.

Even as these thoughts spewed forth, there was a deep sinking feeling in my stomach. The truth was that the national Remain campaign was not even trying to make the emotional argument for our continued presence in the bloc. Perhaps four decades and more of UK politicians almost instinctively blaming Brussels bureaucrats whenever faced with unwanted rules and regulations was finally coming home to roost.

My objections to the prospect of Brexit were also achingly practical. I doubted from the very outset whether Whitehall, let alone the Westminster political class, had the capacity to extricate itself from almost half a century of complex agreements and close co-operation. Then came the issue of Northern Ireland. As we were soon to discover, the backstop was a negotiating device designed to square the circle by guaranteeing open borders between the Republic and Northern Ireland. Within a short time, however, it became crystal clear that once the backstop had been granted, there would be absolutely no incentive for the EU, and particularly the Irish government, to finalise the trading or political terms of Brexit. This lay at the heart of the doctrinal battles over Brexit that overshadowed the rest of my time in politics.

At a hastily assembled meeting of Tory parliamentary Remainers, Craig Oliver, the man who apparently knew all there was to know about Piggate, brushed aside repeated concerns that our campaign was overly focused on the economic case. The team that in the previous two years had delivered victory in the Scottish independence referendum and the general election knew what it was doing, we were assured. All the Remain campaign's private polling suggested that robust, exaggerated and increasingly hysterical claims that a Leave vote would bring about economic collapse were cutting through. For some, of course, even the rational economic arguments fell on deaf ears. Many of that ultimately crucial 6 per cent of electors, who had not even been bothered to go out and vote at the previous year's general election but now did so at the referendum, felt they had nothing to lose by voting Leave.

As referendum day approached, there was also the nagging concern that Cameron was overly focused on the task of holding the Conservative Party together. He had allowed six ministers to continue sitting around the Cabinet table at the same time, in varying degrees, as they were travelling around the country expressly repudiating his entire renegotiation strategy and package. Understandably perhaps, his eyes were on his plans for the years ahead – why make this much more difficult with an overly rancorous campaign? Surely little was to be gained in winning by a very healthy margin but causing lasting enmity within the party ranks?

• • •

It is now Thursday 16 June 2016. One week to go. The piercing alarm on my mobile phone is ringing, vibrating and irritating at 5.50 a.m. Strewth, why have I agreed to do this? I quickly shower, throw on some clothes and head off to the City of London. First thing, out on London Bridge as the early trains arrive and commuters stream across the river, I am out delivering leaflets and exchanging snippets of conversation in the company of Simon Allison, an old frenemy from Oxford and Kensington politics. He is now a Westminster constituent and as a passionate pro-European, he has been doing this most mornings over recent weeks. We spend two hours briefly interrupting the relentless flow of humanity; the reception we get is broadly positive but essentially apathetic. In the aftermath of what is about to befall the nation and in a valiant attempt at therapy, Simon writes and self-publishes a book entitled *Brexit – A Betrayal of Conservatism?* Having read his outstanding analysis, I could never quite work out why he included the question mark.

Off to the City for lunch with two long-standing friends from the Conservative political family. Marcus Booth is a one-time Tory candidate and sometime Tory treasurer, who still sort-of hankers for a political career but in the meantime, as a partner with international law firm White & Case, is carving out a hugely successful legal career that will shortly take him to Dubai. Andrew McHallam was one of that hardy and exclusive crew of Conservative activists in Islington politics. Our paths first crossed nearly three decades ago, and since then we have met up intermittently but remained in contact consistently. A late entrant to the Foreign Office (FCO), his fate and mine will before long once again become more closely intertwined. He has responsibility at the FCO for the Chevening Scholarship scheme and by this time next year, I will be his supervising minister.

My lunch partners are both staunch Remainers and amidst the chatter about politics, I detect a complacent confidence that all will be well. This is until Andrew, reflecting on some of the unexpected Leavers at his workplace, signs off this part of the conversation with, 'Don't rule out a big surprise here.'

As we are about to leave the restaurant, all three of us start to pick up unconfirmed media and internet reports from West Yorkshire that the Labour MP for Batley & Spen, Jo Cox, has been stabbed and shot whilst carrying out constituency duties. It is a Thursday, so most MPs have already left London, but by the time I arrive back at Parliament there is a ghastly, subdued atmosphere. I watch in disbelief as a Labour MP close to tears whispers hoarsely into her mobile phone: 'I am so, so sorry.' Within the hour, the worst is officially confirmed. Arriving home, the first words from my eight-year-old son as he hugs me close and gives me an anxious look are, 'Are you going to be all right, Daddy?'

When we talk about the ebb and flow of political campaigns, it is best not to be too pious. I am sure I was not the only person whose mind soon turned to the political implications of Jo Cox's brutal murder even as its dreadful details were still becoming clear. The fact that her assailant was a mentally ill man with far-right affiliations was widely assumed to work to the advantage of the Remain campaign. Formal campaigning stopped for a time and was certainly very low key from then on. I shall never forget standing at the back of a packed Chamber of the House of Commons on the following Monday watching the future Chancellor of the Exchequer, Rachel Reeves, with tears rolling down her face, voice breaking as she spoke for all of us as parents of young children: 'Batley & Spen will go on to elect a new MP – but no one can replace a mother.'

Finally, under this cloud of tragedy, referendum day arrived. I took a morning call from the then Austrian Ambassador to London, Martin Keizinger, who had become a trusted contact. He wondered if he and a political VIP from Vienna who was going to be in London over the next couple of days could get access to a count in action after the polls closed at 10 p.m. I was able to sort this out and at the appointed hour met up once again with the youthful and charismatic Austrian Foreign Minister Sebastian Kurz, who even then was demonstrating the flair that would take him to his country's chancellorship at the improbably young age of thirty-one.

It was quite a novelty for me to be there at the beginning of an election count. What immediately struck me was the fact that a sizeable number of Labour and Liberal Democrat activists had pitched up to invigilate the count and all were sporting a wide variety of Remain stickers. By contrast, there was a more depleted group of Conservative councillors and activists, with Leavers outnumbering Remainers two to one. Perhaps I should have felt more awkward, but I was happy to chat away amicably with all and sundry across party lines. It has only been with the benefit of hindsight that I realised that this was probably the moment when the die was cast on the twilight of my political career.

There were masses of postal votes that had come in from both the City and Westminster, and as the count got underway the politicos present were quickly able to calculate from this a representative and reliable sample. Remain was heading for 75 per cent in the City and 72 per cent in Westminster, in both cases three percentage points above what I considered a par outcome. All of this was guesswork, of course. At general elections, even when there have been boundary changes, it is a fairly straightforward process to extrapolate numbers on the basis of previous results. Here, we were all very much in the dark.

Nonetheless, within forty-five minutes I felt confident enough to be able to advise Sebastian Kurz that it was going to be fairly close, but Remain was on course to win. He and the ambassador disappeared into the night with a confident spring in their step. Which must have lasted all of three or four hours. It was a little over two years later, at a Council of Europe meeting in Brussels, that Kurz and I next met. He laughed out loud as we shook hands and he introduced me to a colleague: 'This is State Minister Mark Field, my always optimistic English friend.'

• • •

Events moved quickly the morning after the referendum. As I had always anticipated (in what I had assumed to be the highly unlikely event of a Leave victory), David Cameron promptly resigned. The most memorable image of that crazy morning, however, was seeing Boris Johnson and Michael Gove standing like a pair of dazzled rabbits in the headlights behind a rostrum at Vote Leave HQ. Neither of these normally loquacious and accomplished speakers seemed willing or able to rise to the challenge of even a few inspirational or reassuring words. With good reason, perhaps – the outcome was unexpected and the Leavers had no semblance of an agreed plan of action.

As the Leavers even now craft their own narrative of Brexit betrayal (which makes you wonder who has been in government over all these years), it should never be forgotten that the type of Brexit that most Conservative MPs supported was not the version that was ever sold to the British public during the referendum campaign. This was crystal clear even at the time. The free-wheeling, Singapore-on-Thames, deregulatory economic version of Brexit much beloved by Thatcherite Conservatives would never have won the approval of many of the Red Wall voters who ended up backing Leave. In any case, with some 7 million functionally illiterate adults and over 5 million on out-of-work benefits, it was always a pipedream to believe that the UK's economy was sufficiently geared up to go down this route.

That is why the campaign focus was on 'taking back control' of immigration and higher public expenditure, in the form of up to £350 million weekly additional spending on the NHS. Presumably, most Leave voters understood taking back control to mean lower overall numbers. A tad misleading perhaps, but the only out-and-out dishonesty that Remainers can legitimately point to was over the issue of Turkish accession. This has never been remotely possible. It is nothing to do with our own absolute right of veto; the simple reason is that before it came to that, Greece, Cyprus, Germany and France, not to mention Poland and Hungary, would never have had any truck with allowing the free movement of 85 million Turkish citizens into their countries.

Amidst the pressures and given the personalities involved, it should not really have come as a total surprise that Johnson and Gove would destroy each other's chances of succeeding Cameron. For the handful of days that he was in the running, I backed Boris Johnson. My view then was that I thought it almost essential that the Leave campaign now take ownership of their project. More cynically, I felt that Boris Johnson was also the person most likely to promote a soft Brexit – with a 52 per cent to 48 per cent outcome, I was still hoping it might be possible to negotiate a deal that involved the UK remaining in or closely aligned with the single market and customs union. Having built a reputation for leaning towards one wing would have given Boris licence at that time to reach out towards the other. His credentials as the man whose intervention secured the referendum result probably made him the only contender who could open up lines to remaining in the EU's economic institutions without being accused of betraying Brexit. Easier said than done – for as we soon discovered, this would not have allowed us to escape entirely from free movement or EU judicial reach and jurisdiction.

Nevertheless, it was also obvious to me that Johnson never really believed in Brexit. I was never under any illusions that he regarded supporting Leave as the best way to promote his own leadership ambitions, though I suspect his preferred game-plan in early 2016 was to succeed Cameron, before the decade was out, in his new role as the darling of the thwarted Leavers amongst the Conservative Party membership. What I had not reckoned on was just how comprehensively the EU machine would protect its own interests and totally outmanoeuvre the UK in the Brexit talks. That would have happened whoever was in Downing Street in the aftermath of the vote and is not a reflection on the professionalism or personal preferences of the UK civil service.

To be honest, I also had severe doubts about the suitability of Theresa May, who quickly became the runaway favourite. She benefited from the fact that she had a small and dedicated following and stood distinct from the outgoing leadership team. Once Gove had pressed the detonator under long-time rival Boris Johnson's campaign, the party didn't really have any other serious options.

Nevertheless, I was dismayed that May and her backers seemed to think that having the reputation of being a 'bloody difficult woman' was a positive point in her favour, as we prepared for the testing and gruelling Brexit negotiations. She also prided herself on being an unclubbable loner and having a distrustful and secretive approach to personal relations, even with ministerial colleagues. From the very outset it struck me that these personality traits were the precise opposite of what the nation now required. Whether in Europe or Westminster, if the UK was going to get an optimal Brexit deal over the line we now needed collegiality and flexible, nimble negotiation skills of the highest order.

In time, as one of her ministers, I came to admire May's tenacity, diligence and resilience, but her dealings with parliamentary col-leagues were always marked by a self-righteous tone that over time incensed many of her MPs as they refused to yield to her demands. It is a little unfair to pronounce judgement on the basis only of a two-day Europe-Asia ministerial conference in Brussels where I accompanied her, but this was the only time I saw her up close. She was clearly exhausted by the time we had worked through a full-to-bursting schedule of bilateral meetings and social engagements.

Two things stick in my mind. First, her voracious appetite for work and ability to handle facts and figures; she rightly prided herself on diligently reading and understanding all the voluminous briefings you routinely get at assemblies of this sort. Second, despite having been in post for well over two years by this stage, she appeared to have virtually no personal rapport with her head of government counter-parts. Loosening up a little might have made for an easier, more bearable life and may even have resulted in unexpected negotiating bonuses, but serious-minded detachment had been Theresa May's trademark style over all these years, so why change now?

The more pressing problem that faced Theresa May on reaching the premiership was the converse of the opportunity that Johnson might have been able to exploit. She had always fancied herself as the original party moderniser, rebuking the membership as 'the nasty party' when Cameron was still in short trousers in parliamen-tary terms. She had also backed Remain and so was always some-what on the back foot in her relations with the Brexit-voting right of the party. This meant that she felt the need to criticise publicly the jet-setting global elite as 'citizen[s] of nowhere', clamp down hard on the rights of UK-resident EU citizens and rush to invoke Article 50, which started the clock on Brexit, before properly formulating an exit plan.

As a Remainer, she presumably felt compelled to promote a harder Brexit than many might have thought a 52 per cent to 48 per cent outcome deemed necessary and stood back silently as the tabloid press lambasted the judiciary for purportedly blocking the will of the Brexit supporters. Until the adverse outcome of the 2017 election, she also turned something of a blind eye to the antics of her two joint chiefs of staff, who stretched to breaking point the established civic code between political advisers and either ministers or the civil service. If Boris Johnson was later the master of overturning established institutions and conventions, it is at least arguable that despite the sanctimonious disapproval that she continues to have for her successor, it was Theresa May who taught him almost everything he knew.

The other misfortune May faced was that our historic decision to leave the EU meant we were gearing up to make a substantial global trade pitch at the very moment that protectionism was fast coming back into vogue. That year's US presidential campaign had been dominated by pledges from both sides that US domestic industries should be shielded from foreign competition. This sentiment did not arise from as clear a sky as some might believe. It was President Obama in 2010 who roundly poured scorn on 'British Petroleum' after the Louisiana oil spill, despite the fact that this global company had not used that name for well over a decade. When Donald Trump triumphed in November, it was clear that, despite all his promises that the UK would be at the front of the queue for a free-trade deal, the prevailing winds were for economic nationalism.

There are always new threats and opportunities on the horizon. Such is the nature of life. But over the past three or four decades, the UK has bet the bank (quite literally) on continued globalisation. From this perspective, we have felt reassured that others have skin in the game in our continued economic success. So the UK has willingly allowed our assets, whether in real estate or the shareholdings in many of our leading companies, to fall into foreign hands. Family office and overseas pension funds proliferate in the ownership of central London prime office and hotel developments, as evidenced by the constant presence of cranes across the City and Westminster skylines throughout my tenure. These international allies could well turn into global competitors as geopolitical skies begin to darken. Remember that less than a decade ago, the Cameron government was still hailing a golden era with China and from Tony Blair's time onwards, we welcomed with open arms the flow of money from dubious Russian oligarchs. It would be unwise to assume that pure commercial interest, rather than raw national rivalry, will forever determine the continuation of the current array of cross-border co-operation and collaboration.

• • •

Closer to home, in the City of London bankers and policymakers were still working towards trying to secure as near to a 'business as usual' deal as was compatible with leaving the EU. There was talk of 'enhanced equivalence' and I attended and spoke at some of the almost endless seminars and conferences as City professionals all desperately tried to make sense of what was happening. When I look back now at the content of my speeches and published articles during that frenetic year after the referendum vote, it is striking how many of the themes raised remain essentially unresolved to this day.

It is often observed that some of the more outlandish predictions made before the referendum about City and professional services job losses have not come to pass. This cannot be denied. What is much more difficult to quantify is the lost opportunities that have arisen as a result of years of regulatory uncertainty in what remains Europe's biggest financial services hub. Which of the many new openings in novel financial subsectors that migrated to Dublin and Amsterdam, let alone Frankfurt and Paris, would or should have come to London or Edinburgh?

The UK-EU Memorandum of Understanding on Financial Services Co-Operation, signed after we formally left the EU, has left the EU's autonomy unfettered. Worse still, the EU has made it clear that it will continue in future to set standards and devise protocols in financial services; in this way, as a consequence of the EU's economic scale as a market seven times the size of the UK, the City of London is being further marginalised.

To the relief of the UK financial services industry, no single mainland European jurisdiction has emerged as a serious all-round competitor, but post-Brexit, London's place in global league rankings has dipped and continues slowly to sink. The real competition now comes from New York, Singapore and, increasingly, the United Arab Emirates.

My international party role came with official designation as vice-chairman of the Conservative Party. This put me in something of a halfway house between being a frontbencher subject to collective responsibility and continuing to enjoy the independence to speak and write with the freedom of a backbencher. Naturally, there was a firm expectation that I would always vote with the government, which was scarcely a huge imposition.

Most of my other interventions were in the financial and economic sphere where, as the City's MP, I had little difficulty in aligning closely with new Chancellor Philip Hammond, whom I had known socially for over twenty years before either of us had entered

Parliament. His often-mischievous asides belied his 'Spreadsheet Phil' nickname. Philip was a highly competent technocrat with deep commercial understanding born out of hands-on entrepreneurial experience. As the civil service desperately grappled with trying to make the impending Brexit a success, Philip identified the UK's dismal productivity performance as a major potential stumbling block.

But the more closely I looked at it, the rectification of our supply-side failings, which were firmly in the Chancellor's sights, would also require a quiet disavowal of much of the economic record of the coalition. Inadequate public infrastructure was a key problem that had been caused by low levels of investment over many years. The deep reductions in capital budgets to achieve austerity targets at the outset of the coalition had only compounded the issue.

The desperate misalignment between the needs of the UK economy and skill base of its indigenous population, which even before Brexit was constraining the rate of economic growth, was only going to deteriorate further in the event of a form of Brexit that took us well beyond the EU's orbit. This menu all added up to some hard economic truths for life post-Brexit, but it is sobering to realise how little this debate has really moved on since then.

• • •

One of the things that puts many sensible, politically engaged folk off politics is the prospect of always having to 'vote the party line'. What may surprise many who react with horror at this thought is just how often parliamentary divisions are uncontentious. Lots of legislative changes go through on the nod, and it is not difficult even for those of a moderately rebellious temperament to reconcile themselves to supporting the party line for or against amendments to legislation.

I reckon I can count on the fingers of two hands the number of times over a parliamentary career of almost nineteen years when I felt the need to speak up in Parliament in opposition to the official party position. Normally, this involved a clearly flagged constituency interest on a less than earth-shattering matter such as changes to the regulation of Airbnb. On the basis that you keep the whips appraised of what you are going to do, so as to avoid springing any surprises, all normally works out well. The usual drill is to make your concerns clear in the debate and then make yourself scarce if a formal division is called.

The number of issues that are broadly regarded as matters of conscience has gradually crept up over the years. Allowing free, rather than whipped, votes in debates keeps damaging stories about party splits out of the headlines, to the evident relief of party managers. But there is a flip side to this – the need for legislators to have a mind of their own. Contrary to what I suspect is a commonly held assumption, I was only ever asked my view on the death penalty once, when standing in front of a Conservative Party selection committee. Like most lawyers who understand all too well the vagaries of the criminal justice system, I am resolutely opposed. As I tried to impress upon colleagues who wished to restore the death penalty, doing so would only make juries more reluctant to convict on a murder charge, so perversely more of the guilty would end up going free. Despite my implacable opposition to capital and corporal punishment, I always felt slightly uneasy at preaching the UK's official progressive views when travelling overseas and meeting fellow ministers in sovereign nations where these criminal sanctions were still permitted and being carried out.

Mercifully, abortion has not turned here into the touchstone divisive political issue it has become in the US. I must confess that my occasional visits to the neonatal unit of my local hospital, St Mary's in Paddington, always left me feeling a little queasy as I watched from a distance these tiny scraps of prematurely born humanity fighting for life. Often, I reflected that elsewhere within that medical complex a legal termination of a similarly aged foetus might well be taking place. But it is the entrenched absolutism of arguments on both sides of this debate that is something I have never been able to relate to.

My views on gay rights evolved in my twenties. At university I disapproved of the politicisation of the HIV/Aids issue, which in my opinion should always have been regarded primarily as an issue of public health rather than minority rights. By the time of my final selection meeting at the Cities of London & Westminster, the broader issue of the publicly funded promotion of gay rights was making waves nationally within the party. When asked my views, I made a broader case that the Conservatives had always come late to the party in their support for progressive ideals, whether on votes for women, homosexual reform or the death penalty, but insisted, 'History tells us that we Conservatives have nothing to fear from social change.' The number of times that has been quoted back to me approvingly over the years from those who were present left me with two conclusions. First, that this short and spontaneous sentence probably won me the nomination; second, that for this to be quite so memorable, I must have been a remarkably uninspiring speaker during my subsequent two decades in public life!

Within a few months of my first election, I was one of only four Tory MPs to support civil partnerships in a parliamentary division. I wholeheartedly agreed with David Cameron's formulation in supporting gay marriage a decade or so later. I did so because of, rather than despite, my conservatism. One of the few voting regrets I have had as an MP was when the issue of gay adoption was put to a vote, which turned into a matter of confidence in the then party leadership. At the time, I was a whip and felt that duty overrode my conscience.

Support for euthanasia, or assisted dying, is growing amongst both legislators and the general public. During my time in Parliament, I had always assumed that I was likely to be absent by reason of death many years before fundamental reform in this sphere – but now I am not so sure. The flurry of activity over assisted dying in the early months of the Starmer government suggests it is now probably only a matter of time before it is legalised. I am full of foreboding about this, whilst also being fearful that my own death or that of a loved one will be lingering or painful. Yet nothing has convinced me that any of the legal safeguards that have been proposed would not leave some of the most vulnerable in society at great risk. Sensible and compassionate family doctors already know when life is coming to an end and how best to alleviate pain and suffering for the terminally ill. Many medics will feel it is a breach of their Hippocratic Oath to permit the deliberate procurement even of a terminally ill patient's death. Others will cast aside both pragmatic judgement and doing right by their ailing patients and will stick to the letter of new legislation for fear of the consequences of not doing so. But we seem to be sleepwalking into a fundamental societal change here. Well-meaning but uncompromising supporters of euthanasia have started to accuse opponents of assisted dying of being out of touch and old-fashioned in their objections.

I have little doubt that a narrowly drawn change in the law to permit assisted dying for terminally ill patients with no more than six months to live will quickly be regarded as a precedent. Before long, campaigners will claim similar eligibility for euthanasia for those with chronic but non-life-threatening conditions, as well as the physically healthy whose mental illness apparently makes living unbearable. At a time when the cost of care is rising and medical treatment is becoming ever more inadequate, there is a genuine risk that the elderly, disabled and mentally ill will feel, and be made to feel, that they are no more than an unwanted burden to society. As a former lawyer and now former legislator, I believe, perhaps somewhat perversely, that the law is not the right vehicle for dealing with the deeply distressing end-of-life issue.

The case for reducing the voting age in the late 1960s from twenty-one was that by that age, the vast majority of young people were in the workplace and as taxpayers they were being deprived of their right of representation. That was an era when fewer than one in ten went on to higher education and the school leaving age was fifteen. The opportunistic clamour from virtually all the political parties today to enfranchise sixteen-year-olds comes at a time when the direction of travel to permit young people to smoke, buy alcohol or engage in other risky activity is inexorably moving upwards. You now have to be eighteen to sign a contract or to buy cigarettes, fireworks or a knife. The legal age of marriage has recently been raised to eighteen. Some of the activities that are still permitted at sixteen expressly require parental consent. Drivers who have passed their test at seventeen are still subject to additional restrictions. The right to vote should surely come with some commensurate responsibilities.

One moral issue where Conservatives are perennially playing catch-up is over the enduring appeal of socialism and collectivist thinking. Worse still – and this was always one of the most infuriating aspects of appearing on television or radio on a cross-party panel – the sense that there was some sort of moral superiority that attached to those with left-wing views. It is a tradition that harks back to the 1930s and certainly persists to this day. We Conservatives may regard our political opponents as mistaken, misguided perhaps, but broadly speaking we respect that in the marketplace of political ideas, there is room for more than one potential answer.

In the eyes of many on the left, by contrast, Conservative attitudes and those who hold them are somehow morally suspect; all too often the left characterise and dismiss right-wing views as pandering to the worst instincts of human nature. In their own minds and that of their many cheerleaders in the media, those holding left-wing opinions may be naively idealistic, unrealistic, and impractical, but in their core beliefs they are essentially well meaning. A similar trend applies to younger voters holding and espousing liberal or 'socially aware' attitudes. Curiously, this is often coupled with an unshakeable belief that this marks them out as radical and progressive as they spout their fashionable views on diversity and inclusion. In truth, they are almost achingly conventional, with minds often as narrow as those whose attitudes they publicly condemn in their frequent virtue signalling across social media.

· · ·

I was at Conservative Campaign Headquarters on the morning of 18 April 2017 when Theresa May surprised much of the Westminster village by calling a general election. We should really have seen it coming. The Copeland by-election victory in late February was the first time in over eighty years that this semi-rural, semi-industrial Cumbrian constituency had elected a Conservative MP. The Brexit decks had been cleared by the invoking of Article 50 at the end of the following month. The clock was now ticking towards a formal leaving date in March 2019, but the electoral arithmetic looked tricky as May had inherited a small overall majority on assuming the premiership. Few imagined at this moment that it was about to get a whole lot trickier.

I remember remarking casually that morning to Patrick McLoughlin, who had replaced Andrew Feldman as party chairman, that if Jeremy Corbyn's brand of left-wing populism was going to appeal anywhere it was in London. Our sights in the capital were set on winning back the four seats we had very narrowly lost to Labour in 2015, and it was in two of those districts that my local association was instructed to focus the entirety of our campaigning efforts. In the event, Labour MPs were re-elected in all four with an average majority over 11,000.

At more or less the same time, I learned later that my constituency neighbour in Kensington, Victoria Borwick, had rushed into the Whips' Office claiming that the decision to go to the country was disastrously mistaken and warning them that her seat would be lost. To be frank, at the time I put this down to a not uncharacteristic bout of nervous excitability. I turned out to be wrong and in the event, Victoria's fears were realised as her 7,300 majority evaporated like snow in the mid-summer sun.

We started miles ahead in the opinion polls. But the Conservatives were immediately hampered by the need to bypass the Fixed Term Parliament Act so we wouldn't be reliant on Labour's votes. That meant a seven-week timetable before polling day – not ideal for a snap election. Theresa May was then persuaded by her advisers to front-up a highly personalised appeal, based on her providing 'strong and stable' leadership. This played neither to her strengths nor, I suspect, her instincts. She had walked through the door of Downing Street the previous summer after addressing the nation with a deeply sincere speech about tackling burning injustices.

But this was her first national campaign, and in the months running up to it she had assiduously dampened expectations that she might be tempted to seek her own mandate or take advantage of the disarray in Labour's ranks by going to the country. A more experienced campaigner might have listened less to the party's communications experts and insisted that the right strategy now was to present herself as the candidate of change who recognised and relished that Brexit would mean doing things differently.

Political life is full of such imponderables. The drumbeat in support of a second Brexit referendum was already becoming louder. So even without the well-documented missteps of the 2017 election campaign, it was always unrealistic to imagine that the Conservatives would have been swept to the sort of landslide that the early polls were indicating. Even before things began to go wrong, I remember chatting at a party rally with Phillip Lee, who in the following year would resign his junior ministerial role, later cross the floor and eventually stand as a Liberal Democrat in 2019. He was clearly perturbed: 'What exactly is our message to the almost four million loyal Tories who voted Remain? They believed we should remain in the EU – surely, we cannot simply abandon them all?'

The campaign dragged on and on. Day after day of leaflet delivery and almost random canvassing of target voters. Even as someone vaguely on the inside track, I felt, as always, the huge disconnect between the mundane, local campaigning activity that was taking up most of my waking hours and the national themes that were being covered in the press. I am embarrassed to admit that the pause in campaigning after the Manchester and London Bridge terror attacks came as a blessed relief. But these unspeakable acts of Islamist violence failed to jolt the campaign into a new gear. The widespread assumption was that security alerts of this sort could only play to the advantage of Mrs Strong and Stable, the longest-serving Home Secretary in seven decades, especially as she was up against a lifelong sympathiser of the aims, if not necessarily methods, of the Irish Republican Army and Palestinian Liberation Organisation.

The final week of the campaign began with the opinion polls all over the place but an increasing number pointing to a hung Parliament. This applied particularly to those conducted on a constituency-by-constituency basis under a new-fangled statistical technique called multi-level regression and post-stratification (MRP), which was updated on a daily basis. My tendency is to be a little fatalistic about these things. So, I was not unduly worried that this methodology was suggesting that my own seat, where at the previous election only two years earlier we had led the Labour Party by almost twenty-seven percentage points, was now 'too close to call' and on some days even crept into the Labour column.

My new constituency agent, James Cockram, was a little less sanguine. Four days before polling day, he insisted that we put together a bespoke and high-quality glossy leaflet-cum-magazine. Its content and layout were a world away from the standard fare in the CCHQ pack. It was a highly personal appeal from me, addressed very specifically to the 72 per cent of my electors who had voted Remain, who had, as Phillip Lee had rightly observed all those weeks ago, been totally neglected by the Conservatives' national campaign. We recalled our activists from the lost causes in Chiswick and Ealing, so that within twenty-four hours our constituency had been totally delivered. Our publication was well received and to this day I hold it responsible for ensuring that the swing against me was the lowest of any Tory-held seat in central London. All of this is slightly at the margins, but my majority still slumped by two thirds to 3,148 on a 9.3 per cent adverse swing. Had the nearby Kensington, Putney or Battersea swings been replicated, it would have been a very close-run thing.

It was an uncomfortable election night. The hapless politicians in the TV studios having to comment instantly on exit polls always go through the motions of hedging their initial judgements. The fact is, the methodology is now so sophisticated, and more importantly the decision by all broadcasters to pool resources means the sample is so large, that exit polls these days are invariably pretty much on the money. As the early results flowed in, I thought of the many friends amongst the thirty-three Conservative MPs who were in the throes of losing their seats.

Then it was off to my own count. The national picture was still uncertain, but in my brief acceptance speech I was confident in declaring my intention to continue making my contribution on economic and international affairs. I stood back to allow my opponents to have their say. As I looked down from the stage at the clusters of activists facing us all, many sporting rosettes and stickers that betrayed their political allegiances, I was suddenly and unexpectedly struck by the strange premonition that this might be the last time I would be doing this. The trouble with thoughts of this kind is they have a tendency to be self-fulfilling.

CHAPTER 7

A LATE FLOURISH

13 JUNE 2017

The call, when it came, was not unexpected.

Whatever expansive plans Theresa May might have had for reshaping her government team had been scuppered by the outcome of the election. Survival was now the imperative. The Cabinet had been appointed – in truth, largely reappointed – by the Sunday evening and much of the following day was spent in shuttle diplomacy to secure the support of the Democratic Unionist Party. Their ten MPs represented the difference between an impossibly unstable minority administration and a functioning government, albeit one at the near-permanent mercy of its most maverick backbenchers.

As a result, it was only five days after the election, on Tuesday 13 June, that the great minds in No. 10 finally turned to all the other ministerial appointments. For the first time in over a decade, I had skin in the game on a reshuffle day. Normally safely tucked away in my briefcase or jacket pocket, my mobile phone suddenly had pride of place on the desk in my Portcullis House office as I pretended to give undivided attention to an unremarkable morning of constituency emails. It was just past midday when the all-knowing

Downing Street switchboard made contact with me. Within moments, the Prime Minister was on the line and inside a further thirty-five seconds, having appointed me as a Minister of State in the Foreign Office, she was off it again, presumably to anoint the next on her list.

Just hours later, over dinner with non-political friends who were dying to hear a blow-by-blow account of this personally historic brief exchange, I had to admit that almost every detail had already slipped my mind. All I could recall was what had *not* been discussed. There was not a word of guidance nor any instruction as to what the Prime Minister expected of me, although knowing she was aware of my international office role, I guess she must have reckoned the FCO would be up my street. Not for nothing is it said that the haphazard informality that surrounds appointment as a government minister has few parallels in the world of work.

In fairness, I had some warning of what was to come. A few days after the election had been called but just before we all headed off on the campaign trail, I had been invited to see the Chief Whip, Gavin Williamson. At the time, the universal expectation was that we were heading for a massive victory so it was with a beaming smile and confidence that he assured me that I would be made a minister once the mere formality of the election was out of the way. In these congenial circumstances, I concluded that fortune favours the brave. Desperately trying to avoid sounding either overly presumptuous or ungrateful, I thought it would be sensible to lay down my terms, as in all probability this would be my only chance to do so.

These were simple enough. I had become a privy counsellor two years earlier in recognition of my work on the ISC, so with such seniority I reckoned I should be brought in at middle-ranking minister of state level. I was also only really interested in either the Treasury or the Foreign Office. In essence, these were the two departments in which I had both strong policy interest and hands-on experience; they also attracted the most able civil servants and were regarded as the powerhouse of the UK government. I worked on the basis that if I was going to sell my soul for ministerial office, it ought to be for the highest bidder.

Williamson visibly gulped, claimed that he admired my candour and promised to do what he could. Later in his career, it became fashionable for fellow politicians and the media to put the boot in on Gavin Williamson. It is fair to say that his talents were probably not best served in departmental roles, but he was always a highly accomplished behind-the-scenes operator. He relished the power and influence of the Whips' Office and for so long as the political trade operates as it does, you might as well have competent fixers running the show. All I can say is that for me, as for many others, he delivered what he promised, which in politics is a depressingly rare quality.

This advance notice turned out to be useful on a couple of counts. First, to really think through whether in the circumstances of Brexit I could or should serve in government at all. My views on the substantive issue had not changed. I still considered Brexit to be a geopolitical mistake of historic proportions. I also fretted that even its potential medium- and long-term economic upsides risked being undermined if we went ahead with the hard version of Brexit that seemed ever more on the cards. But I also firmly believed that the very fabric of democratic accountability would be destroyed if the political class now thwarted what had been voted for in the referendum. My position on a second referendum, or People's Vote as it later came to be called, was that it was designed to do just that – to overturn the will of the people. So, those personnel within a

Conservative government implementing Brexit should be made up of a variety of viewpoints on the issue. To be given the offer to serve in government but then choose to stand outside and shout from the sidelines would really be nothing more than self-indulgent.

But this line of reasoning, genuine as it was, was also too self-serving to be the whole story. I felt I had done my time in Parliament, particularly in a demanding party role, and 'deserved' a shot at holding office if it was offered. Although I would not necessarily have minded staying on as chairman of the international office, it was clear that our leaving the EU was about to drastically reduce the funding for its work and severely diminish the role.

I had watched a procession of fairly low-grade politicians have their turn on the ministerial merry-go-round and was pretty sure I could do a better job. Whilst I had never regarded becoming a minister as the be-all and end-all of political life, I knew that in retirement I would look back on my time in politics in a different and more fulfilled light if I had been able to give it a go.

As I mulled over what to do, two recollections from my early years as an MP also came to mind. The first was a tea room conversation with a vastly experienced parliamentarian who had turned down the chance to join the government front bench in the early Thatcher years and almost thirty years later was still clearly regretting his decision because the offer was never repeated. The second was a kind letter I had received after I had been dismissed from the front bench in 2006 from the ex-MP father of a friend from Oxford, who assured me my time would come again and implored me not to give up hope. My university friend had died shortly after his fortieth birthday and there was a small part of me that wanted to honour his memory too.

The other reason why it proved so useful to be forewarned and

forearmed about becoming a minister was that it gave me an invaluable few weeks to think through properly how I wanted to achieve
effectiveness. More important still, how I would go about planning
the management of my core private office team.

I still retain the slightly scruffy sheet of A4 paper on which I
sketched out in biro my personal five-point plan immediately after
that fateful meeting with Williamson. It never fails to bring a broad
smile to my face when I reread it now; virtually all of this exercise
in wishful thinking became a successful template for the pattern of
work my private office and I subsequently adopted when the call
came.

Having run a business before going into public service and,
perhaps even more importantly, having had over fifteen years of
parliamentary experience before taking up government office had
given me a fairly clear-sighted understanding of what the role was
to entail. I realised that some surprises inevitably awaited me, but
many MPs admit that on starting their first ministerial job they
were all at sea and literally clueless about the workings of the civil
service and government departments. I was pretty confident that
would not be my experience.

By nature, I recognised that I was very much a man of routine
and worked best when surrounded by order, discipline and a systematic approach to transacting business. I have always enjoyed and
felt comfortable with making decisions.

From conversations with friends who had already served in
ministerial office, I understood that control of one's diary is par-
amount. This particularly applied to me as a central London MP
with substantial constituency-related commitments taking place
during the week (by contrast, most MPs handle the bulk of their
constituency duties on Fridays, when Parliament rarely sits, and at

weekends). On day one, I insisted on introducing a weekly Monday morning meeting at the FCO, which one or two members of my parliamentary team would also attend. This was to work through all diary and travel commitments and the like, thus avoiding a potentially stressful tussle between competing offices. This led to a genuine *esprit de corps* amongst both sets of Team Field (as they called their WhatsApp group). It also meant that when I was abroad, they would often socialise in my absence – to such an extent that when I left Parliament, one of my parliamentary team promptly joined the civil service.

I was insistent that preserving my general well-being and that of those around me meant that the stress and irritation of an overly packed diary should be avoided at all costs. I sought to carve out time for family and personal commitments beyond public duties.

One of my strongest instincts was to avoid the macho culture of the 'red box', namely the vast amounts of paperwork that many ministers take home to deal with in the late evening after an already long day. It was not that I was averse to hard work or long hours. Rather the opposite, in fact, and I quickly recognised the singular importance that the civil service attaches to the rapid throughflow of paperwork. I instructed that I should work from the ministerial office on all written submissions during the working day, meeting up in person with officials as necessary so that decisions would normally be made there and then. Naturally, larger written submissions and any outstanding papers for decision were placed in a file that I would often be able to read and assess further at leisure over the weekend.

Finally, I was always determined to carve out some 'thinking time' for policy and speeches, even with a packed appointments diary. Slightly less in keeping with usual ministerial practice was my resolve to maintain a small personal network – or Brain Trust – of political- and policy-orientated contacts I had known over the years. I continued to meet these contacts of mine individually, informally and discreetly in Parliament from time to time. They helped provide me with an alternative view on a range of global issues of the day. I felt this approach worked well and it allowed me to feed in fresh thinking to my civil service team. After a while, I suspect my private office became aware that something of this nature was happening, for it was usually very rare that I disappeared during the day other than for parliamentary votes. When I did meet some of this personal network, the tell-tale sign was that I would always come back to the Foreign Office fizzing with new ideas.

Thankfully, the old military saying that few wartime plans survive contact with the enemy did not apply to my own modest plan of action. There is a common misconception that the civil service likes nothing more than to obstruct, obfuscate and delay. My experience with a succession of excellent private office and specialist regional teams was the precise opposite. They responded well to decisiveness and a clear agenda. I shall always be grateful to my close-knit private office for making my time in their care the most enjoyable two years of my political life. Our team at any one time was made up of a private secretary, a fast-track high-flyer on a one-year secondment, an assistant private secretary with regional expertise, a diary secretary and an administrator.

The intellectual calibre of many of the people with whom I worked most closely in the FCO was uniformly high. Only a generation ago, many would probably have pursued a career as a university academic. As the career pyramid, promotion prospects and salaries in academia have narrowed, it has been to the benefit of think-tanks and the elite civil service. But I believe there was – and is – a downside to this. The clear preference of most FCO high-flyers and fast-track graduates is to be involved either in ivory-tower policy aspects of the work or to be attached to ministerial private offices nearest the political action.

Given that civil service promotion is largely in the hands of people with this sort of background, these preferences become self-perpetuating. As a result, I believe too little kudos or attention is paid to the service delivery elements of the departmental brief. How best to set up, manage and run multi-year expensive service programmes is seen by many as the Cinderella aspect of work at the FCO. This important and commercially lucrative work is almost exclusively outsourced to leading strategic consultancies and the Big Four accountancy firms, which almost alone have the capacity to bid for and handle such work. As a result, internal FCO or civil service expertise is no longer enhanced and the sort of men and women who are destined to reach the highest grades in the office have seldom developed project management experience. When things go wrong and all hell breaks loose in the media, it tends to be over mismanaged programmes overseas and generally it is over matters of process rather than policy.

In my own small way, I tried to alleviate this by making clear the personal priority I attached to this aspect of our work by regularly walking the upper floors of the Foreign Office building where the London-based service delivery was located. This also gave me a chance to understand properly the nuts and bolts of what the FCO and its NGO and foreign government partners were doing on the ground.

• • •

My arrival at the Foreign Office came at a time when organisational change was in the air. Two of the new ministerial team were to be given joint responsibilities with the Department for International Development (DfID) and it was widely assumed that in time (as indeed happened in 2020) the departments would merge. This reversed the carving out of DfID that had happened when the Blair government came to office in 1997.

Over the years, the cultural differences between the two departments had gradually expanded; their day-to-day priorities and outlook were increasingly at odds and there were widely diverging trajectories for grading, promotion and pay between civil servants of similar years' experience. Our commitment, by now enshrined in law, to rapidly reach spending of 0.7 per cent of GDP on development work had allowed us, with typical British self-regard, to badge the UK as a world leader in aid. But in a time of austerity, it also meant that the aid budget was almost uniquely protected at the same time as the Treasury was requiring other government departments to severely tighten their belts.

As a result, the stumbling block was over the ever-widening disparity in finances between the two departments. The FCO's annual budget was £2.4 billion, which included staff costs and the maintenance of overseas missions. Meanwhile, DfID boasted an annual income of £13 billion, which by law was rising fast each and every year. At our weekly ministerial meetings, few spectacles amused me more than watching an exasperated Boris Johnson bemoaning bitterly the fact that when visiting countries in Africa as Foreign Secretary, he was treated as a second-tier tourist compared with the most junior DfID minister, whose splashing of seemingly endless largesse guaranteed them the red-carpet treatment. Well before the axe finally fell, it was abundantly clear that DfID's independence – and bountiful income – had long been in Boris's sights.

Even before I had set foot in the magnificent Foreign Office building on King Charles Street, which runs the entire distance between Whitehall and St James's Park, my duties had been determined. I would be taking Foreign Office responsibilities for the entire Asia and Pacific region. For a start, this meant the Indian sub-continent. Because in British diplomatic eyes the history and interests of Pakistan were inextricably linked to Afghanistan (AfPak) this meant the latter was tagged on. I also looked after China and its neighbours, all ten south-east Asian states, Japan, North and South Korea and Australasia, including the bewilderingly large number of sovereign state islands in the Pacific Ocean. What even I had not reckoned on was the sheer volume of travel this would involve, not least as I was also the first port of call for several multilateral organisations.

Two days after my appointment, I had a twenty-minute meeting with my immediate superior, the then Foreign Secretary Boris Johnson, and immediately afterwards wrote him a two-page memo setting out the agreed six priorities on which I would be working. By the time Jeremy Hunt arrived as his successor thirteen months later, I ensured a formal note was awaiting him. By this time, I had whittled down my priority list to a single page and four main heads, outlining where progress had been made and further plans were in train.

One of the eternal truths of ministerial life is the fact that your tenure is subject to a non-existent notice period. Enjoy each day as if it is your last, because it might well turn out to be exactly that. One thing that is absolutely essential is to focus your private office team on practical delivery rather than getting bogged down in activity for its own sake. From my earliest days at the Foreign Office, it was easy to see how every single hour of the working day could easily be filled with worthy meetings and diplomatic courtesy calls. But being a hyperactive and prominent minister was one thing; making an effective difference was quite another.

From the outset I could see that Boris Johnson regarded being Foreign Secretary as a very poor consolation prize to the job he really coveted, which had slipped through his fingers the year before. I could see all too clearly that his irrepressibly competitive instincts were on a different scale even to that I had seen in the cut-throat world of legal recruitment. But I enjoyed working with him. The bane of most ministers is to have an overbearing and constantly interfering Secretary of State. That was clearly never Boris's style, but his door was always open whenever potential political flash-points or problems arose.

About a month after my arrival, I received a WhatsApp message from him asking me to breakfast the following morning at the Travellers Club. I pitched up at the appointed hour in Pall Mall, having swotted over all my current policy briefings well into the early hours. It brought back memories of the adrenaline that used to flow with the eve-of-tutorial essay crises that were the penalty for having too much of a good time at university. I had assumed that Professor Johnson was going to put me through my paces on all matters Asian.

The expansive dining room of this favourite haunt of diplomats was all but empty, except for two members of the Foreign Secretary's security detail who were tucking into a full English breakfast at a nearby table. We quickly followed suit, but our conversation never graduated to discussing detailed matters of state. Instead, he treated me to detailed analysis of his party leadership prospects in the, needless to say, highly unlikely event that the ball were to come loose from the back of the proverbial scrum. He winced when I told him that he would almost certainly have prevailed if only he had continued his campaign despite Gove's intervention the previous year. My advice was that he now needed to be patient and convince his doubters by making an effective fist of his current job. I suspect this was seen as an insufficiently enthusiastic response because he never raised the leadership subject with me again.

There was one other occasion I recall that reflected how sensitive he could be to any perceived criticism. I had appeared on a Radio 4 panel and said something that might just have been construed as mildly disapproving of some element of Foreign Office work. It barely registered in the press cuttings, but a very agitated Boris Johnson was quickly on the phone. He caught up with me as I was waiting at Heathrow Airport on my way to Malaysia and Mongolia, where in the Gobi Desert I had an unforgettable visit to the vast Oyu Tolgoi copper mine. I calmed him down but was left surprised at the contrast between what I had just listened to and the public image of a carefree, bold and buccaneering politician. It was often said of Boris Johnson that he was such a slapdash and ill-disciplined operator that it was virtually impossible for him to stick to the party line. Curiously this never seemed to apply to his own campaigns, where he seemed eminently capable of strict message discipline – and insisted that others were similarly obedient.

Most commentators and a fair few diplomats are scathingly dismissive of Johnson's entire record at the Foreign Office. This takes no account of the way in which, early in 2018, he genuinely led from the front in the aftermath of the poisonings of former Russian military office and intelligence asset Sergei Skripal and his daughter Yulia in Salisbury. In due course, a UK citizen was killed by the Novichok nerve agent that operatives had brought into the UK on the orders of the Russian President to carry out what turned out to be a botched assassination attempt. Johnson had been a long-time critic of Vladimir Putin and had previously denounced the annexation of Crimea when many other politicians had been far more equivocal.

As soon as the Salisbury attack took place, he marshalled support for our position within the UN and international community in response to Putin's aggression. I remember two weekends spent systematically ringing my counterparts in Asia as we built as large a coalition as possible. This was Johnson at his very best. He had long marked Putin and Russia's card as a major national security issue. I have little doubt that this personal commitment was why UK intelligence was so forthright in alerting the world to the imminent threat in the months leading up to Russia's invasion of the rest of Ukraine in February 2022. By this time Prime Minister, his tub-thumping and passionate support as an international cheerleader for Ukraine was both genuine and potent.

• • •

The moment I learned that Brexit Secretary David Davis had resigned over differences in policy and strategic outlook in July 2018, following publication of the Chequers plan, I knew immediately that Boris Johnson would feel obliged to follow suit. There was no way he could allow anyone else to usurp his position in the eyes of Tory MPs and membership as the unassailable defender of the Brexit flame. My old friend Jeremy Hunt arrived in his place after six years' hard labour as Health Secretary. For both the Foreign Office and the new Foreign Secretary, a period of relative calm now descended. Week after week, Jeremy was very open with us all about the increasingly fraught state in Cabinet over the Brexit negotiations. It also became fairly obvious that he saw himself as a serious contender for the leadership and this inevitably had an impact on his approach to the foreign affairs brief. On the plus side he, like his predecessor, left me largely to my own devices to get on with my work plan and overseas visits.

The rest of the ministerial team now worked together harmoniously. My private office shared a huge communal space with that of the Middle East Minister, Alistair Burt, with our own offices on either side. We overlooked the historic splendour of the internal courtyard of the Durbar Court. It was like old times for Alistair and me, as during the party's final term in opposition we had had a similar arrangement with our parliamentary offices – albeit on a smaller and far less grand scale in the functional but modern setting of Portcullis House.

Alan Duncan looked after Europe and the Americas. I had enjoyed his often waspish company over many years, but he had a dislike for Boris Johnson that bordered on the obsessive and frequently made its way into the newspapers. The Hunt regime was much more to his liking. I had known Harriett Baldwin, Africa and International Development Minister, since she was an aspiring candidate. Like me, her background was really more City and finance based, but she approached the brief with exactly the right mix of industry, idealism and scepticism.

She had joined us at the only major reshuffle that occurred during my time as a minister. I had turned up to the department that morning reasonably confident that I was staying put but with that small lingering doubt that is always sensible to have in the unpredictable world of politics. Although no official announcements had yet been made, the moment I walked through the door my mind was immediately put to rest. My private office had already been tipped off that for us at least, it was going to be business as usual.

Harriett replaced Rory Stewart. He was a man who, from the moment he entered Parliament in 2010, had gone to great trouble to cultivate a style, self-mythology and image of his own. It is the sort of thing that goes down well with newspaper and magazine feature writers, who start talking up your prospects to an almost absurd degree. In truth, he never had much of a following amongst fellow Tory MPs. Even his moderate performance in the 2019 leadership election, where he came seventh in the initial ballot and a distant fifth overall, was almost certainly boosted by a campaign of tactical voting – ironically enough, by Boris Johnson supporters keen to ease their hero's path to the crown.

Rory Stewart reinvents his time in Parliament on podcasts today as one prolonged and titanic battle between the forces of good (as personified by R. J. N. Stewart) and the evils of Boris Johnson. This masks the uncomfortable truth that the two men have far more in common than Rory dares admit. Highly competitive, egotistical, hugely self-confident and with an over-developed sense of their own political destiny, they both appeared to believe in their innate right to lead. Two peas in a pod, it is perhaps small wonder Boris has become Rory's sworn enemy. Not that I witnessed even the remotest sign of this when the two men served together in the Foreign Office. In fairness, there was enough open enmity between Boris and Alan Duncan that any other ministerial tensions would probably have been difficult to detect.

What I do remember is Rory's genuine passion for the Africa review that seemed to take up most of his time, energy and attention. Two other episodes stick in my mind. Immediately after he was reshuffled out of the department, I inherited from him the administration of the FCO's Prosperity Fund programmes, to which he had seemingly given next to no attention. Dozens of civil servants were awaiting guidance and the go-ahead to use DfID funds on a series of economic collaboration programmes with middle-income countries, which would not otherwise qualify for development aid monies. To me this seemed an important means of the UK sparking up a strong trading relationship after Brexit with the fast-growing economies we needed to stay closely aligned to. Whether Rory's foot-dragging was from a general lack of interest in economic diplomacy or a deliberate attempt to frustrate the top brass in the FCO, who saw the Prosperity Fund as a timely mechanism to snaffle some of that vast DfID budget, I could never quite work out.

The other matter was altogether more serious. The huge amount of time that was blanked out in the ministerial teams' diaries for rehearsal in advance of departmental questions on the floor of the House of Commons never ceased to surprise me. Perhaps this was understandable, as it was the one hour in the month when the TV cameras were rolling on our activities. But naturally it would only make headline news if a minister had been wrongfooted or misspoken on an already high-profile international matter. This was politics as a high-wire performance, where consistent, timely administration and persistent, worthy competence counts for very little. One of Rory's party tricks was to ostentatiously stride forward to the despatch box and answer questions without the folder full of prepared answers that the rest of us would routinely rest on our laps during these sessions and refer to assiduously in answering the quick-fire follow-up questions.

I was in New York attending the UN Security Council on the day of one of these monthly ordeals. The rest of the team divided up my questions. There was one highly sensitive consular matter in my region involving the detention of a dual national that had been assigned to Rory; my private office briefed his in advance about the way this question, with its delicate intelligence and national security aspects, would need to be handled. Few profiles of Rory these days exclude reference by his publicists to the fact that his CV includes time working in 'the edgier part of the FCO' – fairly clear code for MI6. So, he of all people would have been aware that when this sort of issue was raised, all he needed to do was to recite very precisely the two short sentences set out in the briefing. Just read out the agreed line. No less and no more.

This was not Rory's style, of course. When the moment came, instead of reciting the prepared text he blurted out a response that 'extreme action' would be taken if allegations of torture were proven. This performance was almost directly out of the much-vilified Boris Johnson playbook over Nazanin Zaghari-Ratcliffe, and whilst the facts of the two consular cases were rather different, the outcome was for a time similar: a furious diplomatic spat, chilled relations over all consular disputes with the country concerned and a British passport holder facing prolonged detention without trial overseas.

• • •

Away from the personalities and day-to-day work programme at the Foreign Office, it was clear that in the aftermath of the global financial crisis, much of the framework that had been the foundation of economic growth and co-operation since the fall of communism was becoming open to negotiation. I had already witnessed in my time as the City's MP that there had been a retreat from untrammelled globalisation and a new era of protectionism was beckoning.

Events in more recent years have only accelerated that process, with ambivalence towards the perceived benefits of globalisation turning into outright hostility to the concept, even amongst some traditional allies.

As I write these words nobody can predict with certainty how the war in Ukraine and conflict in Israel, Gaza and Lebanon will end. Vladimir Putin and his gangster government seem dedicated to restoring both Russian pride and some of its lost empire and remaining relentlessly indifferent to the suffering of civilians and military personnel alike, whether at home or abroad. The fact that he also controls a vast nuclear arsenal adds to the difficulties that face those who seek swift defeat and removal from office for his regime. In the meantime, the simmering tensions following the murderous Hamas attacks of October 2023 have already sparked a broader regional conflagration, in which uneasy alliances throughout the entire international community will be interlinked.

Geopolitically, the outcome appears more clear. A deep and prolonged division between the west and a bloc centred on China and Russia and hostile to democratic norms such as the rule of law, open elections and a free press. Economic turmoil and divisions seem set to follow.

China's leadership have tried to make their tacit support as senior partner to their rogue neighbour compatible with continued economic relations with the US and European countries and businesses. The swift departure of a vast swathe of western brands and service providers from Russian markets in the aftermath of the declaration of war in Ukraine is being slowly followed by many of those US and European entities who have painstakingly invested time and energy in building up operations in China over recent decades. Some have already been forced by the energies of activist investors not to source cotton picked by forced Uighur labour in Xinjiang province.

Protectionist sentiment has never died, even during the heyday of globalisation and the emergence in recent decades of ever more complex and interconnected supply chains. Witness our own highly active farming lobby, always keen to close down debate as to their domestic methods of production but ready to drum up consumer distaste at minor differentiation in competitors' means in order to block imports. High-profile campaigns here in the UK against GM foods, animal welfare standards and industrialisation of agriculture are little more than blatant protectionism wrapped up as consumer safeguarding.

Whilst 'America First' has been the US trade watchword since Theodore Roosevelt's days over a century ago, there is little doubt that the neo-protectionists were invigorated by Donald Trump's rhetoric. Announcing that the US and its people have been 'screwed' by China, he sought to 'bring jobs home' and impoverished the US consumer by launching a trade war. At the same time, the general critique in the US against China developed from self-serving accusations of unfair competition to that of a national security risk, especially in the highly competitive field of technology. This analysis has been enthusiastically shared by an increasing number of frontline politicians in the UK and EU, who now regard China as a hostile, systematic threat rather than the fast-growing trading partner being welcomed into joint venture arrangements until the end of the last decade.

The trend towards deglobalisation – or 'reclaiming national sovereignty', according to your taste – was naturally accelerated by the pandemic and its aftermath. The vulnerability of global supply chains and the demand for resilience and self-reliance will only increase, with businesses sourcing the most local suppliers available. Linked closely to this is the ongoing challenge of implementing climate change and net zero decarbonisation policies, which will inevitably force national economies to become more local. A good thing in the main, perhaps, but watch as many western governments adopt being 'good environmental citizens' as a pretext for taxes and regulations that are flagrantly protectionist.

History records that adopting a policy of self-sufficiency in the aftermath of the First World War led to an increase in tensions that it was designed to alleviate. The era of globalisation that had come to an end with the outbreak of hostilities was superseded by widespread adoption of tariffs and 'beggar my neighbour' policies in the 1930s, a collapse in global trade and a deep worldwide depression, as countries became increasingly alarmed about their inability to access scarce resources. Ultimately, the sentiment and the emergence of dictatorship governments in Germany and Japan led to a rush to grab land where minerals and foodstuffs were more plentiful.

Today, trading links with China and countries in its orbit are regarded as a source of increasing strategic and security risk, with many commentators questioning Germany's over-reliance on China as a market for its industrial exports. Experts fear that globalised communication links are a signal of vulnerability, and we have already discovered the inherent problems with reliance on Russian oil and gas and the risks of pressure being exerted on western democracies by nations able to restrict supply at such short notice. All of this comes at a time when the protectionist impulse is on the rise everywhere. President Macron of France has been able to publicly implore the EU to start favouring its own industries and this has given licence to free trade sceptics across the continent to speak more openly themselves. Even President Biden, who de-escalated the rhetoric of his predecessor, actively promoted a return to the US's 'managed trade' policies of the 1960s and 1970s, which many of us assumed had been consigned to history with the creation of the General Agreement on Tariffs and Trade and subsequently the World Trade Organization (WTO).

Populist politicians across the world have grasped that trade deals are seldom supported by voters, who see them as beneficial only to large multinational corporations; new disputes in this arena might easily arise as a consequence of electoral domestic politics.

Most worrying has been the progressive breakdown in the international co-operation that might sensibly tackle imminent and future economic and political challenges. When London hosted the G20 summit in April 2009, a new era appeared to be dawning. The developed economies of the time – the US, Germany, Japan, the UK and France – determinedly acted in concert with rapidly emerging markets, such as China, India and Russia to co-ordinate a reflation of the global economy.

Yet this show of G20 unity frayed as the world's economy stabilised. It has now disappeared almost entirely. Renewed military tensions have prompted a cycle of economic sanctions that have curtailed gas supplies and provoked a global energy crisis. Meanwhile, tensions between the US and China have reached an all-time high over Taiwan, resulting in an almost self-fulfilling fatalism about today's great power competition leading inexorably to armed conflict.

• • •

When I was serving as Foreign Minister, it was rare for a month to pass without my making a speech robustly supporting the ideals of the rules-based international system (RBIS). Whether at a think-tank in London, out in New York at the United Nations or on the road in Asia, these timeless ideals of the rule of law, democratic elections and a free press were central to the thinking of the UK, our western allies and the Anglophone world. I would often explain from first principles that it has been a fundamental precept of western political philosophy since the mid-1600s writings of Thomas Hobbes that the weak and the strong benefit equally from the existence of a structure of rules and laws that define and regulate acceptable behaviour.

In its absence, life for everyone risks becoming solitary, poor, nasty, brutish and short. Efforts to codify acceptable forms of international conduct in a multilateral format date back to the Congress of Vienna at the conclusion of the Napoleonic Wars. This laid down the rudiments of the RBIS – a web of values, principles, alliances and conventions, which, barring a few regional skirmishes, underpinned ninety-nine years of European peace until the calamity of the First World War.

Successive emerging great powers have sought to shape and adapt these elements to suit their own perceived best interests, but over the past two centuries none rejected them outright. Instead, even new kids on the block accepted implicitly that their hard power dominance would be protected and enhanced by an agreed system that sustains the predictability and widely recognised stability of the global order.

The last major revision to this rules-based system arose with the foundation of the United Nations in 1945 and the creation of a security council with five permanent members, reflecting the outcome of the second global conflagration that had just concluded.

Pressure on this framework has most recently arisen from three directions. One is familiar, but two are novel. China's emergence as the new kid on the global block has been well tracked by western policymakers. The naive and complacent assumption was that by bringing China into the international system, it would somehow become more western in outlook and culture. Joining the WTO in 2001 would make the Chinese richer and inspire its growing middle class to demand and eventually win a full set of legal and political rights akin to those we in democracies have long taken for granted. Or so we in the west thought.

China has shown no such inclination to play by our rules, with the lessons of the collapse of the USSR weighing heavily on its own internal debate about political reform. There will be no equivalent under President Xi Jinping of Gorbachev's glasnost and perestroika. Indeed, the Chinese leadership seeks to do what other emerging superpowers have done before them – namely, to reshape the rules-based system in a form which unashamedly advances its own interests.

As well as reinforcing Communist Party supremacy, domestic stability, regional dominance and unfettered global trading access, China now challenges and undermines those elements of the system it does not like. Chief amongst these is the 'liberal' or 'enlightened' international human rights architecture, which China and its influential and rapidly expanding roster of associates now openly rebut. At the same time, it has sought to gain greater control over international financial institutions as well as developing parallel structures in parts of the system where technological advances mean there are gaps, such as proposed international regulation and compliance around artificial intelligence and cyber security. With its Belt and Road Initiative, China has sought, with some success, to redraw global norms on sovereign debt forbearance.

This authoritarian wave now extends to the increasingly populist west, many of whose citizens are openly sceptical of the liberal international order, especially over refugee obligations, free movement and conceptions of the universality of rights. Within the EU, openly 'illiberal democracies' rule in Hungary, Czechia, Slovakia and, until recently, in Poland. Even mainstream and longer-established member nations such as Italy and Sweden are now governed by coalitions that include political parties with aggressively authoritarian outlooks on cultural, migration and economic policy.

Suspicion has grown on both the left and right of politics that the west's economic stagnation and flatlining of ordinary living standards has come about as a consequence of the rules-based system being rigged in favour of elites. To this way of thinking, protectionism, isolation and mercantilism offers a better way forward. This acute sense of disenchantment extends even to the intellectual and opinion-forming elites in western societies, who were already aghast at the failure to address a succession of international military crises from Iraq to Afghanistan, Syria and Yemen.

What is unprecedented, however, is the recent challenge to the rules-based system that comes from its principal architect, custodian and beneficiary: the United States of America. It is important to note that whilst this began after Donald Trump first made it to the White House in 2017, the Biden presidency represented a high degree of continuity. The Republican Party has been largely recast in Trump's populist image, and now back in power, it seems set to continue to question global engagement and potentially tear up the structure and alliances of the international system as we have known it.

Regardless of the state of play in the US, the UK will evidently not turn against our single most important security partner.

Nevertheless, if we are capable of re-establishing like-minded diplomatic status with France and Germany in a post-Brexit world, I believe we should try to make concerted efforts to adapt and evolve elements of the international order to better serve the interests of all like-minded democracies.

One regret I have from my time as a minister was not trusting my instincts a little more when it came to questioning the orthodoxy of the content of speeches I delivered on the RBIS. I certainly had my doubts even at the time. The US and the west need to recognise that much of the developing world, containing two thirds of the world's population, regards our conduct of international affairs as hypocritical. We are widely seen as self-interested and insincere, standing up for allegedly immutable principles of international engagement only when it suits us. Our insistence on the universality of our values sounds to many political leaders in the rising powers of Asia and the Middle East as reminiscent of the moral superiority that accompanied colonialism.

It should not have come as such a surprise that our efforts to build a global coalition of condemnation against Russia for its violations of Ukrainian territory fell on deaf ears. Take a closer look at our imperialist past, let alone our twenty-first century incursions into Afghanistan and Iraq. Many beyond the west harbour a deep suspicion that our political leaders care more for saving the lives and communities of fellow Europeans. Similarly, on international trade, climate change and poverty alleviation, when politicians in the west preach to the developing world, our message seems to be, 'Do as we say to make the world a better place, not as we have done in the past to enrich ourselves at the planet's expense.'

I remain hopeful that the essence of our values will endure and in my heart and mind, I believe in the superiority of our system. But we in the west must recognise that there is now keen ideological competition over how the international community should be run. We do not have a monopoly on wisdom, and we must expect robust challenge to our claims of universality and moral superiority in our way of doing things. This will be especially hard to bear in the arena of human rights, where many of the widely supported norms that western societies have developed in recent decades remain alien to a vast majority of the world's population.

· · ·

It hardly needs saying that overseas travel is the highlight of a Foreign Minister's life. Imprisoned by the constant requirement to be available to vote whilst Parliament was sitting, as the government battled to get its business done with a virtually non-existent parliamentary majority, getting away during the parliamentary term time was difficult. Not impossible, though – I always marked out the party conference season and the weeks after the Queen's Speech and Budget as being free to globetrot.

But during my two years in office, I reckoned on travelling throughout most of the summer and Easter recesses. Flights to Asia all being at least four hours in duration meant my private secretary and I would travel business class, and we would often be accompanied by one other diplomat, normally a specialist in whichever sub-region we were visiting.

I was certainly well looked after as one of Her Majesty's ministers of state whilst out on the road. The only downside was knowing that one day when this was all over, the inconveniences and hassles of international travel would return with a vengeance. In the meantime, my private secretary took control of my passport and ensured my landing card was completed. On arrival we were whisked through the diplomatic lane via a VIP lounge, with the fine detail of immigration control and luggage collection all being speedily and invisibly taken care of.

The local UK ambassador or high commissioner would always be there to meet us, even if that meant hanging around at the airport during the early hours of the morning. I had never been able to sleep on planes; this didn't get easier even as I became more accustomed to a diet of almost constant travel. But after a time, it became a necessity. I recall one trip that lasted five days in three countries, which involved three overnight flights, heading straight into a full day's programme on each arrival. For me, the adrenaline flowed as I went into a series of formal meetings with ministerial counterparts. It was the remainder of my team I always felt sorry for – desperately trying to stay awake and be on hand to pass me notes as the diplomatic niceties were carried out.

A day or two before setting out on tour, I would be presented with a comprehensive briefing pack. These were professionally prepared by the relevant FCO regional desk in London and contained information about each country I was about to visit, recent diplomatic telegrams (the regular in-country briefings sent to London by ambassadors abroad, which have in more recent times become less entertaining and forthright as a result of some high-profile leaks) and profiles of all the people I was going to meet, along with 'points to make'.

I made a habit of working my way through the briefing packs before leaving London to acquaint myself with the itinerary and get a clear grip on what we were trying to achieve on the visit. These packs were often over 100 pages long, but it never ceased to amaze me how often, as we chatted on the journey between the airport and the residence, ambassadors or high commissioners expressed surprise that I had evidently read the preparatory paperwork. It soon became clear that this was not always the norm!

More often than not, I would stay at the residence. Sometimes – in places such as Pakistan and Afghanistan – this would be dictated by security considerations, and on these trips, I would also be accompanied by a security detail. In places like Hong Kong, Shanghai and Seoul, the pressure of space meant staying in a luxury international hotel, and this would also apply when visiting places outside a capital city. It was impossible not to allow my mind to drift and imagine the senior politicians and royal VIPs who had previously stayed in the guest suites in some of our smartest residences.

I was fortunate enough to be one of the last ministers to stay in our atmospheric Bangkok residence before its controversial £550 million sale to a global hotel chain. It had been built almost exactly a century earlier on a twelve-acre site of paddy fields then lying on the edge of the built-up area. As Bangkok expanded, our little piece of Thailand became surrounded by the downtown district and was seen as highly desirable – and ultimately expendable – real estate. This was at a time when the cost of the FCO's worldwide estate maintenance had spiralled beyond what austerity funding would allow.

Our embassy in Tokyo is located opposite the Imperial Palace and, like the residence in New Delhi, occupies a prestigious site with an extensive lawn and tranquil garden. Eden Hall in Singapore and our embassy building in Yangon reflected the growth of our nineteenth-century empire. When I was on a visit, high commissioners would always host a small dinner in my honour, attended by prominent locals and leading ex-pats. The only battle I ever had, after several admittedly delicious beef wellington and steak and kidney pie suppers, was in persuading my hosts that having come all this way, I would really prefer to feast on a menu made up of local delicacies.

● ● ●

Burma, or Myanmar as it is now called, took up a significant proportion of my time as a minister. The UK 'held the pen' for this former colony at the UN Security Council. After many years of painstaking diplomacy, we prided ourselves at having promoted and put into place a pathway towards Burmese democracy following almost seven decades of military dictatorship since independence. Central to this was the internationally revered Aung San Suu Kyi, who overcame the privations of spending almost two decades in detention or house arrest to win elections and form a government in 2015.

Her popularity derived from her father Aung San, who had been the nation's founding father. He had negotiated independence with the British as the Second World War came to an end, working with many of the more than 200 distinct ethnic groups to form the Union of Burma. Months before this was achieved, he was assassinated by a political rival. A Buddhist nationalist military dictatorship then took control of the country. His daughter was only two years old, and she spent the next forty years living, studying and raising a family in the UK. Inspired by her father's memory, she returned to her homeland and her plight in captivity captured the imagination of many in the west. She was seen as an icon for human rights and democracy when, after the fall of Soviet Russia, authoritarianism appeared to be in decline across the world.

Eventually, the regime was persuaded to agree to political reforms, but the new constitution still left huge power in the hands of the military. Now that Aung San Suu Kyi was the international figurehead for this deeply compromised democracy, the Burmese military set about a renewed campaign of ethnic violence against the Rohingya, a Muslim minority in the far western Rakhine state. This came to a head in summer 2017 after militant elements within the Rohingya community lashed out against the military, which then accelerated its systematic campaign of brutal suppression, resulting in thousands of deaths and almost a million Rohingya fleeing across the Bangladeshi border.

After these terrible events, which played out before the world media, I authorised our diplomats at the UN General Assembly to help build a consensus for action and justice. This involved working with Islamic countries in the region and across the Middle East. It also meant meetings at the UN in Geneva and making representations at the International Criminal Court in The Hague, where we promoted innovative legal concepts of fact-finding and evidence-gathering that recognised that those in the Burmese military guilty of these systematic human rights violations would be unlikely to face justice any time soon.

Calamitously for her international reputation, Aung San Suu Kyi would not condemn the brutal actions of the military against the Rohingya minority. Indeed, she refused to accept that they had rights of Myanmar citizenship. She cited that community's support for the British during the Second World War against her father's Burmese nationalist freedom fighters who had sided with the Japanese. It was difficult for me to make the case to a restless House of Commons that Aung San Suu Kyi's survival was dependent on a good working relationship with the military. In reality, for all her flaws she was our only hope if Myanmar were to continue down the long road to democracy and freedom.

I met her on two occasions in Naypyidaw, the custom-built administrative capital city in the centre of Myanmar. This soulless place had been constructed out of nothing as recently as 2004; only its utterly deserted streets and roads belied the first impression that the UK equivalent would be to make Milton Keynes our capital city.

Immaculately dressed, speaking perfect but clipped English reminiscent of a strict governess from the 1950s, Aung San Suu Kyi gave little ground when I tried to explain the strength of dismay felt by her staunchest supporters in London. I had been warned about her uncompromising and stubborn approach. From her earliest days in captivity, she had demanded total loyalty and obedience from her followers. It was notable that many of her earliest defenders had fallen out with her since she had assumed political office; the inexperience of her ministerial team was explained by her refusal to delegate and her preference for loyalty over competence.

By the time of my second visit in mid-2018, she was able to hide behind the very public support of the Chinese government for the Myanmar regime and was even more unrepentant. In due course and after my time in office, the leader of the military junta, Min Aung Hlaing, felt able to act with total impunity. With other neighbours like India, Bangladesh and Thailand also refusing to sign up to UN sanctions against his regime, Min Aung Hlaing simply deposed the one-time darling of the west. So it was that six years after she had assumed office, Aung San Suu Kyi was once again placed under house arrest.

Worthy, groundbreaking and painstaking legal work continues behind the scenes at the UN and the ICC, but despite this, gross human rights violations continue daily on Myanmar soil. In my view, one of the unwelcome side effects of the creation of an international criminal jurisdiction is that for every Charles Taylor or

Radovan Karadžić eventually brought to justice, many other genocidal dictators simply continue their domestic belligerence. If the uncompromising message from the international community to anyone accused of crimes against humanity or war crimes is that your only prospect is a criminal trial in The Hague followed by a lifetime in prison, they have little incentive not to double down on their criminality against internal political opponents.

I saw with my own eyes the daily plight of the Rohingya refugees struggling in a vast, sprawling refugee camp near Cox's Bazar, just across the Bangladeshi border. Over a million displaced people were living under precarious canvass prefabs, with dedicated UN and NGO relief workers trying to give children a semblance of education and normality in their young lives. Of all the heartrending experiences in my life, this affected me most deeply. As I watched innocent young girls dutifully learning to read and write in makeshift classrooms, my mind turned to home and my own similarly aged daughter, Arabella. Back in my hotel room that evening, I was overcome by emotion as I reflected on the dreadful contrast in the lives that any loving parents would want for their daughters. The Rohingya's desperate situation is now frozen, if not largely forgotten, with Myanmar's brutal military dictatorship being protected politically and economically by its most powerful neighbour.

China's influence also touches every part of public life in Cambodia. I spent a memorable two-and-a-half days there, visiting Siem Reap and wandering around some of its natural mountain and lakeside beauty and the magnificent twelfth-century Angkor Wat temples, breathtakingly preserved and restored.

As a rare UK ministerial visitor, I had been granted what was supposed to be a quick twenty-minute meeting with long-standing Prime Minister Hun Sen in Cambodia's capital, Phnom Penh. We sat next to one another in large and generously upholstered armchairs at the far end of a ballroom whose walls were covered in ceiling to floor silk drapes. Our respective entourages were placed in similar chairs facing each other and running the length of the room. Two translators hovered behind our chairs and the diplomatic niceties began with Hun Sen and I both sticking to the lines neatly typed out on the cards we had been given in advance.

After the horrors of the Pol Pot regime, hopes had been high that Cambodia might be next in line after Vietnam to turn an economic corner. There were certainly many free-spirited American investors out in Phnom Penh willing to develop its technology and tourism sectors. Hun Sen himself, as a military commander, had spent the Khmer Rouge era in exile in Vietnam. Upon his return he went into politics, becoming Prime Minister in 1985. Whilst he was keen to encourage free enterprise, he had also become more dictatorial, closing down political opposition and restricting the press. As time passed, Cambodia was becoming ever more a client state of China. We went through the motions of my prepared comments on press freedom and open elections and to my surprise, I detected a slight wistfulness in his facial expression. Knowing that he was grooming his American-educated younger son to become his successor, I decided to go off-piste a little.

'Your Excellency, may I speak to you not as a politician but as a father? Like you, I have a beloved son and I want the very best for him. After all that you went through living in exile, surely you want to pass on to your son a country that is free and able to hold its head up high across the world rather than being dependent on one of your near neighbours?'

Our ambassador, who had only recently taken up the post, looked across at me rather nervously and I felt sure that I would owe her an apology afterwards. What I hadn't quite expected was the reaction of the Cambodian leader, who only that week had imprisoned three dissident journalists. Hun Sen leaned across and grasped my hand. Discarding his own notes, he looked me in the eye and over the next hour spoke, via his interpreter, from the heart about his hopes for his country and the struggles and privations he had experienced during the Pol Pot era, never knowing whether he would ever again set foot in the land of his birth.

The family connection also came up in my meeting with Imran Khan, but in his case he was asking after his former brother-in-law and my Conservative colleague, Zac Goldsmith. An election was pending when I travelled out to Pakistan towards the end of 2017. After meetings in Islamabad, we visited the nearby military town of Rawalpindi where I laid a wreath at one of several immaculately cared for Commonwealth War Cemeteries that I came across on my ministerial travels.

We then headed further north to Mardan in the Khyber Pakhtunkhwa province, which was the stronghold of Khan's PTI party. The general expectation was that he might end up as a kingmaker in the event of a close election. Certainly at the time – and we were still almost nine months away from polling day – his political organisation appeared rudimentary. We travelled in a convoy, coming off the main roads and following a dirt track for several miles until we reached a large but non-descript house, which was doubling up as his campaign headquarters.

The cramped front room, dim standard lamps and dark leather sofas made for a cosy, almost homely scene, but it was a world away from the studied formality of most of my meetings in the region. Tea was served and Imran Khan jokingly observed, in a nod to his previous playboy reputation when an international cricketer, that 'nowadays I am not allowed to offer you anything stronger'. He made much of the upsurge in his support amongst younger voters in the big cities and predicted, accurately as it turned out, that he would do well in Lahore and Karachi.

He also confidently told me of his determination to break the stranglehold that the Pakistani Army and its Inter-Services Intelligence agency had on politics. This populist appeal swept him into office, but he was badly compromised by behind-the-scenes manoeuvrings; he made some powerful enemies and like many political leaders in the region, he used corruption allegations as a means of harassing and imprisoning rivals. His economic policies ended up impoverishing many Pakistanis and eventually, after a little over three years as Prime Minister, Khan was ousted, banned from office, and then thrown into jail. It was desperately sad to see the work of this idealistic standard bearer come to a crashing halt, although his zealous supporters in Pakistan and beyond still entertain some hope that his political career may yet be revived.

• • •

I made only one tour to Kabul. Visiting Afghanistan was not for the faint-hearted, but I was accompanied by my assistant private secretary, who was taking the security precautions entirely in her stride. Her sense of adventure was infectious – to a degree, at least. Travelling by road the three miles or so between the international airport and the highly fortified green zone where our embassy was located was strictly forbidden. So, on arrival we were whisked across the runway in an armoured vehicle and uniformed staff fitted us with full body armoured protection. We then clambered up onto a military helicopter.

A door gunner guarded its entrance, concentrating intensely on his automatic machine gun placement in what I had been assured back in London was the 'highly unlikely event of sniper fire from the ground'. What sounded like the remotest of risks in the comfort of my ministerial office suddenly seemed anything but. I glanced across at my private secretary. She was smiling joyfully at the excitement of it all and contemplating a few drinks later with diplomat friends working in our compound. I could only think of my children back home.

The sheer relief when our five-minute flight skimming above Kabul was over was tempered only by the knowledge that I would have to make the same journey in reverse a couple of days later. British troops had long since withdrawn from Helmand province, so the UK's entire military and diplomatic operation was holed up in Kabul. There was still earnest development work being handled by our mainly young diplomats, who lived cheek by jowl in tiny, prefabricated pods within our cramped embassy compound.

But there seemed to be a disconnect between the pragmatic approach of western diplomats who were tentatively reaching out to biddable elements of the Taliban and Afghanistan's President, Ashraf Ghani, who continued to insist that the Taliban lacked any popular support. It was all too easy to come to this conclusion from the standpoint of central Kabul. Posters and billboards of the mujahideen commander and national martyr Ahmad Shah Massoud were everywhere. Ghani himself was an academic who had spent the previous three decades in the US. It was impossible not to admire his dedication to serving the land of his birth, especially as for some years now he had been physically ravaged by stomach cancer. He sipped tea and spoke tentatively. The trouble was that he was almost universally regarded as a stooge of the American government and the nation-building script he was speaking from was fast being unravelled by the newly installed Trump administration.

The UK's influence in Afghanistan was already much diminished by this time. Our military engagement from 2006 in the troubled Helmand region, largely controlled by warlords, had come to an end when we had to be bailed out by US reinforcements. The same had happened in Iraq's Basra province. Back home, a succession of Defence Secretaries talked up our enviable military prowess. On the ground in Kabul, however, our less than stellar military record was well noted by the western diplomats whom I met.

Whenever US generals stopped over in London, I would steadfastly make the case for a continued, long-term western security and training presence on the ground. But, in truth, it was President Obama who first set in train the process that Biden eventually brought to a chaotic close in 2021. Once we had made it clear to the Taliban that withdrawal would happen on the basis of a timetable rather than specified goals being achieved, they simply bided their time.

South Korea was another part of my patch that suddenly became more high profile as a result of President Trump's quixotic approach to foreign affairs. On each of my three ministerial visits, I was struck by the genuine warmth and high regard in which the UK is held. My counterparts seemed to know at least as much as me about the state of Brexit negotiations and they, along with the Japanese, were desperate to see a deal struck that would justify the faith they had shown with the vast amounts of inward investment they had made in the UK.

Seoul shimmered in the winter morning sun; the demilitarised zone at the 38th parallel seemed strangely calm for a demarcation line regarded as one of the world's most dangerous flashpoints.

But it was the day I spent in South Korea's second city, Busan, that lingers most in the memory. There, at the southernmost tip of the peninsula, was the vast and magnificently manicured UN cemetery where most of the 1,106 British soldiers who died in the Korean War lie buried. As we were finalising the Saturday itinerary for my trip, I had asked to visit this memorial almost as an afterthought. Having assumed it would be an essentially private visit, I was taken aback upon my arrival to be met by senior military and municipal figures and a posse of school children who were adamant that the UK's blood sacrifice (second only to that of the US) should be formally recognised. A largely forgotten war it may well be, but not to generations of Koreans, young and old.

Back in London, it was the North Korean ambassador who occupied more of my time. On no fewer than four occasions I formally summoned him to the Foreign Office to remonstrate following President Kim Jong Un's unauthorised nuclear missile tests. The set format of such reprimands involved the removal of all chairs from my private office and then my standing between two senior UK diplomats and reading out a formal note of protest. Facing me and flanked by his deputy and a translator, the North Korean ambassador would then say a few words in response. I certainly had the impression that he barely understood a word of English and his reply was always made through his translator.

Some months later at the annual Buckingham Palace diplomatic reception, with everyone in either white tie or national dress, I caught sight of an especially incongruously dressed guest. Wearing a brown suit, checked shirt and striped kipper tie, he looked more like a small-time gangster from a 1970s TV police drama. Out of context, it took me a moment to recognise that it was my old adversary, the North Korean ambassador. With a beaming smile, he walked towards me and with his arm outstretched greeted me in perfect idiomatic English: 'How lovely to see you, Minister Field, and how nice that for a change you are not giving me a telling off.'

• • •

Understandably, the UK has always taken seriously its contribution to the work of multilateral organisations. We are one of five permanent members on the UN Security Council and speaking at one of its sessions in New York was always a rather intoxicating experience as a Foreign Office Minister. Attendance at the annual UN General Assembly in September was run by my diary secretary like some kind of speed dating gala, as we sought to maximise the number of face-to-face meetings with ministerial counterparts. On three occasions – in debates on Afghanistan, tensions in Korea and on nuclear non-proliferation – I spoke on behalf of the UK at a Security Council meeting.

But there is little doubt that the prolonged conflict between Ukraine and Russia, one of the other fixtures on the Security Council, is fast exposing the UN's limitations. Its role as a middleman in global disputes is waning and may well be beyond repair. The nations of the world seem to be lining up in opposing blocs in a manner worryingly similar to what we saw before 1914 and 1939. Confrontation appears to be the name of the game, and an impotent UN appears to many seasoned diplomats no longer capable of playing the role of global policeman.

The Organisation for Economic Co-operation and Development (OECD), based in Paris, came under my non-regional responsibilities in the box marked 'economic diplomacy'. At a time of economic disintegration and threats of global trade wars, the OECD is the one international organisation of like-minded open and free-market countries where I believed we were best able to promote our economic priorities. My visits to Paris invariably took in a series of fascinating meetings with Fatih Birol, the charismatic executive director of its sister organisation, the International Energy Agency. It was there that I received my first insights as to the strategic importance of Ukraine, which did much to explain subsequent events. Beneath its soil lies one of the richest collections of minerals in the world, from manganese to titanium and nickel, not to mention vast coal deposits, European gas reserves second only to Norway and the phosphates that underpin the global fertiliser industry. It was impossible not to recognise that sources of energy, old and new, lie at the very heart of the geopolitical conflicts that will shape this century.

I also attended COP24 in Katowice, Poland, where I had the diplomatic responsibility for promoting the UK's three main environmental priorities at the time. We continue to seek the City of London becoming a global hub for green finance initiatives. Less certain is whether, without more substantial lithium battery gigafactory capacity, we will be able to fulfil our domestic goals in electric car manufacturing, but I am more confident that in time, the concept of carbon capture and storage will come into vogue. This is one area where the UK has a track record of research expertise, and after several false starts, we seem set to take a lead in its commercial exploitation.

But when I look back at my activity in the multilateral sphere, the two initiatives that bring most pride were both in the Asia and Pacific region. Leaving the EU also meant foregoing our dialogue partner status with the Association of Southeast Asian Nations (ASEAN). Countries like Vietnam, Indonesia and Malaysia are fast-growing middle-income nations. Singapore is now one of the leading global financial and professional services hubs. Our diplomatic connections with Thailand, Brunei and the Philippines are also strong. So, it made eminent sense to apply for dialogue partnership in our own right. My team at the FCO worked tirelessly to achieve this and once Brexit had formally taken place, we were able to secure it.

As soon as the Comprehensive and Progressive Trans-Pacific Partnership (CPTPP) came into force in late 2018, it struck me as an important initiative that the UK would want to align with. Its original members included Japan, Australia, Singapore, Vietnam, Malaysia and New Zealand, and I laid the foundations to all my ministerial counterparts in these nations that the UK was keen to join. Currently its benefits are predominantly diplomatic and geopolitical, rather than a significant post-Brexit boost to trade. Perhaps in this increasingly troubled and unpredictable world, membership of the CPTPP will also ensure enduringly close economic links with the three main security partners we have in the region – Australia, New Zealand and Japan.

What is different and potentially so much more exciting about the CPTPP is that, unlike the EU's single market, it covers goods and services and also includes e-commerce, government procurement and investment. It includes rules and protocols on intellectual property, competition, environmental standards and food safety, which will probably be similar, if not identical, to those that applied when we were in the EU. I was one of the earliest in a long line of UK government ministers to actively promote UK membership of the CPTPP; our accession in December 2024 was a small but important diplomatic triumph for the nation.

• • •

The business of managing our bilateral relationships with China and India was primarily a matter for the Prime Minister and Foreign Secretary. However, they were both countries I had visited on several occasions before becoming a minister and I did so again three times each whilst in office.

The tensions that have arisen in the UK's relationship with China have global implications. As we have seen, at the turn of the millennium the naive assumption from most policymakers in the US and UK was that China's accession to WTO membership and its access to global free markets would inexorably lead to it becoming more accepting of our values. We now know full well that will not happen.

As a result, the predominant challenge facing the current and next generation of western political leaders is how to restrain an increasingly assertive China. This will require tireless diplomatic patience and a commitment to widespread co-operation despite persistent provocation, but it is a road that must start with a realistic assessment of mutual strengths and weaknesses. From the perspective of politicians across the political divide in the US, the goal of global peace and prosperity requires the containment of China and the bringing together of a broad diplomatic and military alliance in the region to halt its designs over the free maritime movement that is so critical to open trade.

Following the fall of communism, the worldwide number of democratic nations increased from around forty to over 100. In the aftermath of the global financial crisis, the western economic model has come under intense pressure, solidarity has frayed and nations (even within the EU) have turned away unvarnished support for this idealised model. To many in the developing world and even for some closer to home, Chinese-style authoritarianism appears a better, and potentially more equitable, system.

Curiously, however, many of China's senior politicians and officials vote with their feet. All too aware of the precariousness of their human and property rights, many continue wherever possible quietly to shift wealth first to Singapore or, better still, to Europe or the US. They continue to educate their children in the west in large numbers and thereby hedge their bets geopolitically. Yet despite this rather back-handed vote of confidence from afar, the narrative of inevitable decline hangs heavily over the US and its allies.

The China challenge is different to the struggle against the Soviet Union. For one, unlike other authoritarian states, it is tightly bound to the world economy. The past two decades of globalisation can only be explained by understanding the role that China's entry into the world economy has played in the process.

But the Belt and Road Initiative, which has brought Chinese infrastructure projects and cultural investment to all corners of the developing world during this time, comes with a price tag. Not just the vast debt pile that many Asian and African countries are building up, but also a simmering resentment towards China for those debts and the sense of dependence they have caused. This has been a rude awakening to Beijing of the colonial grievances that other global powers have had to face previously. As a result, the Chinese leadership, seeing the way the wind is blowing, is determined to make the weather itself. So, it has committed itself to intense efforts to build a more self-reliant, sustainable and inclusive economy at home.

The Communist Party may not need to worry itself about re-election, but it is intensely aware that it needs to constantly retain public legitimacy – economically, culturally and environmentally. This also explains why China intends to pursue an increasingly assertive foreign policy. Within its sphere of influence Hong Kong is arguably already all but lost, but the status of Taiwan will be a major geopolitical headache to the US and its allies in the years ahead. China has ambitions further afield so, unlike his immediate predecessors, President Xi asserts himself as the ultimate guarantor of the rights and interests of the Chinese diaspora worldwide. The west should not take for granted that Singapore or Malaysia, to name only two sovereign Asian states where economic and political power is disproportionately held by Chinese minorities, will invariably side with the US in the event of tensions rising.

However, it was always clear to me that many of the most challenging global problems might only be solved with active Chinese engagement. On nuclear proliferation, climate change, money laundering, financial stability protocols and – yes – tackling pandemics of the future, co-operation between China and the west will be critical. We will all suffer if diplomatic initiatives in these areas are jeopardised.

Nevertheless, a breakdown in trust over long-standing infrastructure collaboration and investment projects has struck at the heart of UK-China relations in recent years. Described as a golden era during the Cameron coalition administration, it is ironic that since the EU referendum, the UK-China relationship has also deteriorated rapidly. Attitudes towards China from UK politicians across the party divide and especially within the Conservative Party have hardened, with some leading figures describing China as an 'acute strategic threat' to UK national security and economic interests.

Intriguingly, Rishi Sunak – acutely aware of the financial implications of distancing the UK from an unfettered trade relationship with the world's second largest economy – tried in his time in Downing Street to bring the pendulum back into balance by instituting a strategy of 'robust pragmatism'. I suspect Keir Starmer will continue trying to achieve economic security without sacrificing prosperity. Essentially, this means following the US government's lead over export controls in order to limit and de-risk exposure to China without provoking retaliatory measures.

The hostility of many UK parliamentarians has arisen primarily over human rights in Hong Kong and Taiwan, as well as the treatment of religious minorities. Concerns about the historic treatment of Tibetans, the home-grown evangelical Christian community or the Uighur Muslims in the Xinjiang region are angrily dismissed by the Chinese government as interfering in internal affairs. National security safeguards in post-Brexit legislation have been enacted that evidently target future Chinese investment in UK technology and critical national infrastructure. This has already resulted in the exclusion of leading Chinese-controlled companies from Huawei to TikTok and Nexperia, whose expertise and ownership of the south Wales-based semi-conductor supplier Newport Wafer Fab now places UK production in this important sector in peril.

Western politicians, even those who strongly disapprove of China, would be wise to avoid provoking a more extensive economic war with China and its allies. The runaway level of US debt seems incompatible with the dollar's near eight-decade run as the global reserve currency. The intensifying geopolitical rivalry between the US and China must give rise to doubts as to how much longer this is sustainable. The vast trade deficits run up by the US and Europe over recent decades have typically been mopped up by China and nations such as Saudi Arabia, the UAE and Qatar, who seek to forge ever-stronger collaboration with the world's second-largest economy.

It is notable that many leading nations in the non-aligned world are quietly making common ground with China as dialogue partners of the Shanghai Cooperation Organisation, currently an informal forum for Eurasian political, economic, defence and security co-operation set up by China and Russia at the turn of the century.

Rather than recognising our vulnerability as holders of fiat currencies drowning in debt, we continue to preach at many of these up-and-coming global players for their failure, as the west would see it, to adhere to our cultural values. It may seem a little far-fetched to predict with confidence that the substantial gold bullion holdings accumulated by China, the Middle East and Russia may one day soon be used to link the value of their currencies to gold. But this would be a game-changing geopolitical development. It would test the resilience of our institutions and businesses and silence those critics of China who claim its influence has peaked and predict only decline ahead.

• • •

India finds itself in a geopolitical sweet spot because of these growing tensions between the US and China. Many global companies, such as Apple, have strong incentives to build India up as a counterweight to China as they seek to deal with potentially vulnerable supply chains. My visits there as a minister naturally always took place in New Delhi to meet political connections. But on each of the second legs of my trips – in Mumbai, Hyderabad and Chennai – the focus was largely on trade development and, invariably, technology collaboration.

India's educational emphasis on science and technology dates back to the Nehru era and has gone from strength to strength since the millennium. It is now well placed to benefit from some of the hostility that US and European politicians feel towards big tech. If this plays out in higher taxes and more stringent regulation, then India will have the chance, with its fast-growing young workforce, to grab an even larger chunk of an expanding market.

The global technology and communication service providers' stratospheric growth over the past quarter century has been achieved in large part by their ability to avoid taxation on an almost industrial scale, though some of this may be as a result of their essential co-operation in national security. Tech giants now strike a public pose standing up for their customers' privacy against big government. Yet their very business models hinge on the exploitation of knowledge and information from their own users – information whose value can easily be calculated and then sold on for profit to third-party advertisers. The patience of many western governments and voters may be wearing thin at the antics of the tech giants, but India stands ready to welcome them with ever more open arms.

Under Prime Minister Narendra Modi, who came to office in 2014, India has become more assertive and self-interested in its approach to global governance. Senior UK politicians have always managed to misjudge how best to deal with India. References to our shared colonial history have always grated as being patronising and so too the constant talk of cricket or India's railways. Even talking admiringly of India as a coming power in view of its economic growth and suggesting that it now needs to assume international burdens to prove this will only irritate Indian counterparts. We *are* a great power will be the quickfire response.

So, any suggestion that the UK has some historical role to intervene or adjudicate in any of India's intractable border disputes, especially with Pakistan, will be quickly rebuffed. The Kashmir and Punjab border disputes may well be a legacy of the 1947 partition, but the view from New Delhi is that this is no longer Britain's business in any way. In both of these intractable disputes, the majority of those from the regions concerned living in the UK are of Muslim and Pakistani origin. The Labour government may feel tempted to pacify MPs in a key voting bloc across dozens of UK inner-city constituencies by making promises that will anger India, especially under Modi's Bharatiya Janata Party.

Above all, Modi's India sees itself as an important global player in its own right. It is comfortable standing alone and refuses to choose between rival power blocs. It sees its economic interests as being best served by not aligning firmly, even in an era of increasingly polarised global politics, with either the US and the west or with China. It has avoided regional economic ties through the CPTPP or the Regional Comprehensive Economic Partnership but has been happy to sign up to a defence pact, as part of the Indo-Pacific Quad grouping, with the US, Australia, and Japan. What we in the UK need to realise is that modern India's strategy is dictated by a hard-nosed assessment of its own interests and benefits rather than any enduring values. I think Lord Palmerston would have understood and approved.

• • •

This type of appreciation of broad geopolitical themes made for an incredibly absorbing two years in ministerial office. I was determined to enjoy my FCO role to the full and avoid getting bogged down in the Brexit furore that now was engulfing British politics. I suspect this would not have been possible in a domestic department. To me, all the early talk of the UK following a Canadian or Norwegian model of Brexit was already largely white noise. The years of strife had begun.

The financial and diplomatic cost of disentangling the UK from the EU became the elephant in the room of British politics. Rather than facing up to this fact, it became easier for government spokesmen, both Leavers and Remainers, to divert the blame onto European negotiators and to those closer to home who wanted to reverse the referendum result. The Chequers plan of July 2018 spoke to the sort of Brexit I felt was optimal – or perhaps, in the circumstances, I should say the least sub-optimal option. But the way the leadership handled things, in an atmosphere of secrecy and distrust, made things worse. From then on it was as if much of the British political class had been infected by a kind of madness. At various times I was approached to join groups of ministers who would meet in private, but never quite in secret, to discuss ways of assisting the Prime Minister. I was never convinced that engaging in any such factional activity would be helpful.

In November came the publication of the Withdrawal Agreement, but it was doomed from the outset. Many in the Cabinet were by now positioning themselves for their future leadership bids. The momentum behind a second referendum was by now so strong that even Tony Blair entered the fray to lambast what at the outset he might have considered a sensible compromise – even if it meant leaving open the possibility that we might depart the EU without a deal. In January 2019 came the first of three votes on the Withdrawal Agreement, and the government lost catastrophically by 432–202. I remember walking through a sparsely filled aye lobby on that night and recalling my earliest days as an opposition MP, when Conservative amendments to legislation attracted similar levels of support.

As the insanity continued, I concentrated ever more on my Foreign Office duties and almost totally zoned out. In the last throw of the dice in March, through indicative and free votes designed to seek out a parliamentary majority for any course of action on the Brexit issue, I supported revoking Article 50. I guess my reasoning was, 'Let's stop the clock and work out collectively from first principles what would be best for the country.' But by then it was far too late. It was only a year or two later, when I reflected on these crazy times, that I realised that in my heart I must have known even then that my time in Parliament was fast coming to an end.

CHAPTER 8

A FULL CIRCLE

3 DECEMBER 2019

'I don't know if you have considered what you are going to do after leaving Parliament, but I wondered if you might be interested in a non-executive chair position with Capital International Bank here on the Isle of Man?'

Greg Ellison's email message arrived totally out of the blue barely a week after I had formally announced my intention to step down. He was the dynamic and resourceful CEO of Capital International Group, the Isle of Man's largest privately owned asset management company. I was but one in a procession of fifty-one Tory MPs returned to Parliament in 2017 who would not be standing again – or at least not as Conservatives. Almost all of us had supported the UK remaining in the EU at the referendum three long years ago; nine were already sitting out their time as independents and the same number would stand unsuccessfully under a different party label at the imminent general election.

Greg and I had already met a few times in the past. For six years before becoming a minister I had been an adviser to Cains, the Isle of Man's largest law firm. They had brought me on board because it was recognised that wholesale change was in the air for its corporate and banking clients in the Crown dependencies following the financial crash. As is often the way after a crisis, the resulting shake-up radically changed the way things got done.

The Vickers Commission was the new broom and its detailed report recommended that the banks should sweep away old practice by 'ring-fencing' their retail, utility functions from the investment and corporate finance activity. For the three Crown dependencies of Jersey, Guernsey and the Isle of Man, this meant the Big Four banks would drastically reduce the size of their operations. The Vickers process dragged on for several years and my job had been to keep the partners at Cains and their clients abreast of political developments in London, as well as playing an ambassadorial role for the firm at conferences in the City and on the island.

It also meant advising the Isle of Man government on mitigating the impact of these changes; ironically, in 2014 this had included casting an eye over proposals to legislate and open up their home-grown banking capabilities. In my new life, I was about to benefit from this experience.

As is the case in any relatively small island (the Isle of Man has a population of 85,000), there is a close-knit community spirit. This applies equally to its commercial sector, where seemingly everyone knows everyone else. Furthermore, the quality of professional services work is uniformly high for such a small jurisdiction. Financial advisers, accountants and lawyers based there will usually have started their careers in London or perhaps worked even further afield; others with some prior Manx connection would typically go to university in the UK before later returning to the island.

There was a widespread assumption from Tory colleagues in Parliament that I must have already had something else lined up before telling my local Conservative Association that I would not be contesting my seat again. Not so – Greg's unexpected email seemed almost too good to be true. It restored my faith that just occasionally in life, things might work out for the best.

But it was not quite yet a done deal. After a flurry of documents and a non-disclosure agreement had been exchanged between us, Greg and Anthony Long, a member of the founding family that are still controlling majority shareholders in Capital International, flew over to London. To this day, I am not quite sure who was selling to whom. But our discussions and lunch went so swimmingly well that by the time they had to head back to Heathrow Airport, thoughts about any other candidates had been shelved. All that remained was to sufficiently impress the Isle of Man regulator, the Financial Services Authority (FSA), that I was a 'fit and proper person' to chair a bank.

My first formal job interview in two decades was set for nine days before the first general election in twenty-seven years in which I would not be standing as a candidate. Tuesday 3 December was a cold and wet day. Plenty of those in and around the Irish Sea, as I would soon discover – and not just in the winter months. Never one to take things for granted, I had devised my own personalised crash course in financial services oversight. In the two weeks' notice that the FSA had given me, I read each day's *Financial Times* more attentively than I had ever done before – literally from cover to cover. The team at Capital International had already provided a guide to my anticipated duties and by the time the day of judgement arrived, I knew more financial acronyms than a world champion Scrabble player.

Whisked over from the airport to Capital International's modern, open-plan offices in the heart of the island's main town, Douglas,

I met up with Greg and Anthony who ushered me the two block, four-minute walk to the FSA's near-identical office building. Their escorting me was reminiscent of proud but slightly nervous parents taking a smartly dressed son to his first day at a new school. The FSA's head of banking and mugs of piping hot coffee were awaiting our arrival. After ten minutes of Isle of Man commercial small talk, my two minders withdrew and I was left alone with the island's regulatory supremo.

Conversation turned to money laundering, business risk assessments, terrorism finance and capital adequacy processes; some were to be avoided, others encouraged apparently. To my surprise, my interrogator had read my second book *The Best of Times* and was genuinely keen to talk through some of its conclusions, especially my theory that the now massively prolonged period of near-zero interest rates meant that much of the risk in the global financial system was likely to have been dangerously mispriced. What was true in 2015 was doubly so four further years on, as we would all in due course begin to discover.

His only abiding concern appeared to be whether I had sufficient time to manage the twenty to twenty-five days per year that was envisaged in the draft contract of employment for my non-executive position. My appointment was given draft approval then and there. This was going to be the first building block in my new portfolio life. It was the first bit of really good news I had received in several months.

· · ·

My time as a minister had come to a slightly premature end in late June when I got caught up in an unpleasant controversy at the annual

Mansion House dinner, which I was attending as the constituency MP. As always, the guests of honour at this black-tie event were the Chancellor of the Exchequer and the Governor of the Bank of England; the 300 or so invited guests had all been called to dinner in the eighteenth-century Egyptian Hall and the first course had been served when all of a sudden, forty protestors unexpectedly stormed the room.

In the commotion, there was a deafening screech as several rape alarms were set off and klaxons blared. Several of the trespassing intruders rushed towards the top table to confront the VIP guests. It was chaos. Only later did it emerge that the disruption had been orchestrated by the environmental group Greenpeace. As a regular attender of around eighty Mansion House events over the years, I was probably quicker than many other guests to realise that there had been a serious failure of security. However, I was by no means the only guest to intervene as the protestors disrupted the event. I got up from my seat and stopped a female intruder who was running towards the top table. As she struggled to rush past me, I grabbed her by the shoulder and escorted her swiftly out of the hall with my hand on the back of her neck.

Order was eventually restored as security belatedly arrived; the formal dinner resumed and to be honest, I thought no more of what had happened. I made my way home by public transport and it was only shortly after I reached my apartment at around 11 p.m. that all hell broke loose. The event was being filmed and footage of my intervention was suddenly all over the internet and television. There is an old saying that the camera never lies, but it is equally the case that it does not always tell the whole truth. Curiously, the broadcast footage was only ever silent – had the sound been transmitted, the sheer chaos of what was happening and the noise of the sirens going off would have been very clear. It had been anything but the 'peaceful protest' that its organisers would later try to claim.

Furthermore, the narrow camera angle only showed me and a solitary protestor, as opposed to the full context of dozens of demonstrators storming the hall and other people intervening to stop them. The footage of the split-second moment of my coming together with the protestor was also broadcast in slow motion. As any football fan viewing the VAR system would confirm, the effect of slow-motion coverage is to make the moment of contact look much more incriminating. That, presumably, was the point.

The almost immediate social media response – anonymous death threats to me and abuse of my family – was predictably vicious. Or, at least, it was initially. Within a matter of hours, as the story ran across the morning news channels, there was an abrupt change of gear. From then on, the overwhelming majority of tweets and emails that were sent to my office account were robustly supportive of my actions.

It is unimaginably dreadful to live through such a media storm. If anything, I became less resilient to this type of coverage as my political career progressed. It is easier said than done to simply switch off from the most toxic social media abuse. I genuinely admire those frontline politicians and celebrities who seem able to cope with an almost constant flow of verbal violence over a prolonged period. I couldn't, and over the next few months the Mansion House incident and its aftermath caused me some serious health issues.

Inevitably, journalists, particularly those I had regularly worked with, rang or left messages to ask whether I would like to 'give my side of the story'. For a split second this was tempting, especially as I regarded the initial coverage of the incident as deliberately misleading. However, the reality is that commenting publicly would only serve to give the story more oxygen. Selected clips of whatever I might say would be broadcast and give licence for others to be interviewed – and those that were selected were unlikely to be supportive. I cannot claim to be an expert in crisis management, although my time in public life has included more than my fair share of scrapes. But when in the days that followed, I was informed by no fewer than three people who had attended the dinner that they had been stood down from TV interviews the next day after they had made it clear that they were going to be sympathetic of my actions. I concluded that staying silent was the right course of action.

After a day or so of a media storm, the caravan moved on and the Mansion House furore died down. Even in the eye of that storm, I was able to raise a smile when the *Daily Express* ran a poll that confirmed that 89 per cent of its readers thought I should keep my ministerial job. Those were not bad odds – I reckoned that at any time there must surely be at least 11 per cent of voters who support the proposition that any minister should get the sack regardless.

What was also very comforting was the reaction of colleagues on the airwaves – on all sides of the House. My most vociferous defenders on the Conservative benches were often fellow MPs whom I barely knew, and I was touched that they were so supportive. Whilst a handful of MPs from opposing parties took to social media in the immediate aftermath to criticise me, my fondest memories were of some prominent Labour female MPs who publicly sought me out over the next few days to express sympathy and ask how I was. The attempts by a couple of vociferous women's rights groups to equate my actions with domestic violence were deeply upsetting. But very quickly, their desperate attempts to make political capital for their cause were made to look foolish by the general, more balanced reaction to what had taken place.

I had been formally suspended as a minister, but by now we were in the middle of the leadership election that would see Theresa May replaced by Boris Johnson. All FCO ministerial travel had been halted and everyone was essentially treading water until the new leader was in place and the ministerial team reshuffled. Within three working days, the City of London Police, having taken eyewitness statements and viewed CCTV footage, cleared me of any wrong-doing and said they would be taking no further action. The Conservatives' investigating officer did not take much longer to dismiss the complaint against me under the party's code of conduct. That really should have been the end of the matter, but, unfortunately for me, the investigation into a potential breach of the Ministerial Code took longer to report.

The superannuated civil servant who was the Prime Minister's independent adviser on the code eventually reported back with the classic civil service compromise opinion. He accepted that I had been justified in intervening but made two minor criticisms of my conduct, which he unilaterally claimed to amount to a breach of the code. I have never met or even spoken to the independent adviser who presumed to pass judgement on me, so at no time did I have the chance to defend myself against his specific criticisms, both of which I would have rebutted had I been given the opportunity.

In any other quasi-judicial context, I would have been entitled to make personal representations. That fundamental denial of a basic principle of natural justice was all the more galling when I later learned that the retired civil servant had himself once been a Permanent Secretary at the Ministry of Justice. Although given the utter disarray in that government department, perhaps I should not have been entirely surprised.

Theresa May declined to endorse these findings before she left

Downing Street. On his first full day in office, Boris Johnson formally dropped the investigation without sanction as I was by then no longer a minister. But all this took its toll. Politicians, like other performers in the public eye, are overly sensitive to any criticism from colleagues or the media. I suspect we would all worry less if we realised just how little most of those apparently hostile critics really care. Many are working to strict deadlines and have to write or blog to order whatever first comes to their mind. It's business, not personal.

I must confess that when people occasionally bring up the Mansion House incident it still makes me inwardly wince, even today. Needless to say, it is only ever raised, with me at least, in the context of wholehearted support for my actions; I guess the recent disruptive antics of Just Stop Oil and Extinction Rebellion, not to mention the murders of Jo Cox and David Amess, have made the public more understanding of the constant security threat that faces those of us in public life. Most sensible folk are willing to give us some leeway when it comes to countering it.

· · ·

With hindsight, it is evident that from the moment Boris Johnson became Prime Minister at the end of July, he – or perhaps more accurately, his Svengali chief of staff Dominic Cummings – was set on a dramatic constitutional rupture that would provoke a general election. Most of us lacked the imagination to see how the country could get out of the deadlocked politics of the previous few years, but he realised that unusually, a single-issue election appeal might just work to his advantage.

Following all the chaotic parliamentary upheaval since June 2016, the voters now simply wanted to Get Brexit Done. The other thing that had changed was the public perception of Jeremy Corbyn as a potential premier – his instinctive refusal to call out Vladimir Putin after the Salisbury poisonings did him untold damage in the eyes of patriotic, working-class voters. This was Boris's route map to a thumping parliamentary majority.

As August 2019 began, my biggest fear was that I was facing almost three years on the back benches winding down my time as an MP and trying to rebuild from scratch my reputation as a commentator on financial affairs. By the end of that month, at a lunch party in Mallorca, one of the leading special advisers in the government had tipped me off that an election was probably on the cards much sooner. Suddenly, I was faced with a whole new set of anxieties. Leaving Parliament and politics had certainly been on my mind, but my working assumption had been that the next election, under the Fixed-Term Parliaments Act, was going to be three years away in 2022. That sort of time frame had lulled me into a false sense of security that no decisions about what might come next would need to be made any time soon.

I realised that my views on Brexit were going to make it very difficult to persuade myself, let alone my loyal constituents, that I could publicly endorse what the new leadership had in mind for the Conservative Party manifesto. A little more selfishly, I also looked at my own prospects outside the warm embrace of the House of Commons. It was one thing to voluntarily give up politics at the age of fifty-five with your party still in government. By contrast, opportunities to carve out a new career might be much more limited if I hung on only to lose my seat at sixty – and by then, public desire for change might have become irresistible and the party might crash into opposition. Back in my recruitment and headhunting days, I remember being asked to meet up after the 1997 defeat with several ex-Tory MP lawyers, all of whom lamented losing their seats at a time when the demand for former Conservative MPs was dismally low. It was a fate I was determined to avoid.

By early September, on returning to London, it was clear that electoral politics was warming up. Local campaigning had kicked off again. Every canvassing session in one of our supposedly safe districts filled me with a mixture of alarm and gloom. Our local core vote appeared to be collapsing – dislike of Brexit, distrust of Boris, despair for the Conservatives. Meanwhile, time spent campaigning in our many social housing estates was far more rewarding. Here our vote was holding up well and there were many Labour switchers coming to us out of a sense of fear of Jeremy Corbyn, something which had been totally absent in 2017. This turned out to be a microcosm of what was in store nationwide.

More importantly, it persuaded me that it was safe to stand down. In the turbulent years that we had been through, I was determined above all not to let my local Conservative Association down. It would not be fair on them or a new candidate to leave the fray if there were a serious risk that the seat might be lost. I was never under any illusions that my personal vote was minimal at best, but in a very close contest it might prove decisive. After I announced that I was not standing, I received scores of letters and emails from supportive and grateful constituents, many insisting that my decision now made it easier for them to vote Liberal Democrat. In the final analysis, I reckon a large number of these folk ended up holding their nose and voting Conservative after they weighed up the risk of letting Corbyn's Labour Party in through the back door.

In Parliament, there was one last throw of the insane Brexit dice. In order to run down the clock to the end of October, which at the time was the designated date for leaving the EU, the government had decided to prorogue Parliament. The idea was to prevent MPs from voting against any motion that would prevent the UK leaving the EU without a formal withdrawal deal. I didn't really approve of these tactics but nevertheless decided to support the government. The bargain I had made with myself once I had entered and left ministerial office was to 'vote the line'.

One class of political operator whom I have always found most nauseous is the brown-nosing loyalist. The sort of person who is a weathervane over policy matters and willing to sell their soul for a sniff of promotion but will suddenly reinvent themselves as men or women of principle the moment they are either fired or their political fortunes sour. Whilst few would ever accuse me of crass careerism of this sort, I also recognised that I had been lucky enough to serve as a minister during a torrid couple of years when getting business through Parliament had required backbenchers to loyally troop through the division lobbies night after night. Now the boot was on the other foot, I felt a strong sense that the right thing to do was to support my party regardless of my reservations over our policy direction.

Enter the Supreme Court, who overrode the judgement not simply of the government but also the monarch and overturned the prorogation. I still regard this judicial intervention as questionable constitutionally. By rights, this decision should have signalled an end to the self-indulgent tearing down of traditional checks and balances. But it wasn't – instead it became the perfect launch pad for the Boris Johnson era, which until as late as autumn 2021, many had assumed would last the entire decade. But this was the moment that I decided to step off the carousel.

For me, being an MP had always been much more than a job or

even a vocation. I had never regarded it as a career as such, but it had become much more of a way of life than I had perhaps realised. I enjoyed its challenges and above all, its variety. Political life was never dull. What I had not reckoned upon when deciding to leave the House of Commons was the extent to which even I had become institutionalised. Not entirely, for up until the time I became a minister I had maintained some outside work interests. But for the first time, I experienced the slight seasickness that must have afflicted my father on leaving the army. It certainly made me appreciate with more sympathy what he must have been through.

The prospect of giving up my seat induced more than a little anxiety in me. It was clear in my mind that once I had gone public with what was a family decision, there could and would be no coming back. Like so many men, I am instinctively resistant to change. On the other hand, once moving on is a fait accompli, I have tended to cope well with it. Fortunately, I am someone who does not often lose sleep over making or accepting decisions. However, being an MP, a public figure, appearing regularly on TV and radio was a big part of my identity throughout my adult life. Funnily enough, in the years since, I have missed that part of being an MP far less than I had anticipated or feared. I am now perfectly comfortable as a private citizen, with views I can express freely to friends and family but without the aching need for a platform or a social media account. I think it was my eight-year-old daughter Arabella who felt the loss of status more – she could no longer proudly tell her school friends that her daddy was an MP and a Minister of the Crown!

But my status as a Member of Parliament was also tied up with a shorthand understanding to anyone I met professionally or socially of who and what I am. In one sense, in the same way as I remain a politically exposed person for life so it has been for my past existence as a frontline politician. I am still routinely introduced by people I have known over the years as 'the former minister/MP/Conservative politician'. Unless I live far longer than either of my parents, being a politician will probably always be seen as an integral part of my identity to the outside world. My entire adult life to date had been spent devoting considerable time and energy to getting into frontline politics or serving as an MP. It would not be easy to shake this off… and perhaps I would never want to.

But the end was now nigh. On 17 October, I was due to be formally readopted at a meeting of the entire Cities of London & Westminster Conservative Association. I wanted to say my thank yous and goodbyes in person. So, having tipped off the senior local Conservatives earlier in the day and sworn them to secrecy as to my intentions, I pitched up in front of several hundred of my most loyal local supporters. Standing on the slightly elevated stage, I cleared my throat and spoke from the heart:

> Twenty years will have passed in December since this association first selected me as its candidate. With your generous but often unsung help, the people of our unique, historic, vibrant Cities of London & Westminster constituency have since entrusted me five times to be their representative in Parliament.
>
> Frankly, over the years I could not have asked for a more tolerant or understanding local Conservative team, always operating smoothly alongside my parliamentary office. Whilst local councillors may have come and gone, I cannot recall a single public disagreement over policy throughout my time. Here, in the heart of our nation's capital, conservatism has been vibrant, outward looking and united. Our two local authorities, Westminster City Council and the City of London Corporation, have been blessed

with consistently outstanding policymakers and flair in an era when we all know city-centre living has become tougher – whether it is antisocial behaviour, round-the-clock noise, daily disruption or protest on our streets. We take for granted this superb local leadership.

Meanwhile, I have been proud of my local reputation as a moderate, consensual MP, invariably keen to work across party lines to the benefit of constituents and communities alike. However, such a pragmatic, co-operative approach to public service has been tested to destruction in the fractious, febrile and deeply divisive aftermath to the EU referendum in 2016. I had dearly hoped that by the time of the next general election these issues would have been resolved. However, it is increasingly clear that divisions over Brexit and our future relationship with the EU-27 will dominate and define domestic politics for many years to come.

As a party vice-chairman and then Minister of State at the Foreign and Commonwealth Office, I was until recently constrained by collective responsibility, although during free, indicative votes in April had the opportunity to express a personal preference for ruling out a no-deal Brexit and for revoking Article 50 – albeit to restart the two-year clock, rather than override the referendum result entirely.

As you will appreciate, these beliefs stand at odds with the current administration's impatient approach to getting Brexit done. Yet even if the current proposed deal passes – and naturally I shall support it – we must be clear that what lies ahead will not be plain sailing. But, having watched many colleagues follow this path in recent torrid months, I have no desire to become a disaffected, dissenting voice from the back benches, undermining a government under whose colours I have been elected. So, the current speculation that a general election may be imminent has forced me to reach the very difficult decision not to offer myself as your candidate for the next election.

I cannot deny that coming to this conclusion has caused me great distress and anxiety in recent weeks. As a Conservative Party member for thirty-five years – and representing it in elected office over the last quarter century – I shall continue from the bottom of my heart to wish it, and especially the members of this wonderful Cities of London & Westminster Conservative Association, the greatest of electoral success.

The truth is that emotionally and geopolitically, I still believe in my heart that the UK would be better served by remaining in or very closely aligned to the EU, not least given our privileged position of opt-outs over immigration and the euro and our hard-won budget rebates.

Nevertheless, from my recent experience as Minister for Asia and the Pacific, I am also confident that in time our people and businesses have the innovation, enthusiasm and drive to make an economic success of Brexit in the decades that lie ahead. On leaving Parliament, I relish the opportunity to contribute active-ly to the vital national mission of ensuring that for the sake of future generations, the vision of a confident, bold global Britain becomes an economic and diplomatic reality.

I cannot thank you and my constituents enough for the un-stinting support you have given me over these past two decades. Please ensure that even amidst these unprecedentedly turbulent political tides you provide as much encouragement, friendship and joy to my successor.

I was deeply touched by the spontaneous standing ovation that followed. Some members looked genuinely upset; others were shocked, and more than a few tears were shed. Several people spoke out openly begging me to reconsider my decision. But the deed had been done and thankfully I have not regretted it for a single moment. In the world of theatre, it is often said that it is best for actors to leave the stage with the audience wanting more. That is precisely where I stood in October 2019, and having just turned fifty-five, there was time to open a new chapter of life. But what would come next?

• • •

The Isle of Man opportunity soon helped force the pace about what my future working life would look like. I suppose one option might have been to put all my eggs in one basket and take a single full-time job, but I am not sure I ever gave that any serious thought. Even if an ideal or suitable role had been available, going down this route would not really have appealed. The more I thought about it, my preference was to go plural – and build a portfolio of mainly non-executive positions. Exactly half a lifetime ago, I had faced a similar fork in the road when leaving the law. Then I had trusted my judgement and entrepreneurial instincts; now, as the main bread winner and with a family to support, there was much more at stake. Then I had the confidence of youth and a sense that the world was, or at least could be, my oyster; now, despite all my accomplishments and experience over the decades, the possibilities offered by the world beyond seemed to have closed in.

Close friends are not always the best of advisers in these sorts of circumstances; in a strange way, it is sometimes easier to speak more openly about your hopes and fears with acquaintances. Friends are either overly desperate to fix your problems then and there or end up slightly embarrassed that you have been so candid; acquaintances will be better listeners and generally can be relied upon to do so without prejudice or any transactional dynamic in your mutual relationship.

Two conversations from this challenging time stick in my mind, both for the quality of advice I was given and what has happened since.

I seemed to have known David Buchler for ever. Unusually, I cannot recall where or when we met, but I know for sure that it was way back in February 2002 that he first took me to the directors' box to watch his beloved Tottenham Hotspur. He is the most accomplished networker I have ever come across but not in a pushy or aggressive way. David had been a Mayfair constituent throughout my time in Parliament. He has had a tremendously successful professional career in the world of corporate restructuring and likes nothing more than bringing together people he knows from different walks of life.

Although it had been a year or so since we had last met up, David responded instantly to my short text message asking for some advice. Coffee at his favourite private corner in the art-deco splendour of the Foyer & Reading Room at Claridge's followed the next morning. He guessed immediately why I wanted to meet and understood why giving up my seat was such a wrench. He listened and teased out what I really wanted to do; he offered advice and reassurance. Bringing me into his firm, Buchler Phillips, it has been a pleasure to work closely with Jo Milner, Katerina Mina and the team. My consultancy there involves some ambassadorial work, speaking about geopolitics at client events as well as assisting in its business development and government relations.

Christopher Mills founded Harwood Capital after a stellar career in investment management and yet more spellbinding financial success has followed. His London home was in Belgravia and our paths would occasionally cross as he was an active supporter of the Conservative Party. He kindly donated to my constituency fighting fund before each and every general election. After announcing that I was standing down, I offered to take him out to lunch by way of thanks for all his past generosity. He would hear nothing of it and insisted on paying – as always. He also let on that I was the only MP, of the several he routinely supported at election time, who would always thank him with a handwritten note afterwards. We talked about my portfolio plans and he gave me some invaluable, practical advice. I plucked up the courage to ask him upfront if he would keep me in mind for any suitable non-executive director (NED) roles.

Some months passed. Then Christopher introduced me to the board of a public company, in which one of his funds was the single largest investor. This was the Salford-based wealth management company Frenkel Topping, and for me it was a great fit and the perfect introduction to learning the PLC ropes. Suddenly, I was linked into the world of brokers, regulators, nominated advisers and communications specialists, not to mention all the legal responsibilities that come with being a public company director.

The non-executive chairman, Tim Linacre, was a well-respected City figure who became an ideal mentor as I got to grips with balance sheets, fluctuating share prices and the constant round of reporting. I am sure it helped that we also shared a near fanatical interest in football, rock and pop music from the 1970s and 1980s and a deepening despair for the fortunes of the Conservative Party, of which he had been a paid-up member even longer than me. Our CEO, Richard Fraser, had been with the company as man and boy, since it was an accountancy partnership, and knew everyone in our ever-expanding market of costs lawyers, expert witnesses and specialists in medical negligence. Frenkel Topping had raised money to fund a series of acquisitions and the oversight of their integration has been a fascinating insight into the nuts and bolts of commercial life.

Very soon, I took up the chance to put some effort into committee work. Remuneration committees are a great way to watch human nature in action. As a relatively fresh-faced NED, I felt this was a tremendous training ground at managing conflict and bringing judgement, objectivity and perspective to the boardroom table. Despite not being an accountant, I then moved on to chair the audit committee, which has become ever more challenging as the regulatory and compliance obligations on directors and auditors alike have tightened.

It really is no exaggeration to say that getting the first public company appointment is always the hardest. In the light of handling my new-found responsibilities at Frenkel Topping well, one of its institutional shareholders put in a good word for me with the founding directors at Lifesafe Holdings as it planned its initial public offering. This is where I came across the charismatic angel investor and entrepreneur Dominic Berger, who was leading the team as executive chairman. If I thought that my career had been varied, it is nothing compared to Dominic's. Starting life as a film director, he moved into the commercial side of online TV, digital media and sport. His enthusiasm, energy and can-do approach to life is infectious.

Lifesafe Holdings developed innovative and environmentally friendly fire-prevention products. I joined the board in early 2022 and was able to take a ringside seat as we devised strategy and overcame untold hurdles on the route to going public in one of the most challenging markets of recent times. Our consumer and industrial momentum have unexpectedly been driven by rapid growth in the US rather than domestic or European markets.

There is still something special about the energy and spirit of commercial adventure that infuses America. For all its problems, not least its utterly dysfunctional politics, there is an ambitious, can-do approach that marks out US businessowners and ensures that ideas there are converted without delay into products and services. Geopolitics aside, this has confirmed one of my earliest observations from my own days starting up new enterprises. Within months, even the most meticulously prepared business plans usually resemble nothing more than a set of random, cascading numbers on the page. The product line you reckon on being the mainstay of your revenues may well be marginalised whilst work that you hope will come on stream two or three years down the line quickly comes to the fore and makes up much of your profits.

I also became informally involved with a waste-to-energy company and the life assurance division of an international professional services outfit. For over two years, I remained in close touch with a prominent European family office leading a consortium of investors, who finally settled on two sustainable infrastructure and electrical vehicle projects in central Europe. I became the non-executive chairman of the special-purpose company it set up to run these $150 million investments.

There are three lessons I have learned from my new life beyond the apparent security of the world of politics. Almost everything took longer to finalise than I thought it would, virtually all the building blocks of my portfolio came about directly or indirectly from contacts I had known for at least fifteen years, and the true benefit of experience in life is a realisation that few problems are entirely novel – the longer you have been around, the more likely that you will be able to pass on wisdom that you have already picked up along life's long journey.

My political background has provided me with a strong understanding of the regulatory challenges that face the organisations whose boards I have joined. I see myself as having the perspective and insight to advise on the economic, political and legislative factors that are shaping its future. Political risk continues to rise up the business agenda everywhere, and in my role with the bank, insights from what I did in the political world have given me a genuine feel for business risk, cyber security measures and all manner of internal controls.

However, my small business background before politics remains vastly more important in giving me that instinctive commercial feel. That said, the advantage of having had a life beyond business is that non-executive roles, especially when chairing meetings, require big-picture oversight. Detail matters, but one of the skills that many successful business executives find most difficult to acquire is the ability to be 'hands off'.

The vast majority of working-age US politicians who lose their seats or retire from politics move seamlessly into political consultancy, public affairs or lobbying. That trend is increasing on this side of the Atlantic. It was something I was always keen to avoid. No disrespect to lobbyists, but one of the saddest sights in Parliament was watching some former MPs hanging around in the public areas, almost wishing to relive what they saw as their glory days. Another reason I was reluctant to put all my eggs into the 'retired politician' basket upon leaving Parliament was that I might be in some demand as a lobbying gun for hire when my party was in office, but that could quickly change when that party looked as if it might be heading into opposition.

In fairness, there are several old friends in public affairs with whom I have enjoyed some fruitful, usually short-term consulting work. But this has almost always hinged on my supposed expertise in either Asia or the Pacific from my ministerial time or in specialist financial services. I knew Andre Ebanks and Charles Parchment from the Cayman Islands government office in London during my time as the City's MP. They brought me in to provide strategic financial services advice alongside their usual public affairs consultancy. This tided me over well for the first couple of years or so after leaving Parliament. Evidently, Andre was not put off by rubbing shoulders with a former politician because he returned to the Cayman Islands, duly got himself elected to its legislature and for a time became its Finance Minister.

• • •

I started this next phase of my working life sitting at the antique partners desk I had bought over three decades ago with virtually my first salary cheque. Little did I imagine that this working from home lark was about to get a lot more popular. No sooner had Boris Johnson swept to a near landslide victory than he got Brexit done (politically at least; some of the economic loose ends are still with us). Everyone, Leavers and Remainers alike, now looked forward to calmer days ahead.

Which is when the Covid pandemic struck. The history of that almost fantastical era of lockdowns is still to be written. What shocked me even then – and slightly disturbs me to this day – is just how compliant the British public were to the repressive rules that they were simply instructed to obey. My instincts have always been broadly libertarian. I am suspicious of large and intrusive government. I am reluctant to support banning things. By the same token, as a rule, I don't take conspiracy theories seriously. But even my mild scepticism about some of the things we were being told about the impact of the virus back in March and April 2020 made me sound slightly unhinged when contrasted with the juggernaut of public opinion that appeared happy with our basic freedoms being curtailed by government decree. In this censorious public attitude lay the seeds of the Partygate controversy that would eventually be a decisive factor in Boris Johnson's downfall. The ruinous impact of lockdown may only now be entirely apparent, but whilst emergency restrictions were in place, public support for it was overwhelming.

My view at the outset was that the restrictions on day-to-day life should have been far less severe. Some form of quarantine for all those in their seventies or older and special provision for younger people at high risk or with prior medical conditions, but otherwise, business as usual. The government deserves some sympathy for where we ended up because it had to move at pace. The counterfactual is also worth considering – was it really practical for the UK to be an outlier compared with all other western European countries and economies of a similar size? Once much of the world went into lockdown, it would have been difficult not to go with the flow.

I suspect the UK Covid-19 Inquiry, when it eventually reports, will tell of a catalogue of institutional failure with the customary – and absurd – government reassurance that 'lessons have been learned'. Presumably, as with the vast array of public inquiries set up over the past couple of decades, it will only be the lawyers who will end up satisfied at their outcome. My main concern is that this protracted and eye-wateringly expensive process will fail to address properly the central issue of future pandemic preparedness or provide a hard-nosed analysis of the wisdom or otherwise of lockdown in the event of another pandemic. Even at the time, I felt the main political failure was the cowardly repetition from ministers that 'at all times we are following scientific or medical advice'. Political leadership is about decision-making and judgement; this means weighing up expert advice but doing so in the broadest possible context rather than cravenly hiding behind so-called independent opinion, however respected or apparently popular it may be.

Predictably, the lawyers and media fixated on sensationalising the personality divisions and profane language exposed by the wholesale release of WhatsApp messages between politicians and their senior advisers. In a classic case of failing to see the wood for the trees, much of the cross-examination in the inquiry missed the utter lack of preparedness or resilience of our 'Rolls-Royce' civil service. I was reassured rather than scandalised upon learning of Boris Johnson's legitimate push back on initial 'expert' advice. He was surely right to pose the question whether a ruinously expensive full lockdown would crash our economy and add massively to the national debt, all in an attempt to ensure that as many 82-year-olds as possible made it to their eighty-fifth birthday. As we now know, the pandemic continues to cast a long shadow on the mental health, lifetime educational and development prospects of a younger generation, despite their having been at minimal risk of the pandemic.

The worship and adulation that many Britons feel for the NHS as an institution was also heightened during the pandemic. Unfortunately, this has only reinforced the innate political conservatism about the urgent reform that is now necessary in healthcare provision for all four nations of the UK. The changes made by Andrew Lansley early in the coalition era were so poorly communicated and received that no one has wanted to touch this issue with a bargepole ever since. But before long, money will talk. At the turn of the century, healthcare accounted for 27 per cent of government spending; this figure is now around 44 per cent and rising fast as a consequence of an ageing population.

The debate about the spiralling costs of social care has still not really graduated beyond arguments about the justice or otherwise of elderly people being required to sell their home to fund some but not all medical conditions. As we all know from Theresa May's failed attempt to find a solution to this conundrum back in 2017, a general election campaign tends to bring far more heat than light to these issues. Nevertheless, the political class needs to put the scaremongering to one side and work as a matter of urgency on devising a viable and lasting framework of funding and social insurance.

The other impact of the pandemic was to place normal party politics into some sort of cryogenic deep freeze for as long as it lasted. Millions of workers were furloughed, with their wages being paid by the state. The national debt leapt by a further half a trillion pounds and the Bank of England recommenced its quantitative easing (or money printing). None of this seemed to matter for so long as interest rates remained at the near-zero level we had all become used to for over a decade.

The low-tax, small-government, free-market wing of the Conservative Party within Cabinet (never normally reluctant to amply brief private conversations to compliant journalists) was strangely silent as all this played out. Only later and with 20/20 hindsight did it regain its voice. In May 2021, on a massive swing, the Conservatives won the traditionally safe Labour seat of Hartlepool at a by-election. The near universal assumption then was that the 2020s would turn out to be the Boris Johnson decade. Most commentators wrote off the prospects of Sir Keir Starmer, confidently predicting that he would end up as just another name in a lengthening list of former Leaders of the Opposition before Labour eventually made it back into office.

But politics did return to normal – and how! The pendulum began to swing back over reported breaches of pandemic regulations that had taken place in 10 Downing Street at the height of lockdown. This was the Partygate scandal, the event that began the slow and painful demise of the Johnson government.

I must confess that I shared the overly optimistic view of many then at the heart of government when the story broke, and even when fines were later imposed, that this whole episode would simply blow over. After all the other career-threatening controversies that Boris Johnson had bounced back from over the years, Partygate seemed at first blush relatively trivial. I had reckoned without the strong sense of resentment felt by many whose lives had been turned upside down by the same politicians and civil servants who apparently saw fit to behave as if blissfully exempt from these new draconian rules they had imposed on everyone else.

• • •

Ironically, Boris Johnson's administration had just started to seriously unravel when the military conflict that he had long warned of began in Ukraine. UK intelligence services had for some months warned that President Putin now had Russia's western neighbour firmly in its sights for a full-scale military invasion. But it still came as a surprise to many when in February 2022, after months of patient preparation, Russia finally launched its attack.

In the immediate aftermath of the Soviet Union's collapse in the early 1990s, the signs of communism's failure had been inescapable.

Along with admission of ideological defeat – made all the more painful given the importance of face and pride to the Russian psyche – came financial meltdown. A sharp downgrading of Russia from global superpower to diminished, weak, failing state followed.

But there remained hope that Russia was a nation firmly on the path to multi-party democracy, rule by law and press freedom. It was a hope stoked in 2000 by the election of Russia's second President, Vladimir Putin. In contrast to his predecessor Boris Yeltsin, Putin was keen visibly to demonstrate Russia's willingness to become an important ally to the US in areas of mutual interest. He accepted a second stage of NATO enlargement to the Baltic states, allowed the US to withdraw from the Anti-Ballistic Missile Treaty and stood shoulder to shoulder with George W. Bush after 9/11 in the battle to defeat global terrorism. Conveniently, this also provided him with an alibi to continue his nation's brutal suppression of dissidents in Chechnya.

Two decades on, as Ukrainian cities either side of the strategically critical Dnieper River were targeted by Russian fighter jets and artillery, the cautious optimism of those years seemed hopelessly misplaced. Yet it was the west's failure to respond robustly and push back against Russia's annexation of Crimea in 2014 that led Putin to believe that there would be little western appetite for prolonged conflict over Ukraine. The cost in terms of restricted oil and gas supplies, economic disruption and a renewed refugee crisis on a scale not seen in Europe for over seven decades had the clear capacity to divide opinion in the west. On the other hand, Putin underestimated that with authoritarianism on the rise since his incursion into Crimea, the risk of not intervening against Russian aggression was that fellow autocrats would have felt emboldened to act with impunity.

In practical terms, Putin had long feared encirclement by nations no longer within the Russian orbit. In taking a firm stance over Ukraine, which at various times since its independence had been encouraged that it would be absorbed into Europe's economic and defence arenas, he set down a marker that Russia would not tolerate further encroachment into what many Russians had long regarded as its sphere of influence.

What we in the west have continually failed to understand is that most Russians regard the eras of Mikhail Gorbachev and Yeltsin with disdain, as a time of chaos, uncertainty and utter humiliation. Despite economic difficulties, Putin has been able consistently to maintain a semblance of domestic popularity by telling the Russian story, filling the vast ideological vacuum left by the disintegration of communist ideals with the notion of a Russian civilisation based upon patriotism, selflessness and deference to a powerful state. More worryingly he presented himself to a global audience as the champion for the interests of all those with Russian connections throughout the region.

In doing so, Putin tapped into a pool of resentment that extends well beyond Russia's borders, encapsulating many of those who despise the US hegemony of recent decades. The elite that has surrounded him remains keen to preserve its powerful business interests, dazzling wealth and access to the luxury goods, lifestyle, properties and educational excellence offered by the west. The prospect of being placed on an international blacklist by the US and Europe, with assets frozen and visas cancelled, has been a sobering one for Putin's cronies and apologists.

Understandably, the west has remained reluctant to directly engage its military might in Ukraine, but we must at least continue to show the Russian President that we will remain resolute when it comes to the implementation of sanctions, even if this harms our own short- and medium-term financial interests. It may prove inconvenient, unpredictable and economically painful, but Russia and its people need to know that the benefits of the west's outward-looking, free-trade and liberal economic institutions must not extend to its companies and countrymen if it continues to test our resolve. Putin's aggression must fail – and must be seen to fail.

In the longer term, it is also vital that Europe reduces its reliance on and exposure to Russian oil and gas. We knew this full well back in 2014 when Crimea was annexed and did very little to mitigate the situation, either then or in the meantime. The US must urgently assist in this regard, removing all barriers to exporting its own energy resource to the continent and encouraging Europe to achieve its own energy independence by sharing new technologies, such as those around shale gas.

The appalling scenes of the suffering endured by ordinary Ukrainian men, women and children still being broadcast across international TV and social media are nothing short of heartbreaking. Ironically, Breslau, the city where my own forefathers had lived for generations, was subsequently inhabited by ethnic Poles, who had themselves been displaced from Lemberg, later known as Lwow and now Lviv, today the most prominent city in western Ukraine. As this frequent changing of names affirms, the borders in these parts have never been quite as fixed as many partisan politicians would have us believe.

More controversially, I believe NATO should recognise that its eager attempts over the past three decades to draw Ukraine away from Russia's orbit have on balance been both misguided and unwise. In the euphoria following the collapse of communism and the Cold War triumph, such initiatives were understandable. They were also mistaken. At this time of unimaginable sacrifice in Ukraine, this message is unwelcome and in no way reflects what the hapless and long-suffering citizens of Ukraine deserve. Modern-day Russia is an authoritarian, kleptocratic aggressor and a near-constant threat to its neighbours and to global stability. Nevertheless, Ukraine's fledgling – and let's be frank – flawed democracy should never have been allowed to believe it would imminently be ready to join the west.

One of the many ironies in UK reporting since Russia's invasion is that those elements of our media normally so relentlessly critical of populist right-leaning governments in central Europe have been strangely muted when it has come to analysing Ukraine's track record. President Volodymyr Zelensky has been masterful in his public relations, but for all his talk of clamping down on corruption, it remains endemic in Ukraine. Even today it is estimated that one in every five dollars of aid is spirited away through graft. Meanwhile, both before and since the conflict began, Zelensky himself has quietly taken control of much of Ukraine's media in order to consolidate his political power base and marginalise internal opposition.

Vladimir Putin spent much of the eight years after annexing Crimea preparing for this military re-engagement in Ukraine. He has known from the outset that Ukraine was a conflict western leaders wished would simply go away. Most commentators assumed that the west's resolve in supporting Ukraine would soon be tested by internal conflict when it became apparent that the impact of sanctions and energy embargoes would fall much more heavily on some European nations than others. Germany's over-reliance on Russian oil and gas, the Baltic states' technology vulnerabilities, the UK and Switzerland's role as bankers to sanctioned Russian citizens and entities. This has not yet happened, but it is also clear that this resolve is beginning to fray, especially amongst those EU and NATO members with historically close ties to Russia. Of much greater concern has been the wavering of support in America and not only within the traditionally isolationist faction of the Republican Party.

The fate of Ukraine has understandably been the first-order geopolitical priority here in the UK and on mainland Europe. Yet, as ever, it has been left to the US to take on the bulk of NATO's financial commitments and fund European continental security. Even before the latest atrocities in Israel and Gaza, with their threats to relative stability in the Middle East, support in Washington for ongoing financial commitment to Ukraine was on the wane. Many US policymakers and think-tanks calculate that strategic tensions in the Indo-Pacific are a more pressing political risk. From this perspective, to guarantee future global peace and prosperity requires the containment of China, as well as bringing together a broad diplomatic and military alliance in the region to halt China's designs on Taiwan and maintain the free maritime movement that is so crucial to open trade in the region.

The assumption promoted in the European media up until the end of 2023 that the war was going Ukraine's way was never widely shared in the US. Perhaps it is memories of the grinding stalemate in Vietnam that has produced fears that something similar is happening in Ukraine – US military commanders assured their political masters in mid-1964 that troops would be engaged on the ground in south-east Asia for no longer than a year. It has always been crystal clear that time was on Russia's side. If Ukraine could not repel and then regain Donbas and neighbouring territory quickly, then stalemate, attrition and political reality would bite.

The bullish public stance of European politicians is for an endgame that sees the Ukrainian state restored at the very least to its pre-2022 borders. Indeed, some support President Zelensky's view that Crimea must also be returned. This is highly unlikely to happen. In the US there is the more modest ambition that a military stalemate leaves open the possibility of a diplomatic settlement. In the eyes of many American foreign affairs specialists, this realpolitik outcome might even result in a chastened, weakened Vladimir Putin remaining in post. Better that than a whole new set of uncertainties, especially in the sphere of the nuclear escalation that might arise if the Russian state were to unravel or break up chaotically.

This erosion in political support from an increasing number of Washington insiders has come about largely as a consequence of irritation, bordering on anger, at the continued freeloading of many European members of NATO. Overall US military and aid expenditure in Ukraine still dwarfs the contribution made by all other NATO nations put together. All this to underpin a collective security guarantee in Europe's own backyard. Fighting talk and ever-bolder long-term defence spending promises by European politicians comes cheap in the eyes of an increasing number of their US counterparts. Especially when it is their electors, beset by an array of domestic concerns of their own, who are expected to foot the immediate bill for such European showboating and bravado.

Pending a ceasefire, which may still be many months or even years away, the UK should now use our frankly limited diplomatic and security expertise to make common cause with those Russian citizens who are committed to the path of resistance to the current regime. The long and winding road to free and fair elections, the rule of law, universal property rights and a pluralistic press cannot simply be imposed by the international community. This pressing priority needs to be proposed by brave Russians themselves, and we must stand ready to support these initiatives from both within and beyond.

If our collective resolve weakens at the prospect of a military stalemate and an endless humanitarian catastrophe, the likeliest outcome is probably a negotiated settlement. But after the eternal security assurances set out in the Budapest Memorandum of 1994 and the proposals to recognise the autonomy of designated sub-regions as part of the ill-fated Minsk agreements in 2015, we should not be surprised if Ukrainian politicians and people alike doubt the reliability of even a UN-brokered deal to bring an end to hostilities.

Predicting that endgame is highly speculative at this point, but some sort of partition between Russian and central European spheres of influence may provide the relief of a ceasefire. Despite all the rhetoric of total victory from both sides, this may be the only way to avoid ever more human carnage and misery, as Ukraine's towns and cities head into a further period of brutal, attritional warfare. However, as we know full well from the Korean peninsula, Cyprus, Israel and Palestine, Bosnia and Herzegovina and even Northern Ireland, such expedient and apparently temporary arrangements have a distinct tendency to turn into permanent sources of tension.

Nevertheless, history records that wars do not always end in peace. Stalemate and a frozen conflict may be where Ukraine ends up. This would be sub-optimal for Ukraine and especially its Baltic and Nordic neighbours, perhaps, but also little short of a disaster for Russia's geopolitical goals. It would tie up huge resources and paralyse Russia's regional ambitions, as well as making it clear to other would-be hostile powers that military invasions do not pay.

• • •

The UK's steadfast support for Ukraine's military and our diplomatic leadership within NATO from the start of 2022 stood in stark contrast to the political turbulence that was engulfing the government domestically. When speaking at a conference on the Isle of Man in the early weeks of 2023, I noted that it was difficult to imagine a more economically and politically tumultuous year than the one that had just come to a close.

Three Prime Ministers had held office in a single calendar year for the first time since 1868 – and even in that year of change at the top, the outcome of a general election was responsible for one of the handovers. The impact of the long-overdue but abrupt Bank of England decision to start unwinding over a decade of ultra-loose monetary policy had been compounded by a sharp spike in energy prices as Russia went to war in Ukraine. Inflation re-emerged with a vengeance as the most pressing priority for policymakers and households alike, with millions engulfed in a cost-of-living crisis. Unease in the financial markets turned to genuine anxiety that the historic mispricing of risk during the decade or so when the cost of money had been so cheap might lead to a more general economic unravelling.

Relatively little remarked upon was the fact that the UK now had, in Rishi Sunak, its first Prime Minister of south Asian heritage. He was absolutely right to observe that in the multiracial Britain of the 2020s, it really was 'not a big deal'. But it was a far cry from attitudes that still held sway as recently as the turn of the century, when many Conservatives had played down Michael Portillo's chances of making it to No. 10 because of what they termed his foreign-sounding name.

In my final term as an MP, I had got to know Rishi as well as busy ministerial colleagues in different departments can. But our paths crossed from time to time when he was a junior minister. He immediately struck me as likeable, bright without being in any way overbearing and never too busy not to stop for a quick chat. Clearly industrious and analytical, he evidently enjoys nothing better than dealing with data and detail. Regrettably, proficient administration is not as universal a quality in government ministers as it should be.

The sense of reassurance provided by the incoming Sunak administration, after the dramatic implosion of the Boris Johnson premiership and the disorderly Truss interlude, was short-lived. Economically, the clouds were darkening. That rise in the cost of energy and much else besides had left most Britons to look much more carefully at their spending. In a consumer-led economy, this is always bad news. As for the politics, it was impossible not to conclude that the Conservative Party's long incumbency was probably coming to an end, with the toll of countless thwarted ambitions and deep policy and personality divisions making it virtually ungovernable. Any new leader, but especially someone who had been so recently rejected by the party membership, would have faced an uphill struggle. Sensible Tory MPs could see what Sunak was trying to do in the aftermath of the carnage that had so comprehensively trashed the party's brand. Sadly, by this time sensible folk in the parliamentary Conservative Party were in decidedly short supply. This proved to be Rishi Sunak's fate as the sands of time drained away towards the general election.

His time as Prime Minister had begun with his personal ratings comfortably outstripping those of the Conservative Party. It ended, after an error-strewn election campaign, with his polling numbers having plunged to levels that compared unfavourably even with his two unlamented predecessors when they had been ousted from the premiership. Diligent, administratively competent and with a ferocious work rate, Sunak had been badly hamstrung by what had come before him. Yet even his keenest advocates had to admit that he showed little sign of projecting a coherent or convincing vision of where the Conservative Party, let alone the nation, should be heading.

As I watched election night unfold in July 2024, for once from the comfort of an armchair, naturally my feelings were of sympathy for old friends who were clinging on desperately or suffering electoral reverse in supposedly safe seats. This was tempered in part by the irony (cruel or delicious, according to taste) of the fate that befell some of the self-regarding Spartans who had made life hell for the government I had been part of between 2017 and 2019. These self-appointed guardians of doctrinal Brexit purity suddenly found themselves outflanked by the re-emergence of Nigel Farage and his latest franchise, Reform UK. Perhaps it was my Germanic roots that brought a sense of *Schadenfreude* to the fore as many Brexit hardliners saw their vote shares plunge and sometimes their majorities go up in smoke, not least when the margin of many of their defeats was smaller than the vote secured by their Reform opponent. As the preposterous Five Families of the Tory right preened themselves over their disruptive antics during the torrid years after the Brexit referendum, little did they realise how many of them were signing their own post-dated death warrants.

The simmering anger from the party membership, thwarted by MPs in their two previous picks for leadership, will continue to make life difficult for the parliamentary leadership as it contemplates the long road to electoral recovery. As the 2024 election approached, I reminded old friends of the gallows humour doing the rounds in East Prussia exactly eighty years earlier: 'Enjoy the war, because the peace will be terrible.' The reckoning for the Conservative Party after the unremitting trauma and turbulence of five Prime Ministers, endless leadership challenges and constant melodrama during its most recent spell in government is unlikely to end any time soon.

In the immediate aftermath of the election, much attention was focused on the shallowness of Labour's popular appeal. The party's share of the popular vote was 33.7 per cent, its sixth lowest in the twenty-two general elections since the Second World War. To achieve a landslide majority of 174 on that basis suggests that the UK's party and electoral system is seriously failing to represent voters on a range of economic and geopolitical issues. Meanwhile, the Conservatives' hold on the 121 seats they managed to win is no less tenuous. In only five constituencies do the Tories have a majority of 10,000 or more (and in sixty-six it is less than 4,000). The fevered debate about relations with Reform UK and how to bring about the urgent necessity of reuniting the divided right-of-centre vote in domestic politics will probably overwhelm the time at the helm for more than one Conservative Leader of the Opposition by the time the current decade has concluded.

We have become accustomed to writing off the chances of any new party seeking to overturn the century-long dominance of the Conservative-Labour duopoly. Four decades ago, the SDP failed to break the mould of UK politics because to do so it needed to destroy the Labour Party. Back then, Labour never fell below 207 seats, even in its cataclysmic 1983 defeat. Today's Conservative Party, as we have seen, has no reliable bedrock of support to ward off the advance of Reform UK – though in the short term, the Tories may be too historically entrenched to die yet too weak to recover as a viable party of government. If polling is to be believed, the British public currently regards Brexit, or at the very least its implementation, as the UK's single biggest strategic mistake of the present century. The chances of rapidly restoring the Conservative brand and any meaningful electoral recovery may be hampered by its authorship of this tale of woe. Paradoxically, this may even play into the hands of Reform UK, which despite being the offspring of the Brexit Party stands ready to mop up the support of right-of-centre voters seeking a credible alternative, untainted by a recent record of failure.

• • •

More fundamental changes may also now be in train. In the fullness of time, I wonder whether historians will look upon the early 2020s in a similar light to the late 1970s – as a period of transition. Each of the last four changes of governing party in the UK followed hot on the heels of major economic upheaval that had helped destroy the credibility of the administration in office. The UK's IMF bailout in 1976, our ejection from the European Monetary System in 1992, the financial crisis of 2007–08 and the colossal costs of the Covid pandemic in 2020–21 were all pivotal economic events. Each and every time the voters had their say after these sudden disruptions, there was a change in government.

The current situation seems to herald a period of even greater refashioning. Indeed, the UK is arguably on the cusp of a new economic era defined by a permanently larger state, enhanced rates of personal taxation and lower rates of economic growth than we have been accustomed to in recent decades. This generalised and lasting increase in the size of the state has not come about as a direct result of the pandemic, but indirectly, the long shadow of Covid has played its part.

The breathtakingly vast debt that was rapidly built up in order to sustain the thousands of businesses and millions of livelihoods that were abruptly halted by government decree when the economy locked down have made it all the harder to question continued higher public spending across the board in the post-pandemic era.

The authoritarian nature of and overwhelming voter support for lockdown have also fundamentally altered general attitudes towards the role of government during times of trouble.

Since the financial crisis we have collectively racked up astronomical levels of debt so that the UK electorate should become protected from economic pain whenever major difficulties strike. As a result, it should not really have come as a surprise that no problem now arises without a clamour that 'the government should do something'. Needless to say, this invariably involves a further financial bailout. Small wonder that public support for an ever-larger role for the state has risen. This is mirrored at Westminster, where the terms of debate are less about the wisdom of government intervention but more about its size and how it should be funded. The spirit of the age has become decidedly social democratic.

Many of the seasoned City of London professionals with whom I have remained in touch bring a deeper perspective to the financial market upheaval that arose after the disastrously executed Truss/Kwarteng mini-Budget in autumn 2022. It is worth remembering that there was already great unease in the markets at the prospect of the vast £120 billion borrowing entailed in the proposed energy bailout scheme they unveiled on taking office. So much for small government and free-market economics…

Meanwhile, a huge mountain of debt remains firmly embedded in the global financial system. Much of this has been propped up by opaque financial instruments. Sounds familiar? Only a small, maverick minority in the financial markets raised the alarm about uncosted derivatives on the eve of the last financial crisis, when conditions appeared to most finance professionals as benign and manageable.

Closer to home, the trouble has been that there have been a

succession of 'one-off challenges' that began with the financial crisis, which have apparently justified ever higher public expenditure. This has never been matched by rising economic growth; nor have politicians levelled with the public that we cannot continue indefinitely down this path. Collectively, we have convinced ourselves that we are entitled to more from the state. Government has simply made up the shortfall by borrowing.

The national debt has tripled over the past fifteen years and only the policy of ultra-low interest rates disguised what was happening. But the days of free money are now behind us, and the reckoning will be painful. Towards the end of my time in Parliament, I would try to respond honestly whenever retired constituents wrote to me complaining of hospital waiting lists on the basis that 'I have paid my dues all through my working life'. Very few of the elderly have paid anything like enough in taxes or national insurance to justify what they believe they are entitled to take out. Public sector pensions are not included in that collective national debt and many of these schemes are not fully funded – yet another set of expectations that will be costly to satisfy.

• • •

So how do we get out of this debt trap? The last time the national debt was as high as 100 per cent of GDP was after the Second World War, when in an act of national salvation, we borrowed against the future. The quarter century that followed was an era of less open capital markets and foreign exchange controls than today. Boosting productivity was a little easier than it is today, but spending cuts were no less politically unpalatable. Successive UK governments were gradually able to reduce the national debt burden by a process of financial repression; governments borrowed indirectly by forcing banks to hold more capital by way of government bonds and savers earned interest at rates lower than inflation. New technology during this period also led to levels of economic growth that have been difficult to emulate since the 1970s.

So, there is a template for recovery. But this will all take time and the generation of Britons who have recently entered the workplace will almost certainly have a worse deal than those of us approaching retirement have taken for granted during our working lives.

For three decades we have relied on low levels of inflation to smooth the path for commercial investment and ease industrial relations. UK businesses and households have taken for granted that whatever the economic headwinds, they have been able to plan on the basis that prices will never deviate much from the central bank's perennial 2 per cent inflation target.

It is now evident that the post-lockdown recovery, such as it was, was built on the shakiest of foundations. The supply-chain hiatus led to a burst of inflationary pressure, a situation magnified by the impact of paying the costs of the pandemic and the Ukraine conflict.

Further fiscal loosening as the pandemic paralysed so many of the UK's service industries has also resulted in money supply becoming dangerously out of kilter. As the pandemic surged, the Bank of England, along with other central banks, resumed its policy of quantitative easing, from which it had barely started the unravelling process after its emergency implementation during the financial crisis. Individual savings had been massively built up during the exceptional circumstances of lockdown and furlough. It should not only have been dyed-in-the-wool adherents of monetarist economics who realised that this pent-up demand was likely to have adverse inflationary consequences.

It is now clear that keeping inflation to recent historic lows will be far more of a challenge than in the past. History also records that inflationary spirals – and their close cousin, wage-price spirals – have a tendency to take hold extremely quickly. Incidentally, this is also why the outgoing Conservative government was so determined to concede little ground to any of the striking public sector workers in the array of recent protracted industrial disputes.

Just over fifty years ago, in the first few months of 1973, inflation in the UK stood at 6.5 per cent, only a little higher than the then 4 per cent level in Germany whose economic success we then hoped to emulate as fellow members of the EEC. Yet within two years UK inflation levels had reached the unprecedented heights of 26 per cent, whilst Germany's remained in low single digits.

The sharp increases in world energy prices, as a consequence of the last major conflict in the Middle East in 1973, impacted comparably on manufacturing economies (this was in the era just before North Sea oil came on tap). However, organised labour in Germany worked in tandem with its government, realising there would have to be a short-term fall in living standards, rather than pushing for large wage hikes. Britain's trade unions took the opposite course and the more powerful were able to threaten and implement strike action. Costs of production rose, further inflation resulted and ever larger pay claims quickly became the norm – those living on fixed incomes or in occupations lacking industrial muscle lost ground, and living standards across the board plummeted.

Those who criticise Treasury orthodoxy also need to reflect that its institutionalised memory is now the single most important element in ensuring that policymakers avoid a repeat of the grim outcome of the 1970s that some of us are just about old enough to remember. Keir Starmer and Rachel Reeves have quickly realised that a painful fiscal reckoning is now upon us. The cost of government borrowing will become much more expensive in the years ahead. Whilst starting down this road did not suit the electoral timetable of their predecessors, battening down the hatches on public spending has become essential as bond market yields rise.

Another potential similarity between the current decade and the 1970s lies with the reluctance of the political class to embrace fundamental change until the restlessness of the electorate forces it upon them. Labour swept back into office in 2024 with a manifesto that spoke to change but offered little beyond continuity. Reassurance rather than radicalism. So, in all probability, the 2028–29 election will offer a more fundamental choice. The question then will be whether Starmer, assuming his administration has not been buffeted by events in the meantime, will follow the lead set by Blair and Thatcher with a more radical second term in office – or if the UK's future lies instead with a populist, right-wing government of the nationalist kind that has come into power in several mainland European countries in the mid-2020s?

• • •

The public finances are not the only thing that government will need to keep under firm control. Immigration was never far from the headlines during my time in politics. I have witnessed massive demographic change whilst living in London since the late 1980s. This has taken place without public assent and continues as a result of differential birth rates, large-scale family reunion and the granting of leave to remain. There are also our obligations under international refugee and asylum treaties – and, of course, the free movement provisions that applied until we voted to leave the European Union. But above all, this continues as a direct result of persistent government failure to invest in domestic development and training to plug glaring capacity gaps in the UK workforce.

In 2011, I led a parliamentary debate into the plight facing vast numbers of domestic staff arriving in central London legitimately, on a working visa, but then having their passport confiscated by their employer and being mistreated. Once in London, many of these hapless victims of exploitation seemed to disappear into thin air in the eyes of the authorities. My own constituency casework forewarned me of this serious issue, and it was a local councillor representing one of the most affluent districts whose dedicated work alerted me to the extent of the abuse. The Modern Slavery Act followed in due course; regrettably, the terms of this legislation have all too often been used by specialist lawyers as a loophole to evade restrictions on entry rather than to protect people already here.

As a Conservative representing an inner-London constituency with a majority of residents – even when I was first elected – born outside the UK, it was no surprise when Sunder Katwala of think-tank British Future sought me out. This was the genesis of an initiative called Conservatives for Managed Migration, which we launched in 2014 in an attempt to promote a calm, reasoned debate within the party about immigration. I argued that the then notional cap on numbers was not only unattainable but was certain to lead to an unhealthy focus on headline figures, disconnected from economic or geopolitical reality.

Since the UK government at the time had precious few tools at its disposal to stem the tide of EU nationals, refugees or asylum seekers coming here, efforts to decrease numbers inevitably rested on deterring many of the most economically productive types of non-EU migrant. People like talented entrepreneurs, academics, businesspeople and research students. When government fails to meet its own unrealistic targets, voter distrust is only reinforced.

I also made the more overtly political case that politicians had consistently ducked having an honest discussion with voters about immigration. Public resentment and anger, quite understandably, has fast filled the policy vacuum. As that sense of resentment has boiled over and with the electoral threat from UKIP at the time (later from the Brexit Party and now from Reform UK), the Conservative Party has seemed ever more fixated by the issue.

Party leaders were perennially tempted to deal with the immigration issue as a problem that could be solved by a retail offer. Cameron devised the 'restrict annual immigration to tens of thousands' policy, Theresa May threatened a 'hostile environment' for illegal immigrants and Rishi Sunak promised to 'stop the boats'. All were widely regarded as failing to deliver on these pledges. In truth, all were probably undeliverable from the outset.

Even the Brexit clarion call to 'take back control' never took account of the UK's economic needs. Since the referendum, a whole generation of Conservative politicians have felt emboldened, perhaps even entitled, to run roughshod over any international treaty or convention that is at odds with 'taking control' of immigration. We simply cannot do this without huge consequences. And as a result, public scepticism and cynicism for politics and politicians (and every promise they make about immigration) is whipped up further.

In order to deal with the skilled and semi-skilled labour shortages that resulted from UK nationals being unable or unwilling to take the jobs that EU nationals had formerly filled, we have ended up issuing record numbers of visas in recent years. Far more workers on construction sites, in hospitality and in seasonal work now come from Commonwealth countries. Since our departure from the EU, the damaging link between race and migration has been more firmly re-established.

By 2021, Lord Sewell, leader of the government's Commission on Race and Ethnic Disparities, argued, 'There are still real obstacles and there are also practical ways to surmount them, but that becomes much harder if people from ethnic minority backgrounds absorb a fatalistic narrative that says the deck is permanently stacked against them.' However, the public debate and political agenda is increasingly dominated by the high-profile activities of groups such as Black Lives Matter, with its advocacy of ideologies such as white privilege and critical race theory. Any attempt at dispassionate debate is closed down by those who insist that 'lived experience' is all that matters.

Meanwhile, the latest demand from many activists in prominent positions is for financial reparations for slavery. This issue is not going away any time soon. Nor is it entirely without precedent, although the payments made by the West German government to Israel in the 1950s for Jewish Holocaust survivors, by the US government in the 1980s to Japanese-Americans interned during the war and even by the UK in 2013 to Kenyans tortured during the Mau Mau uprisings were reparations to living victims. The movement for massive financial reparations for slavery is different in that monies are being demanded for the descendants of victims several centuries after the dreadful ordeal suffered by their ancestors. Man's inhumanity to man has meant that slavery has been adopted as a form of human control and domination over many thousands of years. However, the current proposal applies to only one very narrowly drawn category of slavery, namely enslaved Africans transported across the Atlantic Ocean. It also rests on the tendentious claim that this particular aspect of the slave trade, more than other forms of forced servitude at home or overseas over the centuries, has been responsible for the historic success of the British Empire that is the bedrock of our collective wealth today.

Watching prominent figures from institutions such as the Royal Family and the Church of England falling over themselves to signal their virtue by agreeing to demands for slavery-related reparations, I would urge caution. I am sure there are many millions of us Britons whose forefathers had land and property stolen from them centuries ago by the monarchy and established church. The British Empire got no less rich as a result of the terrible historic injustices our relatives were forced to endure.

If the past is used as a partisan political weapon in managing present-day relationships, we will all suffer – especially if the ever-toxic issue of race is part of the identity mix. Sometimes the understandable demands for justice have to be outweighed by other factors. Spain's transition in the past half century from a military dictatorship with a developing economy to a high-income democratic nation at the heart of Europe came about in large measure by a collective recognition that a firm line had to be drawn under the past. This has not prevented huge amounts of historical remembrance, but the widespread political amnesty after Franco's death in 1975 has ensured that memories of the Spanish Civil War do not poison the modern-day well there.

The attempt to right historical wrongs over transatlantic slavery will not improve race relations. In all likelihood, it would make matters much worse. No one believes payment of reparations will end the divisive culture of grievance or close down once and for all debate over racial identity or privilege. More likely what would follow is a whole new round of feelings of unfairness and resentment to further undermine race and community relations. Who should be made liable for reparation payments? No one alive today was complicit in the transatlantic slave trade. Nor, to the best of my knowledge, were any of my relatives – my research efforts reveal only that when slavery was abolished in the early nineteenth century, my forefathers were either peasant farmers in Devon or semi-skilled craftsmen from Leicester. This is the moral and ethical minefield we face if we go down this route. None of this will end in harmony – or even justice.

• • •

Ultimately, it was the issues of immigration and community re-lations that almost certainly swung the EU referendum. The long shadow of Brexit will be cast across loyalties and alignments in UK politics for some years to come. If opinion polls are to be believed, there has been an intensifying sense of buyers' remorse over Brexit. Since that fateful vote in June 2016, the subject has never been far from the forefront of UK political discourse. After a series of false dawns and three years of political stalemate, we went from an over-whelming desire to 'get Brexit done' – at virtually any cost – to the current state of discontent at the outcome. More recently, it has been an issue that few frontline politicians speak openly to voters about, lest they are accused of wishing to open up an issue that was supposed to have been settled.

For the Conservatives, any admission from the leadership that recovery from our economic malaise might be aided by an engaged, working relationship with the EU risks infuriating ultra-Brexiteers and raising accusations of betrayal. Meanwhile, Labour has in recent years walked a tightrope between pacifying its unrepentant Remain graduate activist base and avoiding any action that dissuades Red Wall Brexit supporters from returning to the fold, having voted Leave in 2016 and then backed Boris Johnson's Tories in 2019. The Liberal Democrats also remember well the outcome of the 2019 election, when they had hoped to appeal exclusively to the 48 per cent of voters who had voted Remain. But in positioning themselves as the party of rejoining, they ended up losing ground from an already very low base.

Even amidst their current travails, the SNP know in their hearts that an unaltered Brexit decision is a crucial part of their case for independence; 62 per cent of Scots voted Remain, so the fact that they were bounced into Brexit by the votes of the English (and Welsh) plays to a sense of grievance that is a mainstay of the SNP's appeal. This will only be enhanced by a sense that the recent adaptation of the Northern Ireland Protocol has given that part of the UK its own special position within the EU customs union and single market set-up.

In short, the universally expedient position across the political spectrum is to claim that the Brexit question is now settled. Instead, the clarion call on matters European seems to be, 'Let's move on…'

Slowly, however, over these years it has dawned on the general public that the political class and civil service were woefully unprepared for the technicalities involved in achieving Brexit. The form of exit we have finally ended up with has sacrificed our economic welfare at the altar of sovereignty and the notional freedom to strike trade deals. In the meantime, our borders seem as far away from effective control as they ever were when we were members of the EU.

Always much overplayed during our half-century membership of what began as a common market and developed into the EU was the persistent irritation expressed by UK businesses, large and small, at the imposition of ever more 'European regulation'. In truth, most of this blizzard of new rules of compliance came about as a direct consequence of the creation of a single market and customs union (of which the UK was both a leading advocate and beneficiary), which by definition required regulatory alignment. As we have since discovered, this harmonisation worked in UK exporters' interests as it allowed British goods to flow unimpeded across the single market.

The consequences of leaving the customs union and single market have been as harsh as they were predictable. Naturally, exporting to the EU has become especially onerous for small enterprises lacking the administrative capacity to deal with the increased regulatory burden. But even large multinationals exporting to the EU have experienced a massive increase in the level of paperwork and bureaucracy. So small or relatively insignificant derogations from EU rules make little sense. It is better for British companies either to maintain total equivalence – and accept that outside the EU we have become a rule-taking supplicant – or seek the benefits, and take the potential risks to reputation, that arise from root and branch deregulation.

The rather obsessive idea that we needed to purge the UK statute book of all remaining EU legislation as a matter of urgency was belatedly recognised as damaging to internationally minded UK businesses. Inward investment will scarcely be enhanced at the prospect of replacing EU standards with British ones, not least as it will likely impose an obligation on companies trading across Europe to comply with two parallel sets of rules.

This reflects one of the unspoken truths about our departure from the European Union – namely, the inherent imbalance in power between the UK and the neighbouring 27-nation bloc, still making up a single market of around 450 million people.

It was – perhaps it still is – fashionable to dismiss the EU as being an institution in terminal decline. Indeed, to many the central premise of Brexit was that Europe was falling apart and that our exit would either precipitate its final collapse or enable us to escape whilst we still had the chance. This has also turned out to be a fallacy – along with the assertion that the act of leaving would signal the end of tensions with the EU. A quick glance at the Swiss experience should have dispelled that particular myth. As we have seen over small boat migration, the Northern Ireland Protocol and euro-denominated City trading, 'leaving' the EU has simply meant starting a whole new set of disputes with our closest economic neighbours.

Yet the British public was assured that the real prize of Brexit would be our ability to strike trade deals on our own terms with economic powers further afield. For sure, we have swiftly been able to cut and paste trade agreements that had already been recently finalised when we were at the EU table. This has worked well with countries such as Japan, South Korea and Vietnam – although there were ominous delays when Japanese trade associations sought to exploit the opportunity to renegotiate clauses to their own benefit.

The US have repeatedly made it clear that they have no current interest in commencing what would be tortuously long negotiations. Presumably they will only do so when it suits them to drive a hard bargain with the UK, in order to use this as a precedent for a US-EU deal.

Meanwhile, the agricultural aspects of the rapidly negotiated UK-Australia trade deal were disowned not only by the UK farming lobby but by the hardline Eurosceptic former Environment Secretary – needless to say, only after he had left office. It is welcome that we have secured dialogue partner status with ASEAN and the CPTPP. However, this is more a post-Brexit diplomatic and geopolitical triumph than symbolic of any significant boost to trade any time soon.

Another misapprehension was that the UK would be able to retain all the benefits of the single market because high-end EU businesses would lobby to retain access to UK consumers. I remember well an almost comical conversation I had with one of Theresa May's three Brexit secretaries, who insisted ever more bombastically that Mercedes and BMW simply would not allow the German government to risk cutting off the British market for their cars in our Brexit negotiations. Predictably, what actually transpired was that UK customers of these upmarket global brands have been forced to grin and bear the imposition of tariffs after we left the EU.

But how does this all play out? Is a return to the EU on the cards?

In reality, despite all the problems outlined above, I still regard this outcome as highly unlikely. After all, as EU members we already had a bespoke deal that was tailored to our interests. The UK's substantial budgetary rebate, amply reflecting our relatively small and industrialised agricultural sector, was entrenched along with opt outs on the single currency, the Schengen common visa arrangements and elements of social legislation. Undoubtedly, the starting point of any attempt to rejoin the EU would be sacrificing these special arrangements. The UK could only expect to be offered a considerably worse deal than the terms on which we left.

Rather more important – would the EU really want us back? As members we were never fully committed or engaged. We stepped aside from the continental engagement that led to the Treaty of Rome in 1957 and only joined sixteen years later in the second wave of membership. Thereafter, we increasingly became semi-detached. Unless and until there is cross-party agreement in the UK in favour of rejoining, it is highly unlikely that the EU would even commence discussions.

Nor should it be forgotten that the UK was comprehensively outmanoeuvred in the exit negotiations. As we now know, those UK politicians who promoted Vote Leave had no plan or strategy from the outset – nor, arguably, ever since – as to what Britain really wanted from those tortuous discussions. By contrast, the EU played a blinder – its negotiators were determined above all that Brexit should not serve as a precedent. Any other EU nation contemplating withdrawal had to be left in no doubt that walking away from the club would leave it worse off. And so it has proved for the UK. This is all the more ironic since we were always rather skilled at negotiating our own best interests when we were members, as that list of historic opt-outs amply attests.

One other great paradox of recent years has come to light more recently with the Windsor Framework that made the hastily and poorly negotiated Northern Ireland Protocol more fit for purpose. Suddenly, it is apparent that the EU Commission had much more discretion to accept our wishes than we had been led to believe after Article 50 was invoked. Their insistence that the rigmarole of getting permission from all twenty-seven member states was a roadblock to progress turned out to have been simply a ploy. When it suited them, the EU was able to use plenty of discretion to act quickly and decisively. Previously, under Prime Ministers May and Johnson, the EU had shown little inclination to make life easier for a UK government, especially whilst it pursued a campaign of public hostility in the media. However, under fresh leadership and at a time when the UK's support of Ukraine was at the forefront of continental priorities, decisive and rapid progress was made. Expect more of the same under the more instinctively pro-EU Labour government.

Small wonder so few of the UK's diplomatic corps have any appetite to go back to the negotiating table with their EU counterparts.

Therefore, it is highly unlikely that Brexit will be reversed any time soon. But that does not mean that we shouldn't continue to rebuild strong diplomatic relations with our continental neighbours. There is enough disorder in the world and enough uncertainty about what happens next in US politics that we need as many strong allies as possible. Events in the Middle East and on the edge of Europe point to chaotic and challenging times ahead.

Since 1941, perhaps even earlier still, the world has relied upon a strong, responsible United States of America to intervene when major conflict arises. Being able to stand behind a global police-man, willing and able to uphold international law, has been the ultimate security for the free world, including for us here in the UK. In the past, troublemaking rule breakers have been called out by American might – albeit not always wisely or proportionately. But unless we have the US there at our side standing up for a rules-based global system, none of us will be able to make plans for the future with any confidence.

• • •

It is sobering to reflect that I entered Parliament almost at the moment when the stable political and benign economic conditions that the UK had begun to take for granted were coming to an end. The terror attacks in New York and Washington took place just three months after I was first elected; afterwards, the near constant military engagement then the economic turmoil after the financial crash meant that my time as an MP was never less than tumultuous. So, there is a small part of me that still feels occasional waves of guilt at being voluntarily missing in action as the political challeng-es continue to mount up. Of course, it is not healthy for the back benches to be full of time servers seeing out their years. But by the same token, Parliament needs to retain some MPs with perspective and experience as to why apparently bright new proposals may not be workable. I fear that a worryingly high level of institutionalised memory is being lost in Parliament before time.

I am not sure I would advise my younger self to go into politics today. I certainly got lucky – and at the risk of sounding entitled, it was simply good fortune – to have represented such a uniquely interesting and prestigious constituency. To be frank, doing so has also helped make my transition out of politics relatively smooth.

From my university days as a student activist, I recognised that politics demanded a thick skin, resilience and stamina galore. But the most stressful aspects of political life have intensified in more recent years with the prevalence of social media and the threats to personal and family security. Naturally, I felt this particularly acutely after my children were born.

My mother's journey had long motivated me to be in public service; I reckon that over the years I was able to make some worthwhile contributions to public life and not only during my time in ministerial office. However, on reflection, I am not sure that getting elected to office was necessarily the only way to have achieved much of this.

Politics has never been a meritocracy, but the prevalence of professional politicians without any meaningful experience beyond the game of politics has evidently neither been beneficial for the country nor the reputation of political and public service. Nor has it provided much incentive for those men and women with substantial and worthwhile prior expertise to put themselves through the stressful process of getting into Parliament.

Even when I was in Parliament, I never accepted the widely held view that we would get a higher calibre of legislator simply by paying MPs more. In reality, doubling the salary of MPs is likely only to make a career in politics even more attractive for the same group of political obsessives who are already well represented within the worlds of public affairs, policy research, political communications and amongst the cadre of special advisers.

I believe a much more serious hurdle to attracting the highest calibre of people into elected politics has arisen as a result of successive governments caving into pressure for external regulation of MPs and political parties every time there has been major public controversy. These so-called independent regulators are entirely unaccountable but regard their statutory function as being beyond reproach. In the name of transparency and openness, their work is faithfully reported in the media. The new regulatory bodies have quickly demanded larger budgets and increased staffing. An expensive bureaucratic structure has been created, along with a strong incentive for the newly empowered body not only to investigate alleged misconduct by MPs but to establish new forms of wrongdoing. In this brave new world, elected politicians are regarded as fair game by regulators and the media alike, with the benefit of the doubt invariably being given to complainants.

This entire regulatory ecosystem began with the creation of the Electoral Commission after public disquiet about political funding. Then, in the immediate aftermath of the expenses scandal, Parliament moved away from its centuries-long, deep, atavistic attachment to self-regulation and its insistence that it should run its own affairs. There was a headlong rush to set up an all-powerful Independent Parliamentary Standards Authority with powers to name and shame. Since 2015, legislation has been in place for MPs to be subject to a recall petition. Almost inevitably there is now intense pressure to expand massively the scope of the misconduct and manner of sanction that might trigger a potential recall – as if frequent general elections were insufficient to hold MPs to account. The Privileges Committee has awarded itself new disciplinary powers and its reports have been given fresh authority by the appointment of a fully staffed Committee on Standards in Public Life. After intense social media pressure over bullying and sexual harassment, an independent complaints and grievance scheme was instituted in 2018. At any one time, this ever-expanding network means there are scores of MPs under one form of investigation or another.

In no way belittling the fact that some of the allegations are of extremely serious misconduct, which in the past would likely have been covered up by the Whips' Offices, most of these inquiries drag on for many, many months. The glare of publicity that attends virtually every investigation makes life pretty unbearable for MPs and their families. Then there is the knowledge that a finding of misconduct – normally only on the balance of probabilities – not only risks ending an MP's political career but is also likely to seriously impair their future employability. This is not a level of scrutiny that even the most prominent businesspeople outside Parliament have to cope with. I suspect it is this new regulatory infrastructure, far more than inadequate parliamentary pay, that is putting many good people off running for Parliament. You have to ask, why would any sane person already in a successful career want to put themselves through this?

If leaving Parliament has felt like coming full circle, this equally applies to the fortunes of the UK when compared to where we were in the mid-1970s, when my political story began. Back then, there was a feeling that nothing much worked, and more than a few commentators have observed that much of what is happening in modern-day Britain is a throwback to those times. This widespread sense is not without foundation. My childhood was spent in the shadow of newspapers stories and TV coverage that suggested that the country was going to the dogs. Industrial strife was endemic; our previous world-acclaimed expertise in manufactured goods, especially cars and electrical products, was derided in comparison to their new Japanese equivalents. Today, public sector strikes are at a thirty-year high and our comparative advantage in the professional service sector seems to be threatened by the rise of Asian and Middle Eastern competition, whose expertise was not so long ago regarded as marginal.

One has to be an optimist of an especially boosterish stripe to believe that over the next few years, the UK will be in a position to emulate the three-decade cycle that gave us the Swinging Sixties (1966) and Cool Britannia (1996) and help put the nation back on the global map as a cultural centre of excellence.

The political class – particularly those on the right of centre – continue to lead the charge with a complacent, ongoing belief in 'British exceptionalism'. We are constantly reassured by many politicians that we 'punch above our weight' in virtually every area of public life and commerce and, perhaps even more absurdly, that 'our best days lie ahead'. Despite this, our relative economic standing has slipped dramatically over the past two decades, with real wages and productivity flatlining since the financial crisis took hold. In the 1970s, our economic eclipse by France, Italy and most shamefully Germany, whom we had either rescued from or defeated in war only a generation earlier, led to much soul searching. By the time this decade is out, our GDP per person may well have been eclipsed by not only by the poorest US state (Mississippi) but also by Poland, less than four decades after it freed itself from the shackles of communism.

We hide behind the myths that our civil service, university sector and healthcare system, to name but three, are somehow the envy of the world. That sense of complacency has seen us preside for well over a decade over policy stagnation in key areas such as labour market reform, energy procurement and adapting the supply side of our economy.

These institutional failures, amongst many others, seriously risk impoverishing future generations of Britons. The unstable and unpredictable business environment the UK has offered investors in recent times will never fulfil the near-universal political ambition of urgent improvement in productivity and economic growth. We all recognise that an ageing population makes ever greater demands on public services and pensions in future, but we continue to spend and borrow as if there were no tomorrow. As we reach the end of an era and cast our eye to the future, I suspect the UK's economic and constitutional model will need to look very different to that which we have grown accustomed to.

ACKNOWLEDGEMENTS

I should like to thank all at Biteback Publishing for their support in this project. James Stephens's wise and thoughtful observations helped crystallise in my mind the thrust of the overriding messages that I have attempted to get across in these pages. Meanwhile, I could not have asked for a more supportive and diligent editor than Catriona Allon. Cat has been invariably upbeat, positive and tolerant of my love of the semi-colon, plentiful adverbs and the split infinitive (even allowing a few to creep into the final text). She has an evident passion for books and publishing that is infectious.

Needless to say, this book would not have happened without the love and support of my wife, Vicki. Doubly so, as she is also my literary agent! The writing of these almost 125,000 words turned out to be remarkably painless; mercifully, I never suffered writer's block for a moment – indeed, if anything, there were some days when I needed to be prised away from my laptop as midnight approached. Thank you for everything.

INDEX